FUNDS OF KNOWLEDGE IN HIGHER EDUCATION

D1715853

To my knowledge this is the first book that addresses exclusively higher education in a variety of social and cultural contexts. . . . And there is more. The book, edited ably by Rios-Aguilar and Kiyama, also represents a challenge to the utility of the original funds of knowledge approach . . . and the need to adapt or supplement its core ideas and methods to a variety of circumstances of study. Congratulations to the editors and authors on the path-breaking volume they have prepared. It is bold work they have undertaken with the goal of helping others access resources in a variety of circumstances and succeed in their advanced studies.

Luis Moll, University of Arizona, USA, from the Foreword

Refining and building on the concept in a sophisticated and multidisciplinary way, this book uses a funds of knowledge approach and connects it to other key conceptual frameworks in education to examine issues related to the access and transition to college, college persistence and success, and pedagogies in higher education. Research on funds of knowledge has become a standard reference to signal a sociocultural orientation in education that seeks to build strategically on the experiences, resources, and knowledge of families and children, especially those from low-income communities of color. Challenging existing deficit thinking in the field, the contribution of this unique and timely book is to apply this concept to and map future work on funds of knowledge in higher education.

Judy Marquez Kiyama is Associate Professor in the Higher Education Department at the University of Denver, Morgridge College of Education, USA.

Cecilia Rios-Aguilar is Associate Professor of Education and Director of the Higher Education Research Institute in the Graduate School of Education and Information Studies at the University of California, Los Angeles, USA.

FUNDS OF KNOWLEDGE IN HIGHER EDUCATION

Honoring Students' Cultural Experiences and Resources as Strengths

Edited by
Judy Marquez Kiyama
Cecilia Rios-Aguilar

Routledge
Taylor & Francis Group

NEW YORK AND LONDON

First published 2018
by Routledge
711 Third Avenue, New York, NY 10017

and by Routledge
2 Park Square, Milton Park, Abingdon, Oxon, OX14 4RN

Routledge is an imprint of the Taylor & Francis Group, an informa business

© 2018 Taylor & Francis

Library of Congress Cataloging-in-Publication Data
A catalog record for this book has been requested

ISBN: 978-1-138-21383-8 (hbk)
ISBN: 978-1-138-21389-0 (pbk)
ISBN: 978-1-315-44732-2 (ebk)

Typeset in Bembo
by Apex CoVantage, LLC

CONTENTS

FOREWORD

It is a pleasure to write this Foreword to a volume extending a funds of knowledge approach to issues and conditions related to higher education. When I teamed up with Carlos Vélez-Ibáñez and James Greenberg, two outstanding anthropologists, who coined the term *funds of knowledge*, and a bit later with Norma González (see González, Moll, & Amanti, 2005), another exceptional anthropologist, to elaborate educational research based on funds of knowledge, we were convinced that we were doing novel and important work. However, we certainly did not anticipate that 30 years or so later, our work would still be cited often and that it would remain relevant, if not vital, to addressing issues in education, writ large, but especially the complexities of diversity and schooling. It is quite gratifying, I must say.

Although our approach has been used, often with adaptations to local realities and issues, in several countries and various locations in the U.S., to my knowledge this is the first book that addresses exclusively higher education in a variety of social and cultural contexts. The readers will go, for example, from the study of the incorporation into higher education of former gang members, to an analysis of the education of African immigrant students, and from there to the study of undocumented students in a private university. And there is more. The book, edited ably by Ríos-Aguilar and Kiyama, also represents a challenge to the utility of the original funds of knowledge approach, especially its emphasis on household visits, developed originally with elementary school students and teachers in mind, and the need to adapt or supplement its core ideas and methods to a variety of circumstances of study.

In what follows, I raise three interrelated issues, among others I could elaborate, that I consider important to the funds of knowledge work, regardless of site or emphasis. One is the idea that education occurs everywhere – it is an everyday activity, and it is certainly not limited to schools, although, in my view, educational researchers have privileged this institution as a primary site for the study of learning and development. Varenne (2007) captured well what I am trying to communicate; he wrote as follows: *As a cultural anthropologist, I argue that education is a fundamental human activity that is infinitely more complex than anything that can happen during learning lessons in school* (p. 1559). In an important sense, that is why we emphasize the study of households, where we can document the social and labor history of families, as well as the cultural practices that help create family life and learning (see, for example, Moll, 2014, Ch. 4). These practices include "exchange relations" that help constitute social and economic activities. It is through networks of exchange that households of modest means can obtain additional resources that may prove essential to their well-being. I am referring here to everyday or mundane activities that form part of the *quid pro quo* of life.

Therefore, when a study avoids, even though it may seem reasonable or advisable, entering a single household and establishing at least the beginnings of social relations of trust with family members, among others who might reside in the household, I understand it but I do not necessarily approve. It is, in effect, the case of educators losing out on valuable opportunities to gather insights on daily life and education, and to learn how to think about culture as dynamic and changing, never fixed or static, and full of agency and versatility, especially in response to the many different and often difficult circumstances of material life. That said, my reservations aside, given the challenges faced by the researchers in the present volume, exemplified perhaps by the work of Giraldo, Solórzano, and Huerta with previously incarcerated, gang-affiliated, men and women of color seeking higher education and the difficulties they have faced, including damaging "micro-aggressions," tailoring the methods to the study's intent certainly makes sense. As such, I also commend the various authors' attempts at openness, at developing novel theoretical combinations and methods befitting their participants and their particular study conditions, as well as the goals of their study.

A second point regards enhancing, through the documentation and understanding of funds of knowledge, representations of families and students. In my view, many teachers, especially those from the middle class teaching in working-class communities, only have a marginal understanding of their students, especially if those students are from the working class and thus vulnerable to stereotypes and deprivation arguments. It is also the case that most teachers do not live in the same community as the students. The household visits, then, are a way of engaging teachers strategically with their cultural environments for teaching. Doing research on funds of knowledge helps create representations of the families based not on some imagined deficit or trait, but on the documentation of cultural practices, such as the presence of biliteracy in household life, among other assets. In other words, rather than a piecemeal or second-hand impression of students and their families (which is, at best, what many teachers have), a funds of knowledge approach offers teachers, or professors, as the case may be, a more thorough understanding of their students, regardless of class background. A good example is found in the chapters in this volume by George Mwangi on African immigrant students, by Montiel on undocumented college students in private universities, and by García on arts education and creative resistance.

The third point regards teacher development and agency. A central aspect of the original work was to create study groups that would enhance the teachers' understanding of the study (including ethical issues that arise in any such study) through the development of their own case studies, which include acquiring a theoretical vocabulary to address study dynamics and findings, and to take the lead pedagogically in how to build on the insights provided by the study (for an elaboration of these practices, see González, Moll, & Amanti, 2005; Moll, 2014, Ch. 4). We came to conclude that as important as creating circumstances for student development is, it is just as important as establishing additive conditions for the development of teachers as educators. Teachers, whether in elementary school or in college, must keep learning from each other, educating themselves, and developing their craft, if they have any hope of addressing pedagogically and fruitfully the changing and challenging circumstances for student advancement.

I close by congratulating the editors and authors on the pathbreaking volume they have prepared. It is bold work they have undertaken with the goal of helping others access resources in a variety of circumstances and succeed in their advanced studies.

Luis C. Moll
University of Arizona

References

González, N., Moll, L. C., & Amanti, C. (2005). *Funds of knowledge: Theorizing practices in households, communities, and classrooms.* Mahwah, NJ: Erlbaum.
Moll, L. C. (2014). *L.S. Vygotsky and education.* New York, NY: Routledge.
Varenne, H. (2007). Difficult collective deliberations: Anthropological notes towards a theory of education. *Teachers College Record, 109*(7), 1559–1588.

PREFACE

Our Funds of Knowledge Journey

The book you are holding in your hands is a collaborative effort of many educators and practitioners who share a commitment to equity and social justice. Our funds of knowledge journeys (FKJ) have different starting points and have taken different routes that converge in this book. It was in 2007 when I (Cecilia Rios-Aguilar) had completed my dissertation, titled *"An Examination of the Relationship between Latina/o Households' Funds of Knowledge and Latina/o Students' Reading Achievement and Literacy Outcomes,"* and became an Assistant Professor at the Center for the Study of Higher Education at the University of Arizona. I was starting my academic career with so much excitement because I was going to be in the same building as Norma González and Luis Moll. They had inspired much of my scholarship, and I was about to collaborate with them on several projects that involved describing how families' funds of knowledge (FK) could be used to improve the education of many underrepresented students in Arizona. I was concerned, though, that I may not succeed in a higher education department while embracing a funds of knowledge approach in my scholarship. I was not sure the field of higher education would appreciate and understand my research.

Also, in 2007, I met Dr. Judy Marquez Kiyama. She was then a graduate student in the Center for the Study of Higher Education. She was conducting her dissertation, titled *"Funds of Knowledge and College Ideologies: Lived Experiences among Mexican-American Families."*

We connected immediately in our interest to conduct research from a funds-of-knowledge perspective. We engaged in many thoughtful conversations about funds of knowledge and how it related to other concepts, such as cultural and social capital. As a result of our many interactions and interests, we decided to embark on this FKJ together. We wrote and published our first paper on the relationship between funds of knowledge and the forms of capital (*Funds of Knowledge for the Poor and Forms of Capital for the Rich?*).[1] We then began to conceptualize how funds of knowledge could be used to study Latina/o students' transitions into college.[2] After publishing these manuscripts, we felt compelled to continue thinking more systematically about what it meant to conduct research on funds of knowledge in a higher education context. So, we continued exploring, both theoretically and through research studies, the connection between students', families', and communities' FK and students' transition to college. Here we are, ten years after our initial encounter, offering this book to scholars and practitioners who are committed to combating deficit thinking in higher education contexts.

How This Book Is Organized

This unique book for both educators and researchers discusses these contributions and maps the future work on FK in higher education. Part 1: Enriching the Concept of Funds of Knowledge discusses the need of a FK approach in postsecondary contexts, summarizes the vast empirical literature on FK, and presents the conceptual refinements to the notion of FK in relation to other frameworks (e.g., forms of capital, critical pedagogy (CP), and critical race theory (CRT)). Specifically, Chapter 1 argues that in order to help underrepresented students persist and succeed in college, we must focus our efforts on recognizing, validating, *and* utilizing the wealth of resources they bring to college campuses. Chapter 2 offers a detailed conceptual analysis of the relationship between FK and economic, social, and cultural capital (including the notions of habitus and field). Our goal is to illuminate tensions and similarities between these concepts. Chapter 3 presents a thorough and extensive content analysis of the existing literature on FK and the forms of capital to help our audience understand the existing knowledge gaps and how to fill them. Chapter 4 examines the relationship between FK, community cultural wealth (CCW), and CRT, and uses data from a case study on the educational and occupational trajectories of formerly incarcerated men and women to illustrate the need to intersect FK with CCW in careful, intentional, and meaningful ways. We end this section with Chapter 5, which offers a presentation of the concept of *creative resistance*. This notion is a form of arts-based resistance that is developed when FK, CP, and CRT are used, simultaneously, to combat deficit thinking. The chapter explains how the creative resistance is structured and the role it has in developing sociopolitical awareness, resistance, and resilience for working-class students.

Part 2: College Access and Persistence summarizes the work on FK and the transition to college among underrepresented students (e.g., Latinas/os and immigrants). Because the scholarship on college access has been published in other venues, Chapter 6 is a reprint of a published article that explores how FK in Mexican American families contributed to the development of educational ideologies.

Unique to this study is the extension of FK beyond traditional K–12 discussions and the incorporation of outreach literature into this framework when studying issues of college access. Chapter 7 explores the educational experiences of the children of African immigrants from a funds of knowledge perspective. Specifically, this chapter examines how African immigrant families communicate about academic expectations and college going to their children. This section ends with Chapter 8, which focuses on examining the college experience of undocumented students in the context of private colleges and universities.

Part 3: Funds of Knowledge as a Pedagogical Tool for Student Success in Higher Education introduces FK as a pedagogical tool for student success in higher education. Chapter 9 examines the FK existent in community college contexts, and how faculty can utilize them to alter their pedagogical practices and help students succeed in college. Chapter 10 examines how students' FK could be used in Career and Technical Education (CTE) programs to improve the educational and career trajectories of underrepresented students. And Chapter 11 examines the role of FK as a culturally relevant pedagogy in higher education classrooms. The final chapter of the book, in the form of a conclusion, offers reflections on the contributions of the chapters and focuses on highlighting the challenges and opportunities to utilizing a FK approach in higher education.

ABOUT THE EDITORS

Judy Marquez Kiyama is an Associate Professor in the Higher Education department at the University of Denver's Morgridge College of Education. Dr. Kiyama's research examines the structures that shape educational opportunities for underserved groups through an asset-based lens to better understand the collective knowledge and resources drawn upon to confront, negotiate, and (re)shape such structures. Her research is organized into three interconnected areas: the role of parents and families; equity and power in educational research; and underserved groups as collective networks of change.

Cecilia Rios-Aguilar is Associate Professor of Education and Director of the Higher Education Research Institute in the Graduate School of Education and Information Studies at the University of California, Los Angeles. Dr. Rios-Aguilar's research is multidisciplinary and uses a variety of conceptual frameworks—funds of knowledge and the forms of capital—and of statistical approaches—regression analysis, multilevel models, spatial analyses and geographic information systems (GIS), and social network analysis—to study the educational and occupational trajectories of underrepresented minorities. Dr. Rios-Aguilar's research interests include critical quantitative research methods, big data, social media, community colleges, and educational policies. She obtained her PhD in Education Theory and Policy from the University of Rochester, her MS in Educational Administration from the University of Rochester, and her BA in Economics from the Instituto Tecnológico Autónomo de México (ITAM).

ACKNOWLEDGMENTS

We would like to express our gratitude to Luis Moll and Norma González for inspiring thousands of scholars, like us, to conduct research that highlights the wealth of resources embedded in all students' lives. Documenting the funds of knowledge that students (and their families and communities) bring to colleges and universities is not an easy task. We have to be open to learn from and with students, and we have to be committed to working with faculty and practitioners to find various ways of strategically utilizing these resources to improve the educational experiences of underrepresented students.

Thanks to Judy Marquez Kiyama, a mother scholar who has shared with me (Cecilia) her brilliance, her strengths, and her vulnerabilities. She has a heart of gold. She is an amazing mother, a superb scholar, and a loyal and generous friend who has always been with me. I am a better scholar and person because of you. You know that I would have never been able to do this work by myself. Gracias por todo.

Thank you to Cecilia Rios-Aguilar, who from our meeting on day one, has been excited and willing to go on this funds of knowledge journey. Cecilia has shared with me (Judy)—and countless students—kindness, a giving spirit, and scholarly brilliance. Cecilia is more than my funds of knowledge partner; she has also taught me about being a strong mother, about believing in your worth, and pursuing your dreams. Thank you, my friend.

Thanks to all our students (and colleagues) who contributed to this book— you are challenging deficit thinking in higher education. You have the capacity, courage, and corazón needed to change the status quo. You have and you will continue to positively influence the academic and occupational trajectories of thousands of students. Gracias por todo.

We also want to thank our families in Mexico and Arizona for their uncondi
tional love and support. Thanks to our husbands and our children for being our
sources of inspiration. Gracias a Arturo, Liliana, Raul, Frank, Francesca y Frank Jr.
por su paciencia y apoyo. We love you.

Notes

1 Rios-Aguilar, C., Kiyama, J. M., Gravitt, M., & Moll, L.C. (2011). Funds of knowledge
   for the poor and forms of capital for the rich? A Capital approach to examining funds
   of knowledge. *Theory and Research in Education, 9*(2), 163–184.
2 Rios-Aguilar, C., & Kiyama, J. M. (2012). Funds of knowledge: A proposed approach
   to study Latina/o students' transition to college. *Journal of Latinos and Education, 11*(1),
   2–16.

PART 1
Enriching the Concept of Funds of Knowledge

1

INTRODUCTION

The Need for a Funds of Knowledge Approach in Higher Education Contexts

Cecilia Rios-Aguilar and Judy Marquez Kiyama

It has been over 20 years since the term funds of knowledge—the existing resources, knowledge, and skills embedded in students and their families (Moll, Amanti, Neff, & González, 1992)—emerged in the literature. The term was very well received in the field of education, particularly in the K–12 context. Indeed, the research on funds of knowledge (FK) has become a standard reference to signal a 'sociocultural' orientation in education that seeks to build strategically on the experiences, resources, and knowledge of families and children, especially those from low-income neighborhoods (Moll, Soto-Santiago, & Schwartz, 2013). After decades of research, what we know is that the FK generated, accumulated, and transmitted by students (and their families and communities) bring abundant possibilities for facilitating the success of under-represented students' education (Moll et al., 2013; Rodríguez, 2013). Indeed, it is the connection between teachers (and their pedagogical approaches and practices) and families' sociocultural, linguistic, and intellectual resources that makes the funds of knowledge approach appealing, relevant, meaningful, possible, and very much needed (Moll et al., 2013).

Since the concept appeared in the literature, the scholarship on FK has inspired a wealth of research and practice in many different places throughout the world and fields. And, recently, it has also been used to examine issues related to college access and transition among Latina/o students (see Rios-Aguilar & Kiyama, 2012; Kiyama, 2010). Funds of knowledge, as a concept, was first introduced in the higher education scholarship by Estela Bensimon. In her 2007 presidential address to the *Association for the Study of Higher Education*, she highlighted the role that FK play in helping faculty to see students and families in terms of possibilities (Rios-Aguilar & Kiyama, 2012), thus countering the negative representations of under-represented students that plague the field of higher education.

Unfortunately, the available literature on college access, persistence, and success is rife with reasons why under-represented students disproportionately fail. The predominant view is one of individually based deficits. Furthermore, the scholarship in higher education tends to assume individuals are able to control their own circumstances, have the freedom to make a variety of choices, and can respond to challenges in predictable, linear, and logical ways (Bensimon, 2007). As a result, when under-represented students appear to make choices that do not lead to successful outcomes (for example, stop or drop out of school in order to take care of family members or to find employment), it is through this individualistic deficit paradigm that they are assessed. Our concern is that the field of higher education is perpetuating the idea that under-represented students (and their families and communities) are lacking or deficient simply because they are not doing what 'successful' students do. Since this is the lens through which services, programs, and policies were and are created, it is no wonder why participation, retention, and graduation rates remain painfully low for under-represented college students around the country.

Another area of research in which a deficit paradigm persists in higher education is related to teaching and learning. For most college students, the main point of student contact and connection occurs within the classroom context (Chang, 2005; Cotten & Wilson, 2006; Deil-Amen, 2011). Most importantly, the ties created within the classroom are key sources of students' sense of belonging in college, which can improve students' persistence and success (Deil-Amen, 2011). Also, researchers have found racial/ethnic minority students are especially receptive to frequent and meaningful interaction with faculty (Chang, 2005; Kim & Sax, 2009). Scholarship that supports increased interaction between students and faculty has also found that the quality of student-faculty relationships is a stronger predictor of learning than student background (Lundberg & Schreiner, 2004; Cotten & Wilson, 2006). The far-reaching and significant value that faculty contribute to the college experience of their students should not be underestimated.

The pedagogical choices faculty make are, indeed, determined by specific perceptions of the students they teach. Similar to the K–12 context, the dominant narrative of under-represented students, particularly those attending community colleges, is that they are unprepared and not as committed to their educational endeavors as other, more successful college students (Mora, 2016). Poor academic performance is often couched in explanations that reinforce the perspective that student deficiencies are the reasons for low academic achievement (Valencia, 2010). Rather than exploring alternative explanations for low student performance, it is often easier for faculty and their respective institutions to explain academic failure as student deficiencies (Mora, 2016). Barnett (2010) correctly points out that extant research on college persistence has neglected to expound on the role of faculty and their pedagogical choices in student success and persistence decisions.

While the importance of interaction between faculty and students is well documented, we know very little about actual teaching and learning processes in higher education contexts. And sadly, despite the escalating evidence on the low persistence and completion rates in colleges in general, and in community colleges in particular, classroom instruction and teaching practices and pedagogies have been, for the most part, under-investigated and under-theorized. We argue that research on classrooms in postsecondary contexts must be conducted from a non-deficit approach. Scholars should investigate more than simply students' attitudes; they must pay attention to the ample resources and knowledge that students bring to their classrooms, and how these can be strategically utilized to improve their learning and academic outcomes. Furthermore, we need to challenge the perceptions faculty have of the students they teach by inviting faculty to get to know students more deeply. According to Grubb and Cox (2005), "faculty are generally sympathetic to the 'busied up' conditions caused by work and family responsibilities" (p. 95). Unfortunately, however, being sympathetic only reinforces their deficit perspective of the students they teach (i.e., their capacity to learn) and the ways such students should be taught.

We argue in this book that a funds of knowledge approach can help faculty to consider students' backgrounds and living conditions as sources of valuable knowledge rather than mere impediments to college-level learning. Furthermore, it is important to move beyond knowing that students are busy and have many responsibilities. Instead, faculty could learn in a deeper way about how students (and their families) navigate their resources (i.e., FK) and vulnerabilities (i.e., periods of unemployment, taking care of family members, financial scarcity, illness, etc.) in order to succeed in college.

In sum, to combat existing deficit thinking that plagues the field of higher education, we propose the use of FK to examine issues related to the transition to college, college persistence and success, and pedagogies in higher education. The goal of the present volume, therefore, is not to recapitulate work done previously, but to elaborate a FK approach for the context of higher education. In doing so, we advance an understanding of funds of knowledge by relating it to other key conceptual frameworks used in the field of higher education, including the forms of capital, critical race theory (CRT), community cultural wealth (CCW), and critical pedagogy (CP). To our knowledge, no other publication or scholarship exists that has refined the concept of FK in a careful, sophisticated, and multidisciplinary way. Finally, our goal in this book is to offer a balanced perspective. This concretely means that we do not suggest that using FK are the panacea to the problems related to college access, persistence, and success. Indeed, there remain a host of structural issues that affect students' decisions and the way they see themselves as college students, thus complicating their academic success. Instead, in this book, we critically examine what FK can (and cannot) do to improve researchers' and practitioners' understanding of under-represented students' trajectories and experiences in college.

References

Barnett, E. A. (2010). Validation experiences and persistence among community college students. *Review of Higher Education, 34*(2), 193–230.

Bensimon, E. M. (2007). The underestimated significance of practitioner knowledge in the scholarship on student success. *Review of Higher Education, 30*(4), 441–469.

Chang, J. C. (2005). Faculty-student interaction at the community college: A focus on students of color. *Research in Higher Education, 46*(7), 769–802.

Cotten, S. R., & Wilson, B. (2006). Student-faculty interactions: Dynamics and determinants. *Higher Education, 51*(4), 487–519.

Deil-Amen, R. (2011). Socio-academic integrative moments: Rethinking academic and social integration among two-year college students in career-related programs. *Journal of Higher Education, 82*(1), 54–91.

Grubb, N., & Cox, R. (2005). Pedagogical alignment and curricular consistency: The challenges for developmental education. *New Directions for Community Colleges, 129*, 93–103.

Kim, Y. K., & Sax, L. J. (2009). Student-faculty interaction in research universities: Differences by student gender, race, social class, and first generation status. *Research in Higher Education, 50*(5), 437–459.

Kiyama, J. M. (2010). College aspirations and limitations: The role of educational ideologies and funds of knowledge in Mexican American families. *American Educational Research Journal, 47*, 330–356. doi:10.3102/0002831209357468

Lundberg, C. A., & Schreiner, L. A. (2004). Quality and frequency of faculty-student interaction as predictor of learning: An analysis by student race/ethnicity. *Journal of College Student Development, 45*(5), 549–565.

Moll, L. C., Amanti, C., Neff, D., & González, N. (1992). Funds of knowledge for teaching: Using a qualitative approach to connect homes and classrooms. *Theory Into Practice, XXXI*, 132–141. doi:10.1080/00405849209543534

Moll, L. C., Soto-Santiago, S., & Schwartz, L. (2013). Funds of knowledge in changing communities. In K. Hall, T. Cremin, B. Comber, & L. Moll (Eds.), *International handbook of research on children's literacy, learning, and culture* (pp. 172–183). West Sussex, UK: Wiley-Blackwell.

Mora, J. (2016). *Aligning practice with pedagogy: Funds of knowledge for community college teaching.* Unpublished doctoral dissertation, Claremont Graduate University.

Rios-Aguilar, C., & Kiyama, J. (2012). Funds of knowledge: An approach to study Latina(o) students' transition to college. *Journal of Latinos and Education, 11*, 2–16. doi:10.1080/15348431.2012.631430

Rodriguez, G. M. (2013). Power and agency in education: Exploring the pedagogical dimensions of funds of knowledge. *Review of Research in Education, 37*, 87–120. doi:10.3102/0091732x12462686

Valencia, R. (2010). *Dismantling contemporary deficit thinking: Educational thought and practice.* New York, NY: Routledge.

2

A COMPLEMENTARY FRAMEWORK

Funds of Knowledge and the Forms of Capital

Cecilia Rios-Aguilar and Judy Marquez Kiyama

Our interest in examining the relationship between funds of knowledge and the forms of capital started very early in our academic careers. Our scholarship started to highlight the connections between these frameworks, and our interest in understanding these links grew over time. We wrote our initial ideas on the link between these concepts in a paper titled, "*Funds of Knowledge for the Poor and Forms of Capital for the Rich?*" (Rios-Aguilar, Kiyama, Gravitt, & Moll, 2011). Our article was very well received in various academic circles. Since then, our thinking about these frameworks has evolved, and we feel compelled to offer education scholars (both in K–12 and higher education) a more careful and expanded analysis of these frameworks. The goal of this chapter, then, is to clarify the disciplinary origins of the forms of capital and funds of knowledge, and to highlight the strengths, as well as the tensions, that complicate the understanding and the use of these notions to study issues of equity, power, and pedagogical change in the field of education. Furthermore, we elaborate on important aspects and distinctions that educational researchers must understand and acknowledge when utilizing these concepts. We start by discussing the notion of social capital; we then turn to the concept of cultural capital and include a careful discussion of habitus and field. Next, we present the concept of funds of knowledge. Finally, we conclude with a discussion of how the frameworks can be used collaboratively to assist educational researchers in developing a better understanding of power relations and change in educational institutions. In suggesting a new approach to conduct educational research, we also recognize the need to further understand how, when, and why the concepts are used interchangeably and are often (mis)used. One contribution in this chapter is the early formation of a complementary framework that builds on the strengths of each conceptual framework. However, as we demonstrate in Chapter 3, educational researchers have begun to reference, compare, and/or use these frameworks together; therefore, a complementary framework can prove to be useful in the study of educational inequities for marginalized populations.

The Theory of Social Capital

Social capital has become a key concept in policy-making and academic spheres (Edwards, 2004). Generally, social capital is concerned with the resources that individuals (and organizations) can access, which both result in, and are the result of, collective and socially negotiated ties and relationships (Edwards, 2004). Particular notions of social capital have become dominant and influential in the field of education. A definition of social capital that has permeated the scholarship in education is the one offered by James Coleman (1988). He defined social capital as "a variety of entities with two elements in common: they all consist of some aspect of social structure, and they facilitate certain actions of actors . . . within the structure" (Portes, 1998, p. 8). From this vantage point, social capital can be thought of as any resource that facilitates individual or collective action, generated by networks of relationships, reciprocity, trust, and social norms (Coleman, 1988). Furthermore, Coleman's research on the relationship between social and human capitals focused on the role parental action (or its absence) plays on the transfer of capital to children and its effects on educational performance. As a result of his approach, the idea that parental involvement is a key form of social capital that affects students' educational outcomes has become part of conventional thinking in the field of educational policy and practice (Edwards, 2004).

Another prominent definition of social capital came from Bourdieu (1973, 1986), who noted that people intentionally built their relationships for the benefits they believed would be provided at a later time (Portes, 2000). Bourdieu's (1986) conception of social capital is interdependent with a range of other capital resources (e.g., cultural, linguistic, and symbolic capital) and is rooted in the concept of economic capital—resources and possessions that are immediately convertible into money (which makes them quantifiable). According to Bourdieu (1986), social capital is defined as "the aggregate of the actual potential resources which are linked to possession of a durable network of more or less institutionalized relationships of mutual acquaintance or recognition" (p. 246). Bourdieu (1986) sees clear profit as being the main reason that actors engage in and maintain links in a network. That profit is not necessarily economic, but according to Bourdieu, it can be reduced to economic profit. For example, there are goods and services to which economic capital gives immediate access to; others can only be obtained by the virtue of a social capital of relationships, which cannot act instantly, unless it has been created and maintained over a certain period of time. Furthermore, Bourdieu (1986) posits that an actor's potential for accruing profit and control of social capital are differentially distributed (Tzanakis, 2013). This concretely means that actors occupy distinctive positions in social space and, therefore, have different opportunities to access and activate social capital. This differential distribution of potential and control is a central notion in Bourdieu's theories of social reproduction (Tzanakis, 2013).

There exist important political and theoretical distinctions in Bourdieu's and Coleman's definitions. Coleman's definition follows the *functionalist* perspective, while Bourdieu's is aligned with the *conflict theory* tradition. Functionalism is a broad perspective in sociology that sets out to interpret society as a structure with interrelated parts (Collins, 1971). Functionalism addresses society as a whole in terms of the function of its constituent elements, namely, norms, customs, traditions, and institutions (Collins, 1971). The pioneering work on functionalist analysis of education was that of Durkheim. Despite many differences of detail and emphasis, functionalist approaches to education, as argued by Morrow and Torres (1995), share a number of key analytical arguments. The characteristic emphasis is on the selective functions of education (i.e., academic, distributive, economic, and political socialization functions) and their overall positive influence upon social development, despite the ongoing need for reform and adjustments (Morrow & Torres, 1995). In sum, from the functionalist perspective on social reality, social capital is looked upon as a central condition of social integration and cohesion, academic and economic success, and the well-being of people (Schultheis, 2014).

Conflict theory, on the other hand, sees social life as a struggle and focuses on the distribution of resources, power, and inequality (Collins, 1971). According to Collins (1990), the basic themes in conflict theory are the following: (a) the central feature of social organization is stratification, (b) the causes of what happens in society are to be sought in the interests of groups and individuals, (c) who wins what in these struggles depends on the resources controlled by each faction, and (d) social change is driven by conflict. Conflict theory is rooted in the ideas of Marx, Engels, and Weber, who believed that society is a dynamic entity constantly undergoing change driven by class conflict (Collins, 1971). This perspective is deeply rooted in a sociological vision of social and economic relationships as being largely based on power, domination, inequalities, and class structures. One of the most important features of conflict theory is that it does not take norms, values, and standards as givens (Collins, 1971). Instead, conflict theorists show the conditions under which ideas and ideals are generated, how they produce solidarity, when they aid domination by giving them legitimacy, and when these processes generate conflict (Collins, 1990). Having these considerations in mind, we now move to discuss how these political and conceptual perspectives operate more concretely in Coleman's and Bourdieu's notions of social capital.

Following the functionalist tradition, social and moral norms were important in Coleman's conceptualization. This normative mindset assumes that individuals are bound to the collective via belief systems, commitment to common values, and community engagement (Lin, 2000; Portes, 2000). Therefore, social relations are productive only when people adhere to the norms and values the social structure prescribes (Coleman, 1988). Trustworthiness and obligation, then, are the pivotal foundations of social capital in Coleman's conception. In fact, without a high degree of both of these elements, societies (or communities) cannot sustain themselves (Coleman, 1988). Furthermore, he used this rationale to advance his analysis of the conditions and outcomes of families and communities using a deficit model to compare dropout rates between public and Catholic private schools. Coleman (1988) claimed that Catholic private high school communities were comprised of students in intact families—two-parent families embedded in networks that necessitate intergenerational closure—and that was the primary reason why private high schools were more academically successful than the public ones. In other words, he insisted that absence or lack of social capital is the result of being born (or socialized) into specific family forms (e.g., single-parent homes, households with many members, parents with low levels of formal education, etc.) and not the way educational institutions were structured or organized (Stanton-Salazar, 2004). Following this line of thought, then, marginalized groups of students are only going to be academically (and, we argue, occupationally) successful if they adhere to prescribed norms.

Coleman's conceptualization has pervaded the field of education. For decades, researchers (e.g., McLeod, 1987; Stinchcombe, 1964) have shown how educators have defined (and continue to define) desirable family-school and student-teacher relationships as based on the following values and norms: trust, partnership, collaboration, cooperation, admiration, and respect. Most importantly, research (e.g., Dufur, Parcel, & Troutman, 2013; McNeal, 1999) indicates that students' and parents' compliance with these norms and standards provide them with various forms of social capital, which in turn translate into higher academic achievement and success. Consequently, for scholars who adhere to Coleman's conception of social capital, there is virtually no space for thinking that educational institutions can contribute to produce inequities, particularly for under-represented students.

On the other hand, the central thrust of Bourdieu's work in education is the exploration of the relationship between the education system and social class structure. Bourdieu (1977) claimed that the educational system served to maintain rather than to reduce inequality. Bourdieu, therefore, rejects functionalists' theories that either ascribe the effects of domination to a single, central apparatus or fail to see how the dominated participate in their own oppression (Giroux, 1983). This rejection becomes clear in Bourdieu's theory of schooling in which he attempts to link the notions of structure and human agency through an analysis of the relationships among dominant culture, school knowledge, and individual biographies (Giroux, 1983). Bourdieu argues against the notion that schools simply reflect the dominant society. Instead, he claims that educational institutions are relatively autonomous and influenced only indirectly by more powerful economic and political institutions (Giroux, 1983). Rather than being linked directly to the power of an economic elite, educational institutions are conceived as part of a larger universe of institutions that do not overtly impose compliance and oppression, but reproduce existing power relations more subtly through the production and distribution of a dominant culture that quietly confirms what it means to be educated (Giroux, 1983).

From research that adheres to Bourdieu's notion (e.g., Stanton-Salazar, 2004; Lareau, 2000), we have learned that actors' social class and positions within the field of education provide them with unique opportunities to access, to possess, and to activate certain forms of social (and cultural) capital. This line of scholarship concentrates on illuminating how specific institutional and ideological forces make access to social capital and institutional support within schools and other institutional settings incredibly difficult for under-represented children and youth (and for their families), thus perpetuating educational inequities (Stanton-Salazar, 2004). This conception of social capital also provides some clues as to how some under-represented students are able to manage their difficult participation in multiple worlds, how they develop cultural strategies for overcoming various obstacles, and how they manage to develop sustaining and supportive relationships with key agents in and out of the educational system (Stanton-Salazar & Dornbusch, 1995).

The Theory of Cultural Capital

Bourdieu (1977, 1986) first used the concept of cultural capital—the different sets of linguistic and cultural competencies, knowledge, and dispositions that are passed from one generation to another by way of the class-located boundaries of their family—to analyze how culture and education interact, thereby contributing to the theorizing of the social reproduction of inequality (Roscigno & Ainsworth-Darnell, 1999). For Bourdieu (1986), cultural capital can exist in three different forms. *Embodied* is an essential component of an individual and cannot be purchased because it requires specific competence closely linked to the person, bound to a cultural or class community; *objectified* separates the dominant from those who are marginalized because it requires possession of valued cultural goods (e.g., books, instruments, and paintings); and *institutionalized* predisposes value and qualification for possession, hence exclusivity (Bourdieu, 1986).

Bourdieu drew on Weber's theories of exclusionary processes, and Durkheim's theories of social classification, to develop a theoretical framework explaining the influence of class culture on social privilege and individual outcomes (Lamont & Lareau, 1988). Concretely, Bourdieu applied his theory primarily to schools, which he viewed to be the institutions with the most significant influence in perpetuating the relationship between class and culture (Kingston, 2001). Research has shown that socially privileged children generally perform better academically and go further in their education (Lareau, 2000). Because education is seen as the "predominant pathway to economic success" (Kingston, 2001, p. 88), the importance of cultural capital should not be ignored. One of Bourdieu's main arguments was that schools are not neutral settings created to provide equal opportunities for its students. Instead, they are reproducers of social structure and class relations (Kingston, 2001).

As is the case for social capital, we cannot forget that for Bourdieu, cultural capital is inextricably linked to the notion of economic capital. In fact, Bourdieu crafted what Erickson (1996) refers to as a "two-capital model" (p. 218), including a vertical and horizontal ranking of cultural and economic capital. The vertical ranking is determined by "cultural volume" (Erickson, 1996, p. 218), that is, the amount of both economic and cultural capital held by each class. Based on Bourdieu's theory, both forms of capital are smallest for those at the bottom of the class structure, and increase with class levels. Horizontal differences account for "the composition of capital, or the strength of cultural capital versus economic capital" (Erickson, 1996, p. 218). That is, for Bourdieu, the acquisition of cultural capital is facilitated by economic capital, thus allowing economic elites to purchase and/or to access more cultural capital, which in turn increases their access to social capital, and then assists in accumulating more economic capital. In sum, for Bourdieu, the acquisition and exercise of cultural and social capital help to explain how economic capital is maintained and reproduced from generation to generation. Thus, theoretical and empirical analyses of Bourdieu's forms of capital and, consequently, of social class must include a discussion of economic capital and how it reproduces and/or exacerbates inequities.

A constant tension permeating the field of education is related to the fact that several scholars have engaged in efforts to relativize or 'multiculturalize' the concept of cultural capital. In an attempt to celebrate the concept's diversity (see Lubienski, 2003, for an elaborate discussion), scholars argue that all groups of students (and families and communities), including marginalized and under-represented groups, possess some forms and some degree of cultural capital. In fact, a proliferation of cultural capitals has emerged in the literature. These include "familial capital" (Yosso, 2005), "resistant capital" (Yosso, 2005), "hip hop capital" (Clay, 2003), and "intercultural capital" (Pöllmann, 2013). Researchers argue that these various forms of cultural capital are part of under-represented students' repertoire of resources, strengths, and assets that they utilize to combat educational, social, and racial inequities. Unfortunately, these alleged forms of cultural capital cannot be considered capital within Bourdieu's theory. Educational scholars need to be clear about the fact that subaltern forms of cultural practice are *not* forms of capital per se. These forms of cultural practice may have their worth or internal logic, but they need to be placed within the struggle over power as defined by the rules of a particular field, as Bourdieu elaborated on his theory. This field, then, needs to be placed in a relationship with other fields, and not detached from them in order to get a clearer picture of social power. For example, cultural practices in highly segregated neighborhoods do not garner enough power outside of their local expression to be considered forms of capital. Consequently, claiming that *all* groups of students, particularly those that are lower in status, have cultural capital only contributes to reinforce achievement ideologies. If cultural capital is emptied of its relational, explanatory import, then power is confounded or not integrated appropriately into theoretical and empirical analyses.

In sum, scholars in the field of education need to reflect on the value and purpose of calling cultural capital the various resources, knowledge, and skills that under-represented students (and their families and communities) possess. Without any doubt, reacting to deficit models that have systematically denied under-represented students of equitable educational opportunities is important. However, we cannot only aspire to counter dominant paradigms by speaking the language of the dominant group. This strategy contributes to misusing Bourdieu's notion of cultural capital. Thus, instead of instilling in students the ideology that acquiring and activating more and more capitals (e.g., social and cultural) will make them successful in school and in life, education scholars and practitioners must develop strategies and practices to make students aware that the process of domination is a strategic game. At the same time, educators must find ways to empower low-status students to figure out how to empty capital of any meaning through the demolition of the systems that sustain it. By focusing exclusively on the "capital" illusion in our scholarship, we are simply trying various ways to make the existing social arrangement work without any payoff. We recognize that while strategies for change may exist, we are likely not using fruitful strategies. Designing and implementing effective plans to change the status quo is going to require more careful thought and action.

To conclude this discussion on social and cultural capital, we elaborate on the centrality of the notion of economic capital in any discussion of social class. Education scholars must be aware that any invocation or use of the idea of social class (in relation to cultural and social capital) that does not incorporate an analysis of economic capital is inaccurate. In other words, when social class is bracketed off from economic capital, scholars lose the ability to capture the importance of how reproduction actually works. This becomes an important point as educational institutions become more segregated along lines of race/ethnicity, language, and class, thus guaranteeing that certain educational spaces are sites of concentrated economic capital, while others (by design) have an utter lack of economic capital. Thus, the tendency to focus exclusively on social and cultural capital viciously ignores that, for example, wealthier public and private educational institutions are able to raise large amounts of money to be shared only among a student body made up almost entirely of the children of affluent families. To be sure, that may be a concentration of cultural and social capital as well, but we should not neglect analysis of this concentration of economic capital, and the political-economic processes that contribute to it.

Capital in Relation to Habitus and Field

Capital, habitus, and field, together, provide a powerful conceptual tool in which method and theory converge as "a way of understanding the world" (Reay, 2004

p. 439). However, most often, educational research takes on the theoretical tool of the forms of capital without engaging or explaining field or habitus. With some exceptions (e.g., McLeod, 1987), the concept of habitus in particular is given little attention in research—when, in fact, field and capital have no meaning without habitus, or as Emirbayer and Johnson (2008) suggest, these concepts "make no sense" and are misappropriated when the three are not considered together (p. 1). In sum, researchers miss out on their potential methodological and theoretical usefulness (Emirbayer & Johnson, 2008; Reay, 2004) when ignoring habitus and field. We turn first to a brief overview of field.

Field

Bourdieu emphasizes that capital in its various forms "does not exist and function except in relation to a field" (Bourdieu & Wacquant, 1992, p. 101; Emirbayer & Johnson, 2008). Fields are more than an organization itself; fields are "structured spaces of positions whose properties depend on their position within these spaces which can be analyzed independently of the characteristics of their occupants" (Bourdieu as cited in Emirbayer & Johnson, 2008, p. 6). A field must be considered beyond relationships with organizations, but between the nodes that organizations occupy with a larger field network.

We can add to this definition the idea Emirbayer and Johnson (2008) developed about the need to think of organizations not as one field, but as a cluster of fields. In higher education, for example, one would not only consider a single university as the field, but the network of different postsecondary institutional types, the K–12 schools a student attended, the funding agencies responsible for providing means for students to attend, the families and communities, etc. The networks and structures found within a particular field are linked to their state of power relations; a state represents an ongoing struggle for domination over the field (Emirbayer & Johnson, 2008). Therefore, one must not only view field as a sum of agents or entities linked by interaction; we must also understand how objective relations are constitutive of the structure of the field which orient the struggles to conserve or transform it (Emirbayer & Johnson, 2008). With this perspective, we are pushed to look beyond the individual actors in organizations. Yet, most of the available scholarship in education reduces capital to what an individual possesses or lacks in relation to a field, often without explaining or identifying the field itself and how the field relates to access and activation of various forms of capital.

Habitus

Bourdieu defines habitus as a durable, but not entirely inflexible, system of learned attitudes, perceptions, and behaviors towards one's probabilities and possibilities in life (Bourdieu & Wacquant, 1992). Habitus, as Barrett and Martina (2012) explain, is developed through socialization within families and social groups, and ultimately contours one's understanding of one's position—and subsequent practices and actions—within a given 'field,' or site of struggle for various resources (Bourdieu & Passeron, 1977). Barrett and Martina (2012) suggest that while one's habitus is shaped early on, most often by family experiences, habitus is not deterministic. It is a generative embodiment that can be altered in different fields and social spaces by educational institutions, peers, and other organizations (Barrett & Martina, 2012; Reay, 2004). Yet, others (see Calhoun, 1993) argue that although habitus is generative and can be adjusted, its social position remains similar across trans-historical contexts, reinforcing the deterministic role of habitus in the theory of reproduction across different fields over time (Calhoun, 1993). Thus, habitus becomes an interplay between past and present (Reay, 2004). Furthermore, the type of one's capital and habitus imported into a field by each member has been created through past and present experiences in other fields (Emirbayer & Johnson, 2008). Therefore, habitus is acquired in certain conditions, like the social class of a family, and subsequently modified in other fields as individuals belong to multiple organizations both sequentially and simultaneously, resulting in an individual's primary and specific habitus (Emirbayer & Johnson, 2008; McLeod, 1987).

For Bourdieu, then, habitus links social structure and individual agency: "It is at once structured, by the patterned social forces that produced it, and structuring, [giving] form and coherence to the various activities of an individual across the separate spheres of life" (Wacquant, 2008, p. 268). Another way to think about habitus is offered by Emirbayer and Johnson's (2008) interpretation of Bourdieu's work: "habitus is a mechanism linking individual action and the macro-structural settings within which future action is taken" (p. 4). The (re) conditioning and modifying nature of habitus allows for new spaces of possibility and new position-taking within fields to be opened up, while at the same time structuring the perception of some of these possible positions as more desirable than others (Emirbayer & Johnson, 2008). Small signals embodied by individual habitus and behaviors then illustrate how organizational habitus structures such possible position-taking (Emirbayer & Johnson, 2008). We suggest that a student's stock of capital—and his or her understanding of the worth of these resources in a social field—are constitutive of their habitus, which, in turn, form a "matrix" of possibilities (Bourdieu, 1977, p. 83), and is generative of their actions within that field. Because habitus has a duality of being both collective and individualized, the concept offers an opportunity to explore and understand habitus of a field or class and a social space within a class (Reay, 2004), and an opportunity to understand how persons within that field or class internalize and construct dispositions of individual habitus (Emirbayer & Johnson, 2008; McLeod, 1987). Thus, there exists collective and individual trajectories that habitus embodies (Reay, 2004). Others would suggest there is a third conceptual use of habitus—that of organizational or institutional habitus (McDonough, 1997; Reay, 2004), which might represent a sub-space within a given field.

While the interpretation and application of Bourdieu's concept of habitus in educational research has been either deterministic or simply absent, researchers (e.g., Barrett & Martina, 2012; Emirbayer & Johnson, 2008) argue for the need to reconsider habitus and its relation with capital and field to actually appreciate the usefulness of Bourdieu's framework. By doing so, researchers will highlight the critical role that educational institutions play, not only in reproducing the system, but in actually providing concrete opportunities for under-represented students to succeed academically and in life. Bourdieu and Wacquant (1992) stated that "the habitus transformed by the action of the school, itself diversified, is in turn at the basis of all subsequent experiences . . . and so on, from restructuring to restructuring" (Bourdieu & Wacquant, 1992, p. 134). While habitus can largely be a self-perpetuating mechanism with a tendency towards reproduction, it can indeed be altered (Barrett & Martina, 2012). Therefore, a student's habitus is "permeable and responsive to what is going on around them" (Reay, 2004, p. 434) and is continually modified through socialization experiences in the world outside of the family (DiMaggio, 1982), including educational institutions. If researchers are not engaging the concepts of field and habitus in conjunction with capital, an important opportunity is missed. Namely, when an individual becomes conscious of their habitus within a certain field, important interplays between structure and agency abound (Barrett & Martina, 2012; Reay, 2004). Not only are educational institutions spaces of recognizing and reshaping one's habitus and capital, individuals within those spaces recognize and reshape their own habitus and capital, leading to the possibility of more equitable educational opportunities and outcomes (Barrett & Martina, 2012).

The Conceptual Framework of Funds of Knowledge

During the early 1990s, the concept of funds of knowledge emerged in the literature in relation to scholarship documenting the resources of working-class Latina/o families, mostly Mexican American in the U.S. Southwest, thus countering deficit perspectives common in depictions of these and other low-income families (Rios-Aguilar et al., 2011). The approach, rooted in anthropological studies of working-class Latina/o households, documented the varied bodies of knowledge that underlie families' productive activities. Central to this line of work were household visits to ethnographically document the families' life experiences, social and labor history, household practices, division of labor, ideologies about childrearing, and values about education that captured what was broadly referred to as their funds of knowledge (Rios-Aguilar et al., 2011). The research on funds of knowledge has become a standard reference to signal a 'socio-cultural' orientation in education that seeks to build strategically on the experiences, resources, and knowledge of families and children, especially those from low-income neighborhoods (Moll, Soto-Santiago, & Schwartz, 2013).

The essential idea in the research on funds of knowledge is that households, especially those in the working class, can be characterized by the practices they have developed and knowledge they have produced and acquired in living their lives (Moll et al., 2013). The social history of families, and their productive or labor activities in both the primary and secondary sectors of the economy, are particularly salient because they reveal experiences (e.g., in farming, construction, transborder transactions, institutional assistance, school programs, and occupational opportunities) that generate much of the knowledge household members may possess, display, elaborate, or share with others (Moll et al., 2013). Household survival may involve creating and contributing in social networks, often with friends and kin, through which such funds of knowledge may be exchanged in addressing some of life's exigencies (Moll et al., 2013). In other words, these funds are not only the stock of information and knowledge found among clusters of households, but the *currency of exchange* among such household arrangements (Vélez-Ibáñez, 1996).

The idea of lived experiences found in the scholarship on funds of knowledge is rooted in a Vygotskian perspective of *perezhivanie*, which is often translated into emotional or lived experiences (Esteban-Guitart & Moll, 2014). Esteban-Guitart and Moll (2014) suggest that lived experiences are created through participation in human activities, socialization, and education, all of which contribute to individuals' identities, thus revealing a connection between families' funds of knowledge and the funds of identity that are subsequently developed. These identities are embedded in historical cultural factors like social institutions, artifacts, and cultural beliefs. The funds of knowledge of families represent an intersection of anthropology, psychology, and education, of which they are a result of a Vygotskian notion of people's lived experiences (Esteban-Guitart & Moll, 2014). These lived experiences intersect with the social networks of families' households, or cluster households, which help to establish external resources that mediated life within the household (Moll, 2014). Moll (2014) further suggests that the funds of knowledge approach works to establish social relations with families that help mediate classroom life. Vygotsky's theoretical influence on understanding lived experiences and ideologies is important when presenting the introduction and development of funds of knowledge as pedagogical tools. Vygotsky suggests that "ideologies function as mediating devices" helping to give meaning to the "activities involved in becoming a student in a school setting" (Moll, 2014, p. 97). This connection is linked to Vygotsky's idea of zones of proximal development,[1] in that child development is interdependent and influenced by the social relations that offer resources, inclusive of the lived experiences and ideologies of cluster households, thus establishing a "sociocultural platform for their pedagogy" (Moll, 2014, p. 119).

One of the tensions surrounding funds of knowledge relates to the fact that many scholars have used the notion as "a theoretical validation of the social and cultural capital of communities that had been viewed without resources or capital of any kind" (González, Wyman, & O'Connor, 2011, p. 482). Furthermore, researchers argue that the funds of knowledge approach re-conceptualizes communities from a strength-based perspective, seeing the richness of knowledge and history within economic marginality, and providing a productive cultural setting that has been traditionally conceived as deprived (González et al., 2011). This particular interpretation and utilization of funds of knowledge, we argue, is problematic because it implies that all students (and their families and communities) have some forms of capital, when in fact, that is not the case. The efforts to challenge deficit paradigms through a funds of knowledge approach represent only a reaction to the functionalist usage of capital theories, like the definition of social capital offered by Coleman. There is no doubt that the lived experiences and knowledge of under-represented students are valuable and crucial starting points, but they need to be engaged in what critical approaches (i.e., Freire, 1973) have suggested: the process of understanding hidden meanings; the ones that lie at the unconscious level and are placed there by processes of domination. The point we make is that funds of knowledge do not occur outside of systems of oppression; they are constructed inside an ongoing struggle for and against domination. Consequently, while funds of knowledge offers many theoretical and pedagogical uses, limitations remain.

First, as mentioned earlier, this asset-based approach does *not* account for larger systemic issues of power or social conflict within educational systems. Second, a funds of knowledge approach does not offer a more careful and elaborated analysis of social class. In fact, González, Moll, and Amanti (2005) acknowledge that they concentrated their efforts in documenting the funds of knowledge of low-income Latina/o households. However, this does not mean that middle-class or upper-class families do not possess funds of knowledge. Actually, it is the case that students (and households and communities) from all different socioeconomic strata have funds of knowledge. Furthermore, it could be argued that families from middle and upper classes actually use their repertoire and wealth of funds of knowledge (and of forms of capital) to recreate systems of domination. Third, funds of knowledge has been critiqued for its limited methodological approaches and reliance on adult household practices as the primary unit of analysis (Esteban-Guitart & Moll, 2014; Rios-Aguilar et al., 2011). Fourth, there seems to be discrepancies in the way funds of knowledge are understood and applied in educational research. In a review of academic work drawing on funds of knowledge, Hogg (2011) found that funds of knowledge are being defined as both sources of knowledge and areas of knowledge, and there is variation in how researchers address what and whose knowledge is incorporated. As Moll et al., (2013) argue, scholars need to pay closer attention to the evolving practices that produce funds of knowledge. In other words, educational researchers need to continue elaborating on a funds of knowledge approach by carefully examining how students (and their families and communities) respond to changes in their social conditions for living. Indeed, these conditions necessitate that households generate new funds of knowledge for survival and advancement (Moll et al., 2013).

The Relationship Between the Forms of Capital and Funds of Knowledge

As stated by Rios-Aguilar, Kiyama, Gravitt, and Moll (2011), educational scholars have assumed that the concept of funds of knowledge is related in some way(s) to social and cultural capital. For instance, Yosso (2005) and Rodriguez (2013) proposed utilizing the concept of *community cultural wealth*, which includes the notion of funds of knowledge, to criticize and re-articulate Bourdieu's cultural capital in ways that are more inclusive of the cultural experiences of "communities of color." Similarly, Stanton-Salazar and Dornbusch (1995) suggested that both funds of knowledge and social capital are key to minority students' educational success. Zipin (2009, 2013) engaged in an elaborate discussion about issues of power when studying funds of knowledge and cultural capital. Specifically, Zipin (2013) challenged the ways in which power is assigned, particularly when focusing on knowledge. He argued that knowledge spans across both capital and funds of knowledge, and when knowledge is valued as capital, it results in forms of individualism and perpetuates efforts to "win the game" (Zipin, 2013). Yet, when knowledge is valued as a community resource (guided by a funds of knowledge lens), it works to sustain community and build stronger collaborative capacity in classrooms (Zipin, 2013). Thus, Zipin addresses the issue that educational institutions exercise arbitrary power in determining the kind of knowledge that is valued. These efforts seem to suggest that there is a possibility for the forms of capital and funds of knowledge to build a research base that moves towards a complementary framework that aids in a better understanding of issues of equity, power, and pedagogical change.

In our previous work (see Rios-Aguilar et al., 2011), it became clear that what is defined as funds of knowledge in certain literature is described as social and/or cultural capital in others. However, funds of knowledge and forms are capital are not synonyms. We do find intersections in their use of consciousness. For Bourdieu, discussions of consciousness are found within the idea of habitus. Although Bourdieu falls short in acknowledging broader social ideologies and the ways in which social consciousness influences one's habitus or individual consciousness, an embodied form of cultural capital can be found in habitus. In tracing the theoretical foundations of funds of knowledge, one can see that "behavior is mediated by consciousness and consciousness means experiencing lived experiences" (Esteban-Guitart & Moll, 2014, p. 14). These lived experiences are captured conceptually by funds of knowledge, which understands that individuals and their social worlds are inseparable (Esteban-Guitart & Moll, 2014). Thus, where Bourdieu falls short in addressing larger social ideologies and consciousness, Moll and colleagues grapple with the idea of how social worlds and social consciousness influence lived experiences.

We recently argued that funds of knowledge can be studied from a capital perspective. Furthermore, we made a compelling argument for future research to carefully examine processes such as (mis)recognition, transmission, conversion, and activation/mobilization of multiple and varied funds of knowledge and forms of capital. However, we did not elaborate on a complementary framework between the forms of capital and funds of knowledge, nor did we document how the forms of capital and funds of knowledge are used in educational research.

A Complementary Framework

We must acknowledge that frameworks have differential power and status in educational research. The issue should not be about which framework is more powerful, but how we can use these frameworks in complementary and more sophisticated ways to understand the educational complexities that continue to plague educational research. One significant contribution resulting from the content analysis detailed in Chapter 3 is the beginnings of, as established by many of the articles reviewed, a conceptual framework that combines capital (i.e., social, cultural, and economic), habitus, field, and funds of knowledge. As previously noted, conceptually connecting funds of knowledge with forms of capital does not represent *the* resolution to the shortcomings of each of the individual frameworks. Yet, as our analysis supports, the foundation of a framework has been established. Research suggests that cross-disciplinary concept building is not only useful but necessary for advancing educational agendas (Foley, 2010; Zipin, Sellar, Brennan, & Gale, 2013). A complementary conceptual framework can also have important practice and policy implications, since empirical analysis, especially equity-based research that informs policy, must be more theory laden (Lucas & Beresford, 2010). If we continue to privilege only social and cultural capital in educational research without questioning the ways in which power is arbitrarily assigned or how these concepts have been reframed, then we run the risk of perpetuating educational deficit models. Furthermore, because the focus of social and cultural capital is not on pedagogical development, we miss important practical and community-building implications that could address issues of equity and power in school settings if funds of knowledge is also considered.

Granted, the utilization of funds of knowledge, from a frequency and magnitude perspective, is not as impressive. Arguably, funds of knowledge are more difficult to measure. Nevertheless, we must not forget that the funds of knowledge approach moves away from deficit functionalist perspectives and invites researchers to concentrate our research on students', families', and communities' resources. Likewise, the pedagogical advances and dimensions of funds of knowledge are becoming more prominently written about in educational research (Rodriguez,

2013). Funds of knowledge pushes the equity agenda (González et al., 2011), and when utilized as a complementary framework with forms of capital, can also address systemic factors that influence educational opportunity (Rios-Aguilar et al., 2011; Zipin, 2013). We are not suggesting privileging only funds of knowledge in educational research, as it does not provide the theoretical grounding to analyze power structures, domination processes, and social reproduction. A complementary framework that encompasses the larger theory of power, inclusive of capital, habitus, and field, while also bringing in funds of knowledge, allows for the advancement of an equity-based agenda in ways not considered before. This complementary framework offers scholars the possibility of analyzing arbitrary power structures and social reproduction, and simultaneously, it offers scholars and practitioners a culturally relevant lens for thinking of pedagogical and community development.

Note

1 The zone of proximal development is understood as the developmental continuum between what a child can do independently and what a child can do with assistance or modeling from others. This represents the proximal level of development (Moll, 2014, p. 33).

References

Barrett, B. D., & Martina, C. A. (2012). Towards a non-deterministic reading of Pierre Bourdieu: Habitus and educational change in urban schools. *Policy Futures in Education, 10*(3), 249–262. doi:10.2304/pfie.2012.10.3.249

Bourdieu, P. (1973). Cultural reproduction and social reproduction. In R. Brown (Ed.), *Knowledge, education and cultural change* (pp. 71–112). London, UK: Tavistock Publications Limited.

Bourdieu, P. (1977). *Outline of a theory of practice.* New York, NY: Cambridge University Press.

Bourdieu, P. (1986). Forms of capital. In J. G. Richardson (Ed.), *Handbook of theory and research for the sociology of education.* New York: Greenwood.

Bourdieu, P., & Passeron, J. C. (1977). *Reproduction in education, society, and culture.* Beverly Hills, CA: Sage.

Bourdieu, P., & Wacquant, L. J. D. (1992). *An invitation to reflexive sociology.* Chicago, IL: The University of Chicago Press.

Calhoun, C. (1993). Habitus, field, and capital: The question of historical specificity. In C. Calhoun, E. LiPuma, & M. Postone (Eds.), *Bourdieu: Critical perspectives* (pp. 61–88). Chicago, IL: The University of Chicago Press.

Clay, A. (2003). Keepin' it real: Black youth, hip-hop culture, and Black identity. *American Behavioral Scientist, 46*(10), 1346–1358. doi:10.177/00027642030460100005

Coleman, J. (1988). Social capital in the creation of human capital. *The American Journal of Sociology, 94*, S95–S120. doi:10.1086/228943

Collins, R. (1971). Functional and conflict theories of educational stratification. *American Sociological Review, 36*(6), 1002–1019. Retrieved from http://links.jstor.org/sici?sici=0003-1224%28197112%2936%3A6%3C1002%3AFACTOE%3E2.0.CO%3B2-6

Collins, R. (1990). Conflict theory and the advance of macro-historical sociology. In G. Ritzer (Ed.), *Frontiers of social theory: The new syntheses* (pp. 68–87). New York, NY: Columbia University Press.

DiMaggio, P. (1982). Cultural capital and school success: The impact of status culture participation on the grades of U.S. high school students. *American Sociological Review, 47*(2), 189–201. doi:10.2307/2094962

Dufur, M., Parcel, T., & Troutman, P. (2013). Does capital at home matter more than capital at school? Social capital effects on academic achievement. *Research in Social Stratification and Mobility, 31*, 1–21. Retrieved from http://socant.chass.ncsu.edu/documents/Parcel_3.pdf

Edwards, R. (2004). Present and absent in troubling ways: Families and social capital debates. *The Sociological Review, 52*, 1–21. doi:10.1111/j.1467-954X.2004.00439.x

Emirbayer, M., & Johnson, V. (2008). Bourdieu and organizational analysis. *Theory and Society, 37*, 1–44. doi:10.1007/s11186-007-9052-y

Erickson, B. (1996). Culture, class, and connections. *American Journal of Sociology, 102*, 217–251. Retrieved from www.jstor.org.ezproxy2.library.arizona.edu/stable/2782191

Esteban-Guitart, M., & Moll, L. C. (2014). Funds of identity: A new concept based on the funds of knowledge approach. *Culture & Psychology, 20*(1), 31–48. doi:10.1177/1354067X13515934

Foley, D. (2010). The rise of class culture theory in educational anthropology. *Anthropology & Education Quarterly, 41*(3), 215–227. doi:10.1111/j.1548-1492.2010.01084.x

Freire, P. (1973). *Education for critical consciousness*. New York, NY: Seabury Press.

Giroux, H. A. (1983). *Theory and resistance in education: A pedagogy for the opposition*. South Hadley, MA: Bergin & Garvey.

González, N., Moll, L. C., & Amanti, C. (2005). *Funds of knowledge: Theorizing practices in households, communities, and classrooms*. Mahwah, NJ: Erlbaum.

González, N., Wyman, L., & O'Connor, B. (2011). The past, present, and future of "funds of knowledge". In M. Pollock & B. Levinson (Eds.), *A companion to the anthropology of education* (pp. 479–494). Malden, MA: Wiley-Blackwell.

Hogg, L. (2011). An investigation of coherence within the literature. *Teaching and Teacher Education, 27*, 666–677. doi:10.1016/j.tate.2010.11.005

Kingston, P. (2001). The unfulfilled promise of cultural capital theory. *Sociology of Education, 74*, 88–99. doi:10.2307/2673255

Lamont, M., & Lareau, A. (1988). Cultural capital: Allusions, gaps and glissandos in recent theoretical developments. *Sociological Theory, 6*, 153–168. doi:10.2307/202113

Lareau, A. (2000). *Home advantage: Social class and parental intervention in elementary education*. Lanham, MD: Rowman & Littlefield.

Lin, N. (2000). Inequality in social capital. *Contemporary Sociology, 29*, 185–195. doi:10.2307/2654086

Lubienski, S. T. (2003). Celebrating diversity and denying disparities: A critical assessment. *Educational Researcher, 32*, 30–38. doi:10.3102/0013189x032008030

Lucas, S. R., & Beresford, L. (2010). Naming and classifying: Theory, evidence, and equity in education. *Review of Research in Education, 34*, 25–84. doi:10.3102/0091732x09353578

McDonough, P. (1997). *Choosing colleges: How social class and schools structure opportunity*. Albany, NY: State University of New York Press.

McLeod, J. (1987). *Ain't no makin it: Aspirations and attainment in a low-income neighborhood*. Boulder, CO: Westview Press.

McNeal, R. (1999). Parental involvement as social capital: Differential effectiveness on science achievement, truancy, and dropping out. *Social Forces, 78*, 117–144. doi:10.1093/sf/78.1.117

Moll, L. C. (2014). *L.S. Vygotsky and education*. New York, NY: Routledge.

Moll, L. C., Soto -Santiago, S., & Schwartz, L. (2013). Funds of knowledge in changing communities. In K. Hall, T. Cremin, B. Comber, & L. Moll (Eds.), *International handbook of research on children's literacy, learning, and culture* (pp. 172–183). West Sussex, UK: Wiley-Blackwell.

Morrow, R., & Torres, C. (Eds.). (1995). *Social theory and education: A critique of theories of social and cultural reproduction*. Albany, NY: State University of New York Press.

Nash, R. (1990). Bourdieu on education and social and cultural reproduction. *British Journal of Sociology of Education*, *11*, 431–447. doi:10.1080/0142569900110405

Pöllmann, A. (2013). Intercultural capital: Toward the conceptualization, operationalization, and empirical investigation of rising marker of sociocultural distinction. *SAGE Open*, *3*(2), 1–7. doi:10.1177/2158244013486117

Portes, A. (1998). Social capital: Its origins and applications in modern sociology. *Annual Review of Sociology*, *24*, 1–24. doi:10.1146/annurev.soc.24.1.1

Portes, A. (2000). The two meanings of social capital. *Sociological Forum*, *15*(1), 1–12. doi:10.1023/a:1007537902813

Reay, D. (2004). 'It's all becoming a habitus': Beyond the habitual use of habitus in education research. *British Journal of Sociology of Education*, *25*, 431–444. doi:10.1080/0142569042000236934

Rios-Aguilar, C., Kiyama, J. M., Gravitt, M., & Moll, L. C. (2011). Funds of knowledge for the poor and forms of capital for the rich? A capital approach to examining funds of knowledge. *Theory and Research in Education*, *9*(2), 163–184. doi:10.1177/1477878511409776

Rodriguez, G. M. (2013). Power and agency in education: Exploring the pedagogical dimensions of funds of knowledge. *Review of Research in Education*, *37*, 87–120. doi:10.3102/0091732x12462686

Roscigno, V., & Ainsworth-Darnell, J. (1999). Race, cultural capital, and educational resources: Persistent inequalities and achievement returns. *Sociology of Education*, *72*, 158–178. doi:10.2307/2673227

Schultheis, F. (2014). Social capital and power: A sociological point of view. In D. Thomä, C. Henning, & H. B. Smith (Eds.), *Social capital, social identities* (pp. 151–164). Germany: De Gruyter.

Stanton-Salazar, R. D. (2004). Social capital among working class minority students. In M. Gibson, P. Gándara & J. P. Koyama (Eds.), *School connections: U.S. Mexican youth, peers, and school achievement* (pp. 18–38). New York, NY: Teachers College Press.

Stanton-Salazar, R. D., & Dornbusch, S. (1995). Social capital and the reproduction of inequality: Information networks among Mexican-origin high school students. *Sociology of Education*, *68*, 116–135. doi:10.2307/2112778

Stinchcombe, A. (1964). *Rebellion in high school*. Chicago, IL: Quadrangle.

Tzanakis, M. (2013). Social capital in Bourdieu's, Coleman's and Putnam's theory: Empirical evidence and emergent measurement issues. *Educate*, *13*, 2–23. Retrieved from http://wh.agh.edu.pl/other/materialy/672_2014_04_23_13_04_24_Spcial_capital2.pdf

Vélez-Ibáñez, C. (1996). *Border visions: Mexican cultures of the Southwest United States*. Tucson, AZ: The University of Arizona Press.

Wacquant, L. (2008). *Urban outcasts: A comparative sociology of advanced marginality*. Cambridge: Polity Press.

Yosso, T. J. (2005). Whose culture has capital? A critical race theory discussion of community cultural wealth. *Race, Ethnicity, and Education*, *8*(1), 69–91. doi:10.1080/1361332052000341006

Zipin, L. (2009). Dark funds of knowledge, deep funds of pedagogy: Exploring boundaries between lifeworlds and schools. *Discourse: Studies in the Cultural Politics of Education*, *30*(3), 317–331. doi:10.1080/01596300903037044

Zipin, L. (2013). Engaging middle years learners by making their communities curricular: A funds of knowledge approach. *Curriculum Perspectives*, *33*(3), 1–12.

Zipin, L., Sellar, S., Brennan, M., & Gale, T. (2015). Educating for futures in marginalized regions: A sociological framework for rethinking and researching aspirations. *Educational Philosophy and Theory*, *47*(3), 227–246. doi:10.1080/00131857.2013.839376

3

A REVIEW OF EXISTING RESEARCH ON FUNDS OF KNOWLEDGE AND THE FORMS OF CAPITAL

Judy Marquez Kiyama, Cecilia Rios-Aguilar, and Molly Sarubbi

Researchers have used the theory of capital (Marx, 1933; Lin, 1999), specifically social and cultural capital, to study variation in educational outcomes and to examine educational inequities. While proliferation in research across different fields that use these theories is enormous, unfortunately, research on the forms of capital is, predominately, "theoretically unreflective" (Sandefur & Laumann, 1998, p. 490). In recent years, scholars have started to utilize alternative conceptual frameworks, such as funds of knowledge, to challenge deficit models and to advance pedagogical practices. Unlike social and cultural capital, funds of knowledge is a relatively new concept used mostly to document the wealth of resources available in marginalized students' (and their families' and communities') lives. While funds of knowledge may not have the same longevity, and perhaps status, in educational research as the forms of capital, the application of each of these concepts has, for the most part, resulted in a lack of clarity and misinterpretation of the potential benefits of using such frameworks for advancing our understanding of issues of equity, power, and pedagogical change in education.

To our knowledge, there is no recent review of research that examines in detail how the forms of capital and funds of knowledge are used in educational research.[1] Since a clear gap in the literature exists, we felt compelled to engage in such an endeavor to clarify the original intent of these concepts and to contribute theoretical advancements that can be utilized to design more nuanced research on equity, power, and pedagogical change in education. We focused our content analysis on seven prominent education journals from the time period of 2002 to 2012: *American Educational Research Journal* (AERJ), *Anthropology in Education Quarterly* (AEQ), *Educational Evaluation and Policy Analysis* (EEPA), *Review of Educational Research* (RER), *Educational Researcher* (ER), *Review of Research in*

Education (RRE), and *Sociology of Education* (SoE). The contribution of our analysis is straightforward: we provide a thorough review of the literature related to three major conceptual frameworks—social capital, cultural capital, and funds of knowledge. Our analysis reveals the imperative need to conduct research that is conceptually sound, and that incorporates complexity in a more nuanced way. Educational research needs to find better explanations for, and actions to address, the inequities in educational opportunities that continue to exist in multiple and diverse ways across educational institutions in the U.S. We argue that a central characteristic of the existing literature that uses these conceptual tools is an ongoing lack of clarity regarding their origins and intentions, the definitions provided (or lack of them), and the mechanisms that explain why inequities in educational opportunities and stratification continue to exist. A review of this type is warranted, as is the exploration of a complementary means of considering these frameworks. This chapter examines the following research questions: (a) How have researchers used the concepts of social and cultural capital and funds of knowledge to advance arguments related to equity and power in the field of education? and (b) How have researchers attempted to refine these conceptualizations to enrich research on equity and power in education? While the focus of this chapter is mostly on equity and power in education, we also made an effort in examining the extent to which these frameworks have been used to produce change in pedagogical and educational practices.

We employ content analysis to examine how these notions have been put to use in research published in leading journals. We conducted a more in-depth content analysis of a smaller sample of journal articles that have, sophisticatedly, utilized these notions to examine issues of equity, power, and in some instances pedagogical change, in educational research, thus leading to theoretical advancements.

Methodology

Our analyses were conducted in several stages. First, we identified and read articles from seven leading peer-reviewed journals in the fields of education, anthropology, and sociology that included any or all of the three concepts of interest: cultural capital, social capital, and funds of knowledge ($n = 367$). Then we conducted a descriptive content analysis to document the patterns of use of these conceptual frameworks. Finally, we conducted an in-depth qualitative content analysis of a sub-sample of articles ($n = 111$), which is a systematic method designed to highlight evidence and extract hidden contents of spoken words and written text (Babbie, 1983; Krippendorff, 2004). Stemler (2001) argues that content analysis is also useful for examining the meaning of patterns and trends contained within documents. We detail our coding scheme and content analyses below. The main purpose of the content analysis was to examine how scholars apply the conceptual frameworks to make theoretical advancements.

Journal Selection

Typically, quantitative reviews of education literature focus on summarizing the results of research in a given area of scientific inquiry as a means of highlighting findings and identifying knowledge gaps (Keselman et al., 1998). Less common, but equally important, are reviews that concentrate on a comprehensive examination of the conceptual frameworks used to study specific issues within educational research. The documentation of patterns and trends in the use of these frameworks has a twofold purpose: (a) it can be used for theory refinement and advancement, and (b) it forms the basis for recommending improvements in the design of future educational research.

To systematically examine how the conceptual frameworks of funds of knowledge and social and cultural capital have been practically utilized to examine issues of equity, power, and pedagogical change in the field of education, we indexed their influence upon empirical research published in the following seven peer-reviewed journals: *American Education Research Journal* (AERJ), *Anthropology & Education Quarterly* (AEQ), *Education Evaluation and Policy Analyses* (EEPA), *Educational Researcher* (ER), *Review of Research in Education* (RRE), *Review of Educational Research* (RER), and *Sociology of Education* (SoE). We chose these journals because we understand these scholarly publications to be the most representative locations of research that involves the application of the conceptual frameworks of interest in this study. Additionally, academic journals serve an important function within most disciplines by offering a mechanism by which educators communicate ideas, stimulate discussion (as well as controversy), and share information (Hutchinson & Lovell, 2004). Our study is cross-sectional in nature and restricted to 10 years (2002–2012), which we believe is an adequate representation of current research on the forms of capital and funds of knowledge. In addition, we chose these years because the number of articles included in the sample was large enough to offer in-depth insights.

Identification of Journal Articles

Several web-based searches were employed to create the best possible database of journal articles to represent the large number of existing studies utilizing the conceptual frameworks of social and cultural capital and funds of knowledge. More specifically, three separate searches were conducted in the SAGE Journals online system for the top education journals. Each search was conducted with the terms *social capital*, *cultural capital*, and *funds of knowledge*. The SAGE Journals online system was searched for the years 2002 to 2012 to examine some of the most recent educational literature published in these journals. In a similar fashion, we used the Wiley Online Library system to identify journal articles published in AEQ. After the initial examination of the abstracts of each of the studies identified, we eliminated from the analyses all commentaries and books reviews. Through this process, we identified a total of 367 published journal articles.

Coding Procedure

We developed a coding system with the goal of conducting a content analysis of journal articles because no existing coding scheme fit our purposes. To ensure accurate analysis, all members of our research team thoroughly read a selected number of journal articles. Each paper was then discussed, with each reader separately presenting his or her findings for all of the questions in the coding scheme. The group then reached consensus regarding each question for each article through discussion and further consultation of the article as needed.

Our coding scheme did not simply identify broad descriptions of the use of these conceptual frameworks in the existing literature on equity and power in education. We also focused on more subtle elements of practice, such as the methodological features and the type of educational issues examined by these frameworks. Our coding scheme contained four major areas: (a) basic information of the article, (b) how concept(s) is/are used in the article, (c) methodological aspects, and (d) what topic is studied or examined in the journal article. We then coded each article as one, two, or three. Articles coded as *one* were those in which the concept(s) does/do appear only on the reference list or notes. Articles were coded as *two* when the concept(s) is/are mentioned in the text, but the concept(s) is/are not defined. We coded as *three* articles in which the concept(s) is/are mentioned in the text and the author(s) provide a definition of the concept(s).

As stated earlier, the major focus of this study involves those articles that have contributed to theoretical advancements. Thus, for the articles coded as *three* (*n* = 111), we developed more detailed categories, which allowed us to more carefully examine how these articles defined the concepts and their contributions to the field. The journal articles were also coded as zero if they mentioned or defined the concept(s) *ceremoniously*—that is, the articles mentioned or defined the concept but briefly and without any engagement with prior research that uses the concept or theoretical discussion (Sallaz & Zavisca, 2008). The articles were coded as *one* if they mentioned/defined the concept *paradigmatically*—that is, the articles tested key assumptions of conceptual frameworks used, or the articles made a substantial contribution to our understanding of the concept (Sallaz & Zavisca, 2008).

In-Depth Content Analysis

After documenting the patterns used in these conceptual frameworks, we conducted an in-depth content analysis of those articles that were coded as three. That is, we selected the articles in which social capital, cultural capital, and/or funds of knowledge was/were mentioned in the text and the author(s) provided a definition or discussion of the concept(s). Of the 111 articles identified, 31 percent were published in AERJ, 18 percent in SoE, 14 percent in RER, 14 percent in AEQ, 10 percent in RRE, 7 percent in ER, and 6 percent in EEPA. Additionally, of the 111 articles, 72 percent of them utilized the concepts paradigmatically, and the remaining articles, 28 percent of them, used the concepts ceremoniously. Based on this initial understanding, we felt it important to re-analyze the articles utilizing a more detailed qualitative coding scheme. The articles were re-read to better understand how the authors engaged in and discussed each of the concepts. First, each member of the research team was asked to re-read two of the articles and to categorize his/her notes. We then came back together, compared notes and categories, and agreed upon the following categories when reading the subsequent articles: (a) article summary; (b) use of concept (i.e., original versus existing/evolving uses of the conceptual frameworks); (c) the relationship between the forms of capital and funds of knowledge with specific attention paid to the similarities and differences in methods, units of analysis, outcomes, and purposes; (d) theoretical developments or extensions; and (e) implications and suggestions for future research on power, educational equity, and pedagogical change. Each of the 111 articles was read utilizing this particular framework and a content summary was created for each.

Results

Our findings are split into four sections: (a) patterns of utilization of social capital, cultural capital, and funds of knowledge; (b) uses of the forms of capital and funds of knowledge in educational research; (c) theoretical contributions made in educational research; and finally, (d) how literature contributes to the broader research agenda on issues of power, equity, and pedagogical change. The findings are organized in this way in an effort to address our broader research questions.

Patterns of Utilization of Social Capital, Cultural Capital, and Funds of Knowledge

We identified a total of 367 articles that utilized the frameworks of interest. One of the most interesting findings of our analysis is the amount of overlap within these frameworks. We found that out of the 367 articles that comprise our database, 88 articles (or 24 percent of the total number of articles identified) used more than one concept to examine issues of equity and power in education. When there is overlap, scholars tend to rely mostly on both social and cultural capital notions (74 percent). Twelve percent of the articles intersect cultural capital and funds of knowledge (e.g., Buendia, Ares, Juarez, & Peercy, 2004), 8 percent combine funds of knowledge and social capital (e.g., Brayboy, Castagno, & Maughan, 2007; Vasquez, 2006), and 6 percent utilize the three conceptual frameworks simultaneously (e.g., Enright, 2011; Kiyama, 2010; McNamara Horvat, Weininger, & Lareau, 2003; Ream & Palardy, 2008; Schutz, 2006).

We also built Table 3.1 to summarize the patterns of utilization of the frameworks of interest. We took into consideration the amount of overlap in the use of these notions. So, instead of using the total number of articles identified ($n =$ 367), we examined the total number of times the concepts were mentioned in our entire database of journal articles ($n = 455$). Table 3.1 shows that social capital was the most utilized conceptual framework compared to cultural capital and funds of knowledge (47 percent, 39 percent, and 14 percent, respectively). In addition, we found that a relatively low percentage of the articles, that is 24 percent of the total, actually defined the concept(s) used. Interestingly, the vast majority of the articles that use funds of knowledge, 82 percent, were coded as one and two, indicating that scholars only referenced the concept or cited articles related to this particular concept. Only 18 percent of the articles actually provided a definition for funds of knowledge. Additionally, only 9 percent of the articles that used the forms of capital as the main framework of analysis related the concept of capital with the notions of habitus and/or field. Finally, a very small proportion of articles (i.e., 4 percent of the total) also referred to the concept of economic capital when examining the notions of social and cultural capital.

Of particular interest to this study are articles coded as three ($n = 111$). Among these, we found that 72 percent of them utilized the concepts paradigmatically, thus contributing to enriching the theory. The remaining articles, 28 percent of them, used the concepts ceremoniously, meaning that they did *not* engage in a meaningful discussion of how the theory works. To provide a clear illustration and justification for our claims, we conducted detailed content analyses of the 111 articles coded as three, discussed in the following sections of this chapter.

TABLE 3.1 Quantitative Summary of the Review of the Literature on Social Capital, Cultural Capital, and Funds of Knowledge

Concept Utilization / Theoretical Framework	Social Capital	Cultural Capital	Funds of Knowledge	Total
1 = Concept(s) does/do only appear(s) in reference list or notes	54	39	16	109 (20%)
	(49%)	(36%)	(15%)	
Percent (%) within concept utilization	(25%)	(22%)	(25%)	
Percent (%) within theoretical framework				
2 = Concept(s) is/are mentioned in the text, but concept is/are *not* defined	100	99	36	235 (55%)
	(43%)	(42%)	(15%)	
	(47%)	(56%)	(57%)	
Percent (%) within concept utilization				
Percent (%) within theoretical framework				
3 = Concept(s) is/are mentioned in the text and defined	60	40	11	111 (25%)
	(54%)	(37%)	(9%)	
Percent (%) within concept utilization	(28%)	(22%)	(18%)	
Percent (%) within theoretical framework				
Total	**214 (44%)**	**178 (38%)**	**63 (18%)**	**455 (100%)**

Uses of the Forms of Capital and Funds of Knowledge in Educational Research

Social capital was used overwhelmingly with respect to relational networks and the resources and navigational properties provided by such networks (Cohen, Raudenbush, & Ball, 2003; Goddard, 2003; Louie, 2005; Ream, 2003). Most authors drew from Coleman's definition of social capital, with only Dika and Singh (2002) offering an overview of the differences between Bourdieu's and Coleman's definitions. When studying relational networks and the resources and properties within, it was Coleman's more deterministic interpretation of social capital that was used, particularly as research examined variables of parent/child interactions within family structures tied to academic outcomes (Dika & Singh, 2002). One exception to this was Daly and Finnigan's (2011) examination of educational reform-related social networks. Drawing from Lin's conceptualization of social capital, the authors moved beyond social capital as a fixed and static concept.

Understanding networks was not the only way in which social capital was used. Many articles focused on K–12 schooling. There were a few exceptions (Louie, 2005; Park, 2012) that did apply social capital to understand transition and success of students of color in higher education. However, the majority of social capital articles focused exclusively on K–12 education. Social capital was used less frequently for the following topics: parental networks (McNamara Horvat et al., 2003; Ream & Palardy, 2008), teacher networks and socialization (Achinstein, Ogawa, & Speiglman, 2004; Coburn & Russell, 2008; Frank, Zhao, Penuel, Ellefson, & Porter, 2011), the collectivism of marginalized groups (Morris, 2004; Zapata Maldonado, Rhoads, & Buenavista, 2005), and the influence of social capital and socio-economic status on academic achievement (Ream & Rumberger, 2008; Sirin, 2005).

The primary way in which cultural capital was utilized was consistent with Bourdieu's development of the framework as a means of explaining social reproduction. Using cultural capital to explain social stratification and cultural reproduction was found in multiple articles (Achinstein, Ogawa, & Speiglman, 2004; Chiu & Khoo, 2005; LeTendre, Hofer, & Shimizu, 2003; Lubienski, 2003; Warikoo & Carter, 2009; Wiggan, 2007). Again, the majority of these articles focused on social reproduction in K–12 settings. The next way in which cultural capital was used was to explain the ethnic and academic identities of marginalized groups (Nasir & Saxe, 2003; O'Connor, Lewis, & Mueller, 2007; Pearce, 2006; Petchauer, 2009). Similar to Lareau and Horvat's (1999) work on parental networks and parent involvement in K–12 settings, several articles engaged cultural capital to further this research (Jones, 2007; Lee & Bowen, 2006; McNamara Horvat, Weininger, & Lareau, 2003; Morris, 2005; Perez Carreón, Drake, & Calabrese Barton, 2005). Finally, cultural capital was used less frequently for the following topics: a sociohistorical perspective of immigrant versus national students

(Louie, 2005), the collectivism and cultural capital of marginalized groups (Morris, 2004; Zapata-Maldonado et al, 2005), cultural capital as knowledge (Bills, 2003), and the role of class location and class origin in the transmission of class advantages across generations (Roksa & Potter, 2011).

Very few articles engaged in a discussion of a larger theory of power, and instead presented habitus and/or field as distinct concepts. In general, authors (Nuñez & Bowers, 2011) often used different notions of habitus without engaging in the concept. For example, Nuñez and Bowers (2011), while citing Bourdieu, defined different forms of capital and habitus, and moved to a conceptual framing of habitus that utilized McDonough's (1997) organizational habitus. Thus, although Nuñez and Bowers (2011) offered a discussion of organizational level of habitus, the concept was still treated as a discreet variable. In general, habitus was briefly stated, even more briefly defined, and rarely engaged as a concept. For example, Yamamoto and Brinton (2010) and Roksa and Potter (2011) briefly defined habitus as embodied cultural capital, while Meier Jaeger (2011) offered a few examples of the ways in which habitus is embedded. Overall, when habitus was included in the discussion, it appeared to be used primarily to justify the variables chosen (Nuñez & Bowers, 2011) or as a deterministic variable suggesting that habitus is equated with families' cultural notions and cannot be shifted (Park, 2012). Even Dika and Singh (2002), who presented the most in-depth discussion about the necessity of recognizing social capital in conjunction with cultural capital, field, and habitus, did not review the concepts within a larger theory of power, rather as disparate notions. Missing from all of these articles is not only a discussion of habitus as individual consciousness, but also a recognition that habitus is part of the larger consciousness shaping fields and institutions. Therefore, not only are immediate contexts and surroundings influencing habitus often left out of theoretical conversations, but the larger ideologies of institutions and systems shaping such consciousness are void as well, reducing any mention of habitus to an overly simplistic concept.

Similar to social capital, the concept of funds of knowledge was used to explain community–school relations (Schutz, 2006). The biggest difference between the use of funds of knowledge and the use of forms of capital is that funds of knowledge was primarily used to explain K–12 pedagogical approaches or as a way to improve pedagogical action, referred to as a "resource pedagogy" (Paris, 2012). For example, North (2006) drew upon community-based knowledge as a way for teachers to strengthen academic learning for students of color and low-income students. Funds of knowledge as a pedagogical approach was also utilized by Nasir, Hand, and Taylor (2008), who presented funds of knowledge as an example of programs and research that seek to challenge the boundaries between what they referred to as "domain knowledge" and "cultural knowledge." Likewise, Arzubiaga, Nogueron, and Sullivan (2009) offered funds of knowledge as a framework to counter research that presents families as lacking. However, very few articles went into a substantive discussion about the development of funds of knowledge as a framework or how funds of knowledge might be used conceptually as a collaborative framework with forms of capital. The exceptions were Moll (2010), who engaged in a review of how funds of knowledge as a pedagogical and conceptual framework originated, and Kiyama (2010), who brought social and cultural capital in as a secondary framework in her research on the development of educational ideologies in Mexican-American families. While this summative overview provides a descriptive review of the uses of the forms of capital and funds of knowledge, it does not address the theoretical contributions of the studies. For that, we turn to a discussion of theoretical development and advances in the study of educational equity.

Theoretical Contributions: How the Frameworks are Used in Educational Research

The previous section offered a discussion of the uses of funds of knowledge and forms of capital in educational research, inclusive of the 111 articles that were coded both as ceremonious and paradigmatic. In the section that follows, we discuss theoretical contributions which allow for a more in-depth review of those articles (72 percent of the 111) coded as utilizing the concepts paradigmatically.

Theoretical Foundations: Presumptive and Disparate

A substantive discussion about the theoretical underpinnings and the uses of capital and funds of knowledge framed the studies coded as three. Most of these discussions were done in separate sections and only in a handful of journals. Actually, there is no mention of the notion of funds of knowledge in *Sociology of Education*. Thus, while authors often provided a thoughtful critique of these concepts (e.g., Morris, 2004; Schutz, 2006), very few articles offered a discussion on theoretical overlap; those who did provide a discussion of theoretical overlap are reviewed below. Further, authors often presumed that readers were aware of the foundation of the concepts and moved quickly into examples and discussion without defining the forms of capital or funds of knowledge. Missing from these articles were explanations of theoretical origins, assumptions, and relevance for their particular study (see Achinstein, Ogawa, Sexton, & Freitas, 2010 as an example).

In our analysis of theoretical overlap, we noted that in only two instances (Kiyama, 2010; Lubienski, 2003) was there explicit discussion of the potential of integrating forms of capital and funds of knowledge. When more than one theory was used, they generally were limited to presenting multiple forms of capital, sometimes with mention of funds of knowledge, as evidenced in the following examples. The first example is that of Lee and Bowen (2006), who drew from Bourdieu's and Coleman's cultural and social capital to review forms of parent involvement on elementary students' academic achievement. Lee and Bowen explicitly link social capital with human capital, suggesting, in support of Coleman's social capital theory, that human capital found in parents (in the form of educational attainment) is transmitted to their children as they develop their own human capital only if parents direct social capital to their children.

Likewise, Ream and Palardy (2008) addressed social class differences in parental social capital. While the authors drew from Portes (1998), Bourdieu (1986), Coleman (1988), and McNamara Horvat et al. (2003) to create their conceptual framework of social capital, they acknowledge the importance of funds of knowledge. Ream and Palardy's (2008) work utilizes funds of knowledge to highlight the existence of class differences in parent-child interactions. Yet, the way in which Ream and Palardy present funds of knowledge in this article is not the way Moll, Amanti, Neff, and González (1992) have drawn upon funds of knowledge—that is, as resources with educational and pedagogical utility. Therefore, the article is limited in that it does not discuss how funds of knowledge can and should be used (or converted) into diverse forms of capital.

Theoretical Foundations: Conceptual Misuse and Renaming

As Lubienski (2003) predicted, we found that many authors have taken to using one theoretical construct to describe or represent another. In some cases, authors use social and cultural capital to describe what more appropriately would be conceptualized as funds of knowledge. For example, Louie's (2005) use of ethnic social capital is very similar to funds of knowledge. She shared an example of families mobilizing ethnic social capital to obtain a desired return, like gaining access to a high-performance school. In another such example, Perez Carreon, Drake, and Calabrese Barton (2005) described capital found in the home to characterize what we might label as funds of knowledge. This includes repairs on vehicles to save money, growing up on farming communities in Mexico, and growing vegetables in the backyard. These cultural practices are nearly identical to the examples Moll et al. (1992) documented as funds of knowledge. Finally, Morris (2004) engaged cultural capital to describe how Black communities in the South shared their cultural capital with one another to develop "social capital (Black social capital) for survival and success in a segregated world" (p. 102). This renaming of capital also reappeared as "multicultural capital" (Achinstein, Ogawa, Sexton, & Freitas, 2010); "hip hop cultural capital," which inferred a knowledge of hip hop music (Petchauer, 2009); and dominant, non-dominant cultural capital, and "Black" cultural capital (Carter, 2003, 2006). Interestingly, both Morris' (2004) and Moll et al.'s (1992) work with funds of knowledge utilize the terms "survival and success" in describing the processes of cultivating either cultural capital or funds of knowledge, respectively. This discrepant use of concepts was not limited to funds of knowledge. In the case of Perez Carreon, Drake, and Calabrese Barton (2005), we also found that characteristics of both social capital and cultural capital were combined into one concept, labeled as cultural capital.

Theoretical Overlap: Towards a Complementary Framework

We found that only two articles explicitly addressed the overlap between funds of knowledge and forms of capital. The first was Lubienski's (2003) article on celebrating diversity and denying disparities, which offered a thoughtful argument about researchers losing the original meaning and use of cultural capital by adopting or confusing it with new connotations, including funds of knowledge. The second was Kiyama's (2010) article, which examined the development of educational aspirations in Mexican-American families as they promoted a college-going culture. Kiyama drew upon funds of knowledge as a primary framework, with social and cultural capital serving as secondary frameworks.

Specifically, Lubienski discussed how researchers have begun to confuse Bourdieu's cultural capital with Moll et al.'s (1992) funds of knowledge. She argued that what was being called cultural capital in some communities (drawing from the example of knowledge of food stamps) would not be cultural capital under original definitions because it does not facilitate inclusion into high-status groups. She further argued that defining cultural capital in that way resulted in a loss of its original usefulness. Such use suggested that everyone has cultural capital and that "no set of cultural practices should be valued more or less than another" (p. 34). Lubienski cautioned that when this occurs, we forget or hide that those individuals with cultural capital have distinct advantages. Interestingly, Lubienski (2003) did not contemplate the possibility that funds of knowledge, when studied from a capital perspective, can enrich research that utilizes the forms of capital. Lubienski also did not discuss the role that economic capital, habitus, and field play in developing a more complex theory of power and educational equity.

Kiyama's (2010) article did demonstrate the importance of considering a theoretical overlap, particularly when challenging deficit views of underrepresented groups, although she did not acknowledge the importance of economic capital, habitus, and field in the overlap. Kiyama drew upon this overlapping framework to challenge functionalist perspectives that favor the dominant class and examine existing structures that perpetuate inequities. What resulted in combining the frameworks was a deeper understanding of K–12 schooling experiences as it applies to issues of college access and college-going. Such a combined framework recognized the inherent college-going resources in families (i.e., funds of knowledge) while also challenging power structures that reproduce educational inequities (i.e., social and cultural capital). Missing from Kiyama's (2010) research is an extension of this framework to understand how funds of knowledge are converted, transmitted, and activated in different fields, particularly those dominated by traditional forms of capital (Rios-Aguilar, Kiyama, Gravitt, & Moll, 2011). Understanding how funds of knowledge functions within certain fields is imperative to moving towards a complementary framework, as those in dominant positions within the field determine the value and rates of conversion, exercise power over the field, and promote the recognition and legitimacy of distribution among parties (Emirbayer & Johnson, 2008, p. 13). Thus, understanding the field of power is key as it is influenced not only by social class, but race, ethnicity, gender, and language.

Theoretical Extension: A Broader Theory of Power

It is clear that when Bourdieu conceptualized capital, habitus, and field, a theoretical opportunity was provided from which to examine social reproduction and class-based inequities across educational systems while critically considering both structure and agency. Yet, as demonstrated, the theory has been dismantled and reinterpreted time and again. We return to the research that has set in motion a reconsideration of this broader theory of power. Most notably, researchers are urging the consideration of "socio-demographic dimensions" (Lucas & Beresford, 2010, p. 27), including the intersections of race/ethnicity, class, gender, and language (Dika & Singh, 2002; Ek, 2009; Lucas & Beresford, 2010) when addressing issues of power within educational systems. Specifically, Dika and Singh (2002) warn that continuing to draw from Coleman's conceptualization of social capital clouds the intersection of these dimensions and obscures issues of power and domination in school settings. By focusing on these sociodemographic dimensions within a capital framework, the ways in which power manifests and the pathways through which it operates can be better understood (Lucas & Beresford, 2010), thus leading to a greater likelihood of influencing policy and practice.

In suggesting the use of a complementary framework and ultimately, a broader theory of power, we question if the constructs have to be mutually exclusive. Nasir, Hand, and Taylor (2008) note that "viewing culture solely in terms of the variations and similarities among practices and orientations misses the role of power in determining what forms of knowledge are considered competent and productive in different contexts" (p. 193). By eliminating the assumed mutual exclusivity of forms of capital and funds of knowledge, we believe researchers can better understand diverse cultural practices, the role of power, and students' experiences as members of families and larger systems.

Zipin (2013) and Zipin, Sellar, Brennan, and Gale (2015) offer an important theoretical summary of these points and present a sociological framework that connects with anthropological concepts like funds of knowledge to study social-cultural phenomena in education. They argue that conceptual resources must include *and* extend Bourdieu's toolkit, as Bourdieu's work assists in analyzing social-historical underpinnings and the subconscious levels of practical logics and power that constitute habitus (Zipin et al., 2015). Zipin and colleagues (2015) argue that further conceptual resources are needed to explore the materializing of social processes. Funds of knowledge allows for this as it builds capacity for "students to enact their agency" and pursue (and analyze) community futures, "rather than reproduce, historically received social-structural limits" (Zipin et al., 2015,

p. 39). Thus, our call for a complementary framework further supports Zipin et al.'s (2015) work and builds upon the research reviewed in this content analysis.

Addressing Issues of Equity, Power, and Pedagogical Change

One final element served as the basis for our content analysis of the literature. We examined how authors used the frameworks of funds of knowledge and forms of capital to engage research focused on issues of equity, power, and pedagogical change. Our analysis pointed to advances in research studying issues of educational inequity, and further highlighted areas in which a complementary framework would be applicable and provide additional theoretical depth. Although many researchers have utilized the forms of capital and funds of knowledge to study social stratification and cultural reproduction in communities, we sought to understand how studies were extending the research agenda on equity, power, and pedagogical change in new directions.

Challenging Inequities Through Collectivism and Relational Processes

Just as researchers have established that habitus is malleable (Barrett & Martina, 2012), so too are the relational processes embedded within social capital and funds of knowledge. When considering the role of social class, particularly with regard to status, power, and authority, such processes manifest not as absolute and deterministic, but relational, suggesting that no one person in the relationship is bound to be powerful or powerless (Lewis & Forman, 2002). Social class is an active part of everyday relations; in one such case between parents and teachers (Lewis & Forman, 2002), how teacher-parent interactions play out can shift depending on the nature of the field and habitus and how value is constructed within the space. Thus, schools as sites of social class reproduction do not have to be automatic (Lewis & Forman, 2002). Analyzing how such relations are formed would contribute to a better understanding of how spaces, like schools, shift from sites of reproduction to intra-community and collectivist spaces (Wong, 2008).

As is consistent with cluster households in the funds of knowledge framework (Moll et al., 1992), collectivist groups are organized around common values. Some of these values include the development of group norms, interdependence, attachment with families and community members, and valuing needs, goals, and aspirations of the collective (Fox, Lowe, & McClellen, 2005; Triandis, Chen, & Chan, 1998). Thus, agency is manifested and power structures are challenged when groups come together as a collective. As an example, Morris (2004) used a sociohistorical lens to examine the collective agency of two elementary schools in African-American communities in St. Louis and Atlanta. Morris demonstrated how African-Americans can come together in spite of racial inequalities and poverty. Specifically, Morris (2004) drew from Orr's (1999) notion of cultural capital to highlight how "Black people share their [Black] cultural capital with one another and develop their social capital for survival and success" (p. 102). While one could argue that Morris used Black social and cultural capital to represent what might be termed funds of knowledge in other studies, his argument was that the group collectively organized to advocate for opportunity for the community. Central to this collectivism is "fictive kinship" and collective identity that bound the community together (Morris, 2004). Morris expanded the notion of social capital to include the collectivism of marginalized groups in developing agency while confronting persistent racism and poverty. Morris did not, however, address how students manifest agency once they leave the predominantly African-American school settings. Thus, while Morris addressed issues of power and equity, his findings did not challenge the dominant ideal of social capital and its effectiveness outside of African-American settings, nor how those relational processes might be shifted between the African-American community and school personnel.

Yet, Zapata Maldonado, Rhoads, and Buenavista (2005) demonstrated how collectivism within communities can reshift existing power structures and challenge contemporary social integration and multicultural theories of student retention by arguing that such theories do not adequately account for the academic needs of underrepresented students. Drawing on social and cultural capital, collectivism, and social praxis, Zapata Maldonado et al. (2005) demonstrated how underrepresented students develop knowledge, skills, and networks and build community ties and collectivism. In doing so, students move towards praxis and challenge dominant social and institutional norms. Additionally, students were able to build bridges across different racial/ethnic communities for the sake of organizing a united community of color. Zapata Maldonado et al. (2005), like Morris (2004), extended the notion of social capital by suggesting that it can be informed by a focus on collectivism, and that social praxis can result in community empowerment and agency. The authors demonstrated that students operate in a form of "double-consciousness" and highlighted the fact that students are maintaining their cultural heritage while promoting transformative forms of cultural and social capital. In doing so, students begin to both understand the dominant system that misrepresents them and work collectively within the system to change it.

Issues of Activation and Convertibility: Social Exchange Across Class Boundaries

In attempting to understand how activation and convertibility of funds of knowledge and forms of capital might occur, we ground our discussion in an examination of five types of parent involvement on elementary school children's academic achievement (Lee & Bowen, 2006). The authors studied race/ethnicity, poverty, and parent educational attainment, and addressed how differences in involvement are measured. Lee and Bowen (2006) concluded that researchers and educational institutions need to create strategies for overcoming barriers related to parental involvement and that scholars must recognize different forms of involvement. By doing so, the value of non-dominant forms of involvement are established. As this analysis has demonstrated, forms of capital—or in this example, forms of involvement—are often viewed as markers of academic and social (in)adequacy in schools (Corbett, 2004). The educational space (or field) serves as a powerful organizational frame for the influence and abstractions of cultural capital and becomes classed, raced, and gendered when subsequently forming dispositions (i.e., habitus) (Corbett, 2004). Because subaltern forms of cultural practice or funds of knowledge rarely translate from home/community to school and vice versa, we wonder how those forms of involvement, upon entering a space in which they are recognized and validated, might be converted into actual forms of capital that are rewarded within the existing power structures while also providing opportunity to challenge existing power structures.

Continuing with the example of parental involvement, Perez Carreon, Drake, and Calabrese Barton (2005) examined different models of parental engagement and challenged dominant literature around notions of parent involvement. The authors provided examples of activating different types of cultural practices. Perez Carreon et al. (2005) distinguished between capital found in the home, material capital, and formal cultural capital (what we consider Bourdieu and Passeron's cultural capital), and demonstrated how home and material (what we interpret as subaltern forms of cultural practices) can be used in schools for activating traditional capital. The activation represented in this study suggested that parental engagement was a product that led to new opportunities and networks within and outside of the schools (Perez Carreon et al., 2005). The development of new networks also suggests that cultural practices were both activated and converted into new forms of social capital. Similar to the original funds of knowledge study (Moll et al., 1992), the authors asserted that schools are missing the opportunity to learn from families' insights and knowledge about education, and that the practices developed through the hardships of immigration are continuously drawn from when supporting the schooling of their children. The work of Perez Carreon and colleagues teaches us that activation and convertibility of capital is a process and a product.

Given our review of the literature, we understand that findings from various studies (Ream & Palardy, 2008; Lareau, 2000, 2003) indicate that social capital functions differently across different socioeconomic groups. Further, these studies reveal "how social interaction and meaning making between individuals and within groups facilitate for some students, even while inhibiting for others, the accumulation and exchange of various kinds of educationally useful resources" (Ream & Palardy, 2008, p. 240). Additionally, Ream and Palardy (2008) distinguished between the availability of social capital to different groups and its convertibility to other forms of capital. The theoretical questioning posed by Ream and Palardy points to the necessity of deconstructing the reasons behind educational inequity, and how exchange and convertibility amongst different forms of capital can be shared by families across social class boundaries and across different identities, including race, gender, and language. Thus, we must consider that the convertibility of various kinds of social and cultural capital and funds of knowledge depends on embedded social processes, entrenched within systems that arbitrarily decide the value of the capital and/or funds of knowledge, which have traditionally been ignored from educational research. Furthermore, scholars cannot forget the role of economic capital when examining social class differences, as it plays a key role in the process of domination.

Discussion and Conclusion

The findings of this content analysis represent a number of important themes regarding the use of forms of capital and funds of knowledge, particularly when studying issues of educational inequity. The findings also establish the foundation for a proposed complementary framework of funds of knowledge and the forms of capital. The patterns of utilization for these three frameworks demonstrate that social capital is the most used of the three, but how researchers utilize these frameworks is oftentimes inconsistent. The terms are sometimes merely cited, other times defined, and in some cases, discussed and theorized in detail. It is the latter that we were particularly interested in as we began our in-depth content analysis. Findings from the in-depth content analysis reveal how researchers are utilizing the frameworks, the theoretical contributions, and the advances being made in the broader agenda on studying issues of equity, power, and change in educational research and practices.

Implications for Future Research

Many questions and ideas remain that provide opportunities for future research. Although this study is the only review that conducts a content analysis on how researchers have used forms of capital and funds of knowledge, one of the limitations is that we selected only seven leading journals to conduct our analyses. It is likely that scholarship contributing to the advancement of these theoretical frameworks has been published in a variety of different journals, particularly practice-oriented journals. Therefore, future analyses should expand to other journals. Just as is reflective in our hierarchical educational systems, the field also functions in a hierarchical manner with respect to the journals that are considered "leading" or "top tier." Perhaps much of the research addressing funds of knowledge and the power mechanisms we describe appears in lower-tier or practice-oriented journals. Possibly, funds of knowledge research might have a different status in these other journals. Likewise, it might also be the case that the research and publishing paradigm of many U.S. education journals restricts opportunities for in-depth theoretical engagement and interrogation. We must also begin to challenge power systems in the field itself that have produced a theory-averse mindset and have relegated funds of knowledge work into less-prestigious journals. What is it about the framework itself that suggests it is a better "fit" for these practice-oriented journals? Future analyses of the literature should focus on the various elements of the research designs to better understand why it is the case that funds of knowledge does not as frequently appear in leading journals. To be certain, funds of knowledge research has contributed both theoretically and pedagogically. Therefore, we argue that top-tier journals must include equity-minded frameworks like funds of knowledge if we are to continue to advance the field.

Furthermore, findings from our content analysis revealed that within these leading journals, there is a lack of research investigating educational issues in higher education and the transition to the job market—a clear opportunity for future research. It appears that educational research exists in two separate systems: K–12 and higher education. We must stop addressing research as two bounded, separate systems and instead investigate students' educational opportunities from a broader educational trajectory perspective. By only focusing on K–12, we do not understand the power structures throughout the entire educational pathways of students, and it assumes educational responsibility ends at the K–12 level when students graduate from high school. Likewise, by failing to include higher education research, we ignore the responsibility that institutions of higher education, and the actors within them, have in the success of K–12 students. Yet, we cannot end our research questions around educational equity there, at higher education. We must ask, how are power and stratification renegotiated at various steps of the educational pathway, including labor markets? Very little is known, and even less is published about how students' educational experiences influence their transition into and navigation of labor markets post-graduation.

Conclusion

The content analysis presented in this study reveals that the concepts of social and cultural capital and, to a lesser extent, funds of knowledge have become commonplace within the educational lexicon. As such, these concepts serve exclusively as building blocks for larger arguments and are not sufficiently elaborated upon, thus impeding theoretical advancements.

In presenting our findings, we demonstrated how each of the three frameworks were used by educational researchers. Yet, we were left wondering how one would ascertain the value of each. We question, which framework is more valued and has a higher status within educational research? If we were to answer this question solely from a frequentalist and magnitude approach, then social capital clearly warrants higher status. Likewise, if we could determine value by understanding ease in quantifying conceptual elements of the framework in order to create proxies, social capital would again emerge as more valuable. If we understand value by the application of the framework and broader discussion as it extends from original developments and conceptualizations, cultural capital appears to be more valued. However, we argue that a shift is necessary with respect to how the field of education defines value and status of frameworks and understand more broadly how such frameworks might be used. Finally, we found that most of the literature on funds of knowledge centers on pedagogical change, ignoring power structures and inequities. As demonstrated in this book, together funds of knowledge and the forms of capital can offer an important complementary framework for studying issues of educational equity and power (Chapter 2). We also demonstrate how emerging research illustrates the ways in which funds of knowledge can be an integral framework that exposes power structures, particularly when combined with frameworks like critical race theory, critical pedagogy, and community cultural wealth (Chapters 4 and 5). Finally, we illustrate how funds of knowledge can be useful as a pedagogy and lens beyond K–12 education and into postsecondary education (Chapters 6–10). Therefore, in assembling the chapters in this book, we worked to intentionally address many of the shortcomings that emerged from the content analysis reviewed in this chapter.

Note

1 There exist reviews on social capital (Dika & Singh, 2002) and on the pedagogical dimensions of funds of knowledge (Rodriguez, 2013; Hogg, 2011), but not on the three frameworks explored in this study.

References

Achinstein, B., Ogawa, R. T., Sexton, D., & Freitas, C. (2010). Retaining teachers of color: A pressing problem and a potential strategy for "hard-to-staff" schools. *Review of Educational Research, 80*, 71–107. doi:10.3102/0034654309355994

Achinstein, B., Ogawa, R. T., & Speiglman, A. (2004). Are we creating separate and unequal tracks of teachers? The effects of state policy, local conditions, and teacher characteristics on new teacher socialization. *American Educational Research Journal, 41*(3), 557–603. doi:10.3102/00028312041003557

Arzubiaga, A. E., Nogueron, A. L., & Sullivan, A. L. (2009). The education of children in im/migrant families. *Review of Research in Education, 33*, 246–271. doi:10.3102/0091732x08328243

Babbie, E. (1983). *The practice of social research* (3rd ed.). Belmont, CA: Wadsworth Publishing Company.

Barrett, B. D., & Martina, C. A. (2012). Towards a non-deterministic reading of Pierre Bourdieu: Habitus and educational change in urban schools. *Policy Futures in Education, 10*(3), 249–262. doi:10.2304/pfie.2012.10.3.249

Bills, D. B. (2003). Credentials, signals, and screens: Explaining the relationship between schooling and job assignment. *Review of Educational Research, 73*(4), 441–469. doi:10.3102/00346543073004441

Bourdieu, P. (1986). Forms of capital. In J. G. Richardson (Ed.), *Handbook of theory and research for the sociology of education*. New York: Greenwood.

Brayboy, B. M. J., Castagno, A. E., & Maughan, E. (2007). Chapter six: Equality and justice for all? Examining race in education scholarship. *Review of Research in Education, 31*, 159–194. doi:10.3102/0091732X07300046159

Buendía, E., Ares, N., Juarez, B. G., & Peercy, M. (2004). The geographies of difference: The production of east side, west side, and central city school. *American Educational Research Journal, 41*, 833–863. doi:10.3102/00028312041004833

Carter, P. L. (2003). "Black" cultural capital, status positioning, and schooling conflicts for low-income, African American youth. *Social Problems, 50*(1), 36–55. doi:10.1525/sp.2003.50.1.136

Carter, P. L. (2006). Straddling boundaries: Identity, culture, and school. *Sociology of Education, 79*(4), 304–328. doi:10.1177/003804070607900402

Chiu, M. M., & Khoo, L. (2005). Effects of resources, inequality, and privilege bias on achievement: Country, school, and student level analyses. *American Educational Research Journal, 42*(4), 575–603. doi:10.3102/00028312042004575

Coburn, C. E., & Russell, J. L. (2008). District policy and teachers' social networks. *Educational Evaluation and Policy Analysis, 30*(3), 203–235. doi:10.3102/0162373708321829

Cohen, D. K., Raudenbush, S. W., & Ball, D. L. (2003). Resources, instruction, and research. *Educational Evaluation and Policy Analysis, 25*(2), 119–142. doi:10.3102/01623737025002119

Coleman, J. (1988). Social capital in the creation of human capital. *The American Journal of Sociology, 94*, S95–S120. doi:10.1086/228943

Corbett, M. (2004). "It was fine, if you wanted to leave": Educational ambivalence in a Nova Scotian coastal community 1963–1998. *Anthropology & Education Quarterly, 35*, 451–471. doi:10.1525/aeq.2004.35.4.451

Daly, A. J., & Finnigan, K. S. (2011). The ebb and flow of social network ties between district leaders under high-stakes accountability. *American Educational Research Journal, 48*(1), 39–79. doi:10.3102/0002831210368990

Dika, S., & Singh, K. (2002). Applications of social capital in educational literature: A critical synthesis. *Review of Educational Research, 72*(1), 31–60. doi:10.3102/00346543072001031

Ek, L. D. (2009). "It's different lives": A Guatemalan American adolescent's construction of ethnic and gender identities across educational contexts. *Anthropology & Education Quarterly, 40*, 405–420. doi:10.1111/j.1548-1492.2009.01061.x

Emirbayer, M., & Johnson, V. (2008). Bourdieu and organizational analysis. *Theory and Society, 37*, 1–44. doi:10.1007/s11186-007-9052-y

Enright, K. A. (2011). Language and literacy for a new mainstream. *American Educational Research Journal, 48*, 80–118. doi:10.3102/0002831210368989

Fox, M. J. T., Lowe, S. C., & McClellan, G. S. (Eds.). (2005). *New directions for student services: Serving native American students.* San Francisco, CA: Jossey-Bass.

Frank, K. A., Zhao, Y., Penuel, W. R., Ellefson, N., & Porter, S. (2011). Focus, fiddle, and friends: Experiences that transform knowledge for the implementation of innovations. *Sociology of Education, 84*(2), 137–156. doi:10.1177/0038040711401812

Goddard, R. D. (2003). Relational networks, social trust, and norms: A social capital perspective on students' chances of academic success. *Educational Evaluation and Policy Analysis, 25*, 59–74. doi:10.3102/01623737025001059

Hogg, L. (2011). An investigation of coherence within the literature. *Teaching and Teacher Education, 27*(3), 666–677. doi:10.1016/j.tate.2010.11.005

Hutchinson, S., & Lovell, C. (2004). A review of methodological characteristics of research published in key journals in higher education: Implications for graduate research teaching. *Research in Higher Education, 45*, 393–403. doi:10.1023/b:rihe.0000027392.94172.d2

Jones, S. (2007). Working-poor mothers and middle-class others: Psychosocial considerations in home-school relations and research. *Anthropology & Education Quarterly, 38,* 157–177. doi:10.1525/aeq.2007.38.2.159

Keselman, H., Huberty, C., Lix, L., Olejnik, S., Cribbie, R., Donahue, B., . . . Levin, J. R. (1998). Statistical practices of educational researchers: An analysis of their ANOVA, MANOVA and ANCOVA analyses. *Review of Educational Research, 68,* 350–386. doi:10.3102/00346543068003350

Kiyama, J. M. (2010). College aspirations and limitations: The role of educational ideologies and funds of knowledge in Mexican American families. *American Educational Research Journal, 47*(2), 330–356. doi:10.3102/0002831209357468

Krippendorff, K. (2004). *Content analysis: An introduction to its methodology* (2nd ed.). Thousand Oaks, CA: Sage.

Lareau, A. (2000). *Home advantage: Social class and parental intervention in elementary education.* Lanham, MD: Rowman & Littlefield.

Lareau, A. (2003). *Unequal childhoods: Class, race, and family life.* Berkeley, CA: University of California Press.

Lareau, A., & Horvat, E. (1999). Moments of social inclusion and exclusion: Race, class, and cultural capital in family-school relationships. *Sociology of Education, 72,* 37–53. doi:10.2307/2673185

Lee, J., & Bowen, N. K. (2006). Parent involvement, cultural capital, and the achievement gap among elementary school children. *American Educational Research Journal, 43*(2), 193–218. doi:10.3102/00028312043002193

LeTendre, G. K., Hofer, B. K., & Shimizu, H. (2003). What is tracking? Cultural expectations in the United States, Germany, and Japan. *American Educational Research Journal, 40*(1), 43–89. doi:10.3102/00028312040001043

Lewis, A. E., & Forman, T. A. (2002). Contestation or collaboration: A comparative study of home-school relations. *Anthropology & Education Quarterly, 33,* 60–89. doi:10.1525/aeq.2002.33.1.60

Lin, N. (1999). Building a network theory of social capital. *Connections, 22,* 28–51. Retrieved from www.bebr.ufl.edu/sites/default/files/Building%20a%20Network%20Theory%20of%20Social%20Capital.pdf

Louie, V. (2005). Chapter 4: Immigrant newcomer populations, ESEA, and the pipeline to college: Current considerations and future lines of inquiry. *Review of Research in Education, 29,* 69–104. doi:10.3102/0091732x029001069

Lubienski, S. T. (2003). Celebrating diversity and denying disparities: A critical assessment. *Educational Researcher, 32,* 30–38. doi:10.3102/0013189x032008030

Lucas, S. R., & Beresford, L. (2010). Naming and classifying: Theory, evidence, and equity in education. *Review of Research in Education, 34,* 25–84. doi:10.3102/0091732x09353578

Marx, K. (1849) 1933. *Wage-labour and capital.* Reprint, New York, NY: International Publishers Co.

McDonough, P. (1997). *Choosing colleges: How social class and schools structure opportunity.* Albany, NY: State University of New York Press.

McNamara Horvat, E., Weininger, E. B., & Lareau, A. (2003). From social ties to social capital: Class differences between the relations between schools and parent networks. *American Educational Research Journal, 40,* 319–351. doi:10.3102/00028312040002319

Meier Jaeger, M. (2011). Does cultural capital really affect academic achievement? New evidence from combined sibling and panel data. *Sociology of Education, 84,* 281–298. doi:10.1177/0038040711417010

Moll, L. C. (2010). Mobilizing culture, language, and educational practices: Fulfilling the promises of Mendez and Brown. *Educational Researcher, 39*, 451–460. doi:10.3102/0013189x10380654

Moll, L. C., Amanti, C., Neff, D., & González, N. (1992). Funds of knowledge for teaching: Using a qualitative approach to connect homes and classrooms. *Theory Into Practice, 31*(2), 132–141.

Morris, E. W. (2005). From "middle class" to "trailer trash": Teachers' perceptions of White students in a predominantly minority school. *Sociology of Education, 78*, 99–121. doi:10.1177/003804070507800201

Morris, J. E. (2004). Can anything good come from Nazareth? Race, class, and African American schooling and community in the urban South and Midwest. *American Educational Research Journal, 41*, 69–112. doi:10.3102/00028312041001069

Nasir, N. S., Hand, V., & Taylor, E. V. (2008). Culture and mathematics in school: Boundaries between "cultural" and "domain" knowledge in the mathematics classroom and beyond. *Review of Research in Education, 32*(1), 187–240. doi:10.3102/0091732x07308962

Nasir, N. S., & Saxe, G. B. (2003). Ethnic and academic identities: A cultural practice perspective on emerging tensions and their management in the lives of minority students. *Educational Researcher, 32*(5), 14–18. doi:10.3102/0013189x032005014

North, C. E. (2006). More than words? Delving into the substantive meaning(s) of "social justice" in education. *Review of Educational Research, 76*, 507–535. doi:10.3102/00346543076004507

Nuñez, A., & Bowers, A. J. (2011). Exploring what leads high school students to enroll in Hispanic-serving institutions: A multilevel analysis. *American Educational Research Journal, 48*, 1286–1313. doi:10.3102/0002831211408061

O'Connor, C., Lewis, A., & Mueller, J. (2007). Researching "Black" educational experiences and outcomes: Theoretical and methodological considerations. *Educational Researcher, 36*, 541–552. doi:10.3102/0013189x07312661

Orr, M. (1999). *Black social capital: The politics of school reform in Baltimore, 1986–1998.* Lawrence, KS: University Press of Kansas.

Paris, D. (2012). Culturally sustaining pedagogy: A needed change in stance, terminology, and practice. *Educational Researcher, 41*, 93–97. doi:10.3102/0013189x12441244

Park, J. J. (2012). It takes a village (or an ethnic economy): The varying roles of socioeconomic status, religion, and social capital in SAT preparation for Chinese and Korean American students. *American Educational Research Journal, 49*, 624–650. doi:10.3102/0002831211425609

Pearce, R. R. (2006). Effects of cultural and social structural factors on the achievement of White and Chinese American students at school transition points. *American Educational Research Journal, 43*(1), 75–101. doi:10.3102/00028312043001075

Perez Carreon, G., Drake, C., & Calabrese Barton, A. (2005). The importance of presence: Immigrant parents' school engagement experiences. *American Educational Research Journal, 42*(3), 465–498. doi:10.3102/00028312042003465

Petchauer, E. (2009). Framing and reviewing hip-hop educational research. *Review of Educational Research, 79*, 946–978. doi:10.3102/0034654308330967

Portes, A. (1998). Social capital: Its origins and applications in modern sociology. *Annual Review of Sociology, 24*, 1–24. doi:10.1146/annurev.soc.24.1.1

Ream, R. K. (2003). Counterfeit social capital and Mexican-American underachievement. *Education Evaluation and Policy Analysis, 25*(3), 237–262. doi:10.3102/016237370 25003237

Ream, R. K., & Palardy, G. (2008). Reexamining social class differences in the availability and the educational utility of parental social capital. *American Educational Research Journal, 45,* 238–278. doi:10.3102/0002831207308643

Ream, R. K., & Rumberger, R. W. (2008). Student engagement, peer social capital, and school dropout among Mexican American and non-Latino White students. *Sociology of Education, 81,* 109–139. doi:10.1177/003804070808100201

Rios-Aguilar, C., Kiyama, J. M., Gravitt, M., & Moll, L. C. (2011). Funds of knowledge for the poor and forms of capital for the rich? A capital approach to examining funds of knowledge. *Theory and Research in Education, 9*(2), 163–184. doi:10.1177/1477878511409776

Rodriguez, G. M. (2013). Power and agency in education: Exploring the pedagogical dimensions of funds of knowledge. *Review of Research in Education, 37*(1), 87–120. doi:10.3102/0091732x12462686

Roksa, J., & Potter, D. (2011). Parenting and academic achievement: Intergenerational transmission of educational advantage. *Sociology of Education, 84,* 299–321. doi:10.1177/0038040711417013

Sallaz, J., & Zavisca, J. (2008). From the margins to the mainstream: The unlikely meeting of Pierre Bourdieu and US sociology. *Sociologica, 2,* 1–21.

Sandefur, R. L., & Laumann, E. O. (1998). A paradigm for social capital. *Rationality and Society, 10*(4), 481–501. doi:10.1177/104346398010004005

Schutz, A. (2006). Home is a prison in the global city: The tragic failure of school-based community engagement strategies. *Review of Educational Research, 76,* 691–743. doi:10.3102/00346543076004691

Sirin, S. R. (2005). Socioeconomic status and academic achievement: A meta-analytic review of research. *Review of Educational Research, 75*(3), 417–453. doi:10.3102/00346543075003417

Stemler, S. (2001). An overview of content analysis. *Practical Assessment, Research & Evaluation, 7*(17). Retrieved from http://PAREonline.net/getvn.asp?v=7&n=17

Triandis, H. C., Chen, X. P., & Chan, D. K. (1998). Scenarios for the measurement of collectivism and individualism. *Journal of Cross-Cultural Psychology, 29*(2), 275–289. doi:10.1177/0022022198292001

Vasquez, O. A. (2006). Chapter 2: Cross-national explorations of sociocultural research on learning. *Review of Research in Education, 30*(1), 33–64. doi:10.3102/0091732X030001033

Warikoo, N., & Carter, P. (2009). Cultural explanations for racial and ethnic stratification in academic achievement: A call for a new and improved theory. *Review of Educational Research, 79*(1), 366–394. doi:10.3102/0034654308326162

Wiggan, G. (2007). Race, school achievement, and educational inequality: Toward a student-based inquiry perspective. *Review of Educational Research, 77*(3), 310–333. doi:10.3102/003465430303947

Wong, N. A. (2008). "They see us as a resource": The role of a community-based youth center in supporting the academic lives of low-income Chinese American youth. *Anthropology & Education Quarterly, 39*(2), 181–204. doi:10.1111/j.1548-1492.2008.00015.x

Yamamoto, Y., & Brinton, M. (2010). Cultural capital in East Asian educational systems: The case of Japan. *Sociology of Education, 83*(1), 67–83. doi:10.1177/0038040709356567

Zapata Maldonado, D. E., Rhoads, R., & Buenavista, T. L. (2005). The student-initiated retention project: Theoretical contributions and the role of self-empowerment. *American Educational Research Journal, 42*(4), 605–638. doi:10.3102/00028312042004605

Zipin, L. (2013). Engaging middle years learners by making their communities curricular: A funds of knowledge approach. *Curriculum Perspectives, 33*(3), 1–12.

Zipin, L., Sellar, S., Brennan, M., & Gale, T. (2015). Educating for futures in marginalized regions: A sociological framework for rethinking and researching aspirations. *Educational Philosophy and Theory, 47*(3), 227–246. doi:10.1080/00131857.2013.839376

4

FROM INCARCERATION TO COMMUNITY COLLEGE

Funds of Knowledge, Community Cultural Wealth, and Critical Race Theory

Luis Gustavo Giraldo, Adrian H. Huerta, and Daniel Solórzano

United States higher education has seen increased enrollment of Students of Color (American Council on Education, 2011; Chang, Altbach, & Lomotey, 2005). Similarly, the number of people housed in correctional facilities in the United States has reached an epoch-making level (Garland, 2001; Bahena, Cooc, Currie-Rubin, Kuttner, & Ng, 2012). Garland (2001) has referred to this time period as the era of "mass incarceration" for low-income communities of color, as incarceration rates over the past 30 years have seen a 500 percent increase in incarcerated Americans (American Civil Liberties Union [ACLU], 2007). Pettit and Western (2004) further report that the incarcerated population is dispropor-tionately Black and Latina/o. Although tough-on-crime policies and discrimina-tion continue to spread across the criminal justice system, many economic factors are pushing states, including California, to reconsider incarceration policies to change to release more non-violent offenders from prison due to the costs asso-ciated with incarceration (Smith, 2009). As incarcerated individuals are released, they experience numerous social, economic, psychological, and political barriers to personal success, including challenges reintegrating into higher education.

In an era of mass incarceration, there are efforts to release non-violent offend-ers as a result of Proposition 57, voted for and passed in November 2016. Prop-osition 57, proposed by Governor Jerry Brown, set to reduce the state prison population and address the tough-on-crime policies that have filled correctional institutions at disproportionate rates with Black and Latino males (ACLU, 2007; Giraldo, 2016). The measure also reassigns the decision-making process from prosecutors to judges to decide when juveniles should be tried as adults. Con-sequently, this effort creates momentum for some previously incarcerated, for-merly gang-involved Students of Color to seek higher education as part of their reintegration (Giraldo, 2016). In fact, an important number of previously incarcerated formerly gang-involved men and women of color are attending community colleges (Giraldo, 2016). However, we know nothing about their experiences in postsecondary institutions, particularly in community colleges. Therefore, this chapter fills an important knowledge gap and contributes to understanding their experiences in these higher education institutions from a non-deficit perspective through a critical race theory (CRT) lens complemented by funds of knowledge (FK) and community cultural wealth (CCW).

Critical Race Theory

CRT works toward identifying and challenging racism in its historical and contemporary forms as part of a larger goal of identifying and challenging all forms of subordination. This study simultaneously utilized FK to yield new insights and understanding of previously incarcerated, formerly gang-involved students' successful trajectories, or how they successfully reintegrated through their community college experiences.

Ladson-Billings and Tate (1995) are credited with introducing CRT to centralize race to understand the context and critique the persistent educational inequalities experienced by Students of Color. Consequently, Solórzano (1997) expanded CRT by incorporating five tenets, where these tenets stressed the centrality and intersectionality of race and racism with other forms of subordination, which places race at the center of all discourse to understand systematic oppression (Solórzano, 1997; Solórzano & Yosso, 2000). As Solórzano and associates (1997) acknowledge:

- 1st tenet—although race is central to the analysis, the role of other social identities must be considered to fully explain the multiple oppressions one may face (e.g., sexism, classism, eurocentrism, monolingualism, and heterosexism);
- 2nd tenet—the challenge to the dominant ideology calls for scholars to question race-neutral concepts such as objectivity, meritocracy, and equal opportunity within education settings. It also calls on us to challenge cultural deficit frameworks that minimize, distort, and stereotype the experiences of Students of Color. In the end, the funds of knowledge and community cultural wealth frameworks meet that challenge;
- 3rd tenet—the commitment to social justice stresses the importance of educational researchers to be committed to eliminating racism and other forms of oppression that exist within education;
- 4th tenet—the centrality of experiential knowledge recognizes the importance of legitimizing the personal stories and histories of People of Color. Experiential knowledge should stem from the lived experiences of students, who can provide a level of expertise in understanding racial issues through first-hand experience;

- 5th tenet—CRT in education must use an interdisciplinary perspective, which requires a historical and contemporary outlook using various disciplinary perspectives with an emphasis on the history of racism, sexism, and classism.

As a prevailing framework for studying race and racism, CRT has challenged the dominant paradigms in analyzing the history of access and success for Students of Color (e.g., Buenavista, Jayakumar, & Misa-Escalante, 2009; Harper, Patton, & Wooden, 2009; Yosso, Smith, Ceja, & Solórzano, 2009).

Funds of Knowledge

As a counternarrative to deficit models of low-income Latina/o families, FK emerged in the educational literature to highlight the many resources and "wealth" that they possess (Moll & Greenberg, 1992; Moll, Amanti, Neff, & González, 1992). Moll and Greenberg's (1990) research was rooted in a perspective that highlighted that every household is an educational environment, and its members gain knowledge that helps them navigate their life-learning using their social and historical wisdom, stories, and teachings as a road map.

This chapter uses Rios-Aguilar, Kiyama, Gravitt, and Moll's (2011) new approach, which combines FK and capital to enrich research that strives to understand the educational successes of previously incarcerated, formerly gang-involved men and women of color. More specifically, it embeds a capital perspective within the FK approach to explicitly address issues of power, class, ideology, and racism that earlier research on FK had not contemplated.

This chapter also redefines the concept of dark funds of knowledge as introduced by Zipin (2009). He introduced "dark" FK through the Redesigning Pedagogies in the North (RPiN) project, which built curricula to incorporate students' "dark" experiences outside of the classroom into their learning environments at school. Importantly, these experiences included significant life-altering and impactful traumas that ultimately triggered and defined an identity embraced by students. These identities outside of classroom space served as a means of survival and adaptation. Students use their FK to make meaning of their worlds; thus, all these experiences entailed capital that was accessed in the classroom through the RPiN project pedagogy. As such, the FK accessed to embrace this approach came from "dark" topics (experiences) that students brought into the classroom (Zipin, 2009). Ultimately, these FK were used to bridge students' experiences with teaching and learning in academic learning spaces.

Consequently, dark FK are noted and discussed using a CRT non-deficit perspective to reconceptualize the concept of dark FK to FK that exist within dark spaces. This conversion focuses on the light in the darkness that this group of students experienced as they survived a lifestyle that included gangs, incarceration, and the trauma that comes from violence. The change also notes that the spaces frequented by this group of students are dark. It allows for hope and dreams to be acknowledged as existing within these "dark spaces."

Community Cultural Wealth

Yosso (2005) developed the concept of CCW to challenge and extend Bourdieu's use of cultural and social capital—capitals that focus on white middle-class families. She defines CCW as "the array of cultural knowledge, skills, abilities and contacts possessed by socially marginalized groups that often go unrecognized and unacknowledged" (p. 1). Yosso stresses that marginalized and vulnerable students, families, and communities have multiple forms of capital that have been used and shared for survival and mobility. She went on to explain: "It includes aspirational, navigational, social, linguistic, familial and resistant capital. These forms of capital draw on the knowledges Students of Color bring with them from their homes and communities into the classroom" (p. 1).

In this chapter, CCW provides a connection to FK by adding a critical race perspective to the cultural wealth that previously incarcerated, formerly gang-involved students bring to the classroom, and the overall college process that is accessed through their experiences of light in dark spaces as a form of capital. Using CCW also helps provide a clearer analysis of the impact that racial microaggressions have on the educational trajectories of previously incarcerated former gang members in community college. CCW allows for the different forms of capital to include capital from "dark spaces" into the examination of how these forms can be formed and accessed by these students.

Importantly, this chapter explores issues of power, class, ideology, and racism through the experiences of racial microaggressions by this particular group of students. With these various issues in the backdrop, this chapter addresses the following research questions:

1.   What are the experiences of previously incarcerated, formerly gang-involved students as they reintegrate and transition into community college?
2.   How do previously incarcerated, formerly gang-involved students use FK and CCW on community college campuses as they experience racial microaggressions[1]?

Data Collection

This case study combined ethnographic participatory observations of the Chicana/o studies class at Homeboy Industries (HBI) and individual interviews with all 15 of the HBI students who participated in the class. In addition, the case study utilized data from interviews with one program administrator and the faculty member who was in charge of teaching the college course at Homeboy

Industries. We used vignettes to explain racial microaggressions to study partici-pants and to lead interviews into discussion. Last, we reviewed all documents relevant to this study that were publicly available at Homeboy Industries and at East Los Angeles College, Los Angeles City College and Los Angeles Trade Tech.

Data Collection Procedures

The primary researcher took an active participant observant approach through-out the 15-week course. He engaged with 15 course participants during five three-hour class sessions and 10 two-hour study group sessions. Each of the 15 participants completed a one-on-one semi-structured interview. The semi-structured nature of the interviews allowed the students to tell their stories as they related to their educational experiences and occupational goals, and to describe their involvement with the "gang life" and their experiences as previ-ously incarcerated community college students. He maintained particular focus on their experiences of racial microaggressions within these institutions and among their peers.

The principal researcher defined racial microaggressions for the participants through detailed vignettes depicting acts of racism. He then asked questions related to (a) each participant's experiences in community college and how he or she had experienced racial microaggressions on campus, both within the student's own race and among student services and faculty; (b) how the participant had responded to racial microaggressions; (c) how he or she identified significant bar-riers to success in community college; and (d) why the participant felt he or she had experienced community college in the way that he or she had.

To further assess other experiences of previously incarcerated, formerly gang-involved students in community colleges, he conducted participatory observations of five students' interactions with community college student services personnel. This allowed us to discuss the complexities of racial microaggressions, how they had impacted these students, and how the students had responded to these assaults. He also conducted another 17 one-on-one semi-structured interviews with pre-viously incarcerated, formerly gang-involved college students.

Last, he interviewed the faculty member teaching the course at Homeboy Industries and one student services administrator to shed light on how they per-ceived this particular group of students' experiences in a community college set-ting at HBI, on their particular community college campuses, and through their responses to vignettes depicting racial microaggressions experienced by Students of Color.

Data Analysis

All interviews were audiotaped and transcribed. Overarching themes in partici-pants' responses were analyzed in reference to studies of the experiences of Stu-dents of Color with racial microaggressions in higher education (e.g., Smith et al.,

2007; Solórzano & Delgado Bernal, 2000; Yosso et al., 2009). We analyzed the data both inductively and deductively (Coffey & Atkinson, 1996) to generate the coding schemes. More specifically, we analyzed the interviews by first developing initial codes (Strauss & Corbin, 1998). Next, based on the intersection and partitioning of these initial codes, we created data matrices to identify themes and subthemes that we used to organize the final stages of the analyses and interpretation of the data.

The initial codes of racial microaggressions, funds of knowledge, and Community Cultural Wealth were content analyzed and subdivided into themes and coded as racial microaggressions, intergroup racial microaggressions, converting funds of knowledge, and forms of Community Cultural Wealth. These codes were then scanned for content that intersected with the first initial set of codes and subthemes and checked for patterns across students. We triangulated the data to ensure trustworthiness by having more than one subject as a data source. The HBI participant data are shown in Table 4.1.

TABLE 4.1   Homeboy Industries Participant Demographics and Aspirations

Name (Age)	Gender/Ethnic Self Identification	Years Incarcerated	Years in Higher Education	Educational Goal and Occupational Goal
Shena (32)	Female Other	7	5	MA Business/Entrepreneur
Monique (35)	Female Chicana	10	7	MFT Therapist
Adriana (30)	Female Hispanic	6 months	1 (semester)	AA first, then BA or higher Recreational Therapist in Recovery
Geo (18)	Male Hispanic	2	1 (month)	PhD Parole Officer
Pam (30)	Female Hispanic	2	3 (semesters)	BA Business Manager
Xabi (33)	Male Latino	13	1	PhD Drug and Alcohol Counselor for Youth
Fermin (20)	Male Chicano	1 month	2.5	PhD Business Administrator
Felisha (32)	Female African American	3 1/2	6 (weeks)	BA Chef
Mikey (31)	Male Hispanic	10	1 (month)	BA Social Worker
Ingrid (39)	Female Mexican American	6 months	3 (semesters)	MA Substance Abuse Counselor

(Continued)

TABLE 4.1 (Continued)

Name (Age)	Gender/Ethnic Self Identification	Years Incarcerated	Years in Higher Education	Educational Goal and Occupational Goal
Lewis (23)	Male Hispanic	12	2 (months)	PhD / Gourmet Chef
Andy (27)	Male Latino	11	1 1/2	PhD / Rehabilitation Program Director/Owner
Roy (34)	Mexican American Male	20	3 1/2	MA / Art Therapist
Richard (39)	Male Chicano	18	1 (semester)	AA / Counselor
Gab (38)	Male Chicano	13	1 (semester)	BA / Case Manager
Eddie (18)	Male Latino	4	1 (month)	PhD / Graphic Designer
Jose (19)	Male Hispanic	3 1/2	1 (month)	MA / Parole Officer
Abe (18)	Male Latino	2	1 (month)	JD / Lawyer
Louie (27)	Male Mexican/ Latino	7	3	Automotive Technician/ Business owner
Kenny (21)	Mexican American Male	3 (months)	3	PhD / Math Professor
Chris (25)	Male Mexican	10	1 (day)	BA / Therapist
Joseph (42)	Male Mexican	13	1 1/2	MA / Director of Training Programs
Bob (47)	Male Latino	25	1 (semester)	BA / Substance Abuse Counselor
Dave (21)	Male Latino	4	1 (semester)	BA / Parole Officer
Rob (40)	Male Chicano	2	1	BA / Counselor
Lew (37)	Male Latino	7	2	BA / Business Owner
Stew (36)	Male Latino	17	1	BA / Counselor
Meri (39)	Female Hispanic	9	2	BA / Case Manager

Context for the Case Study

Homeboy Industries is a central element to the community college students who were previously incarcerated or former gang members. Homeboy Industries serves as a national model and is the largest gang intervention and re-entry program in the U.S. that provides free services to its constituents (Boyle, 2010). For almost 30 years, the agency has served as a beacon of hope and opportunity for individuals attempting to leave gang life, who frequently experience multiple barriers and challenges, and for whom there is virtually no other avenue to enter the mainstream society due to the social stigma associated with gang membership, incarceration, and tattoos (Boyle, 2010). Homeboy Industries has served thousands of people from various racial and ethnic backgrounds, ages, and life experiences, who search for a second opportunity and to develop a new community or peer and family. The mission is to provide free and holistic services to the former "homeboys," which include tattoo removal, one-on-one counseling, job and technical training, legal aid, life skills courses, General Education Diploma preparation, high school diploma assistance, academic tutoring, case management that helps participants develop "navigational capital" to heal and reintegrate, court-mandated classes (e.g., anger management, parenting, domestic violence, and substance abuse groups), access to postsecondary education courses, and other services (Homeboy Industries, 2014). The culmination of these various efforts and services is to create opportunities to foster hope, kinship, community, healing, and change (Homeboy Industries, 2014). At Homeboy Industries, community is forged, and it holds its participants to identify the truth of who they are—and not the worst thing they have ever done (Boyle, 2010).

Homeboy Industries Onsite College Course

The development of an on-site college course at Homeboy Industries was born out of the interest of formerly incarcerated individuals and gang members wanting to pursue higher education. The community college class, Chicana/os in Contemporary Society, was an introductory course in this particular discipline. All enrolled students were eligible for college units, and the course required one weekly class lecture of three hours for 15 weeks, and 10 weeks of two-hour study sessions, which were hosted in HBI. The additional rationale for the course was to demonstrate viability for other students, including those who previously departed high school early, were over suspended and expelled, and were disrespected by educators.

Findings

This chapter focuses on examining two emergent themes: (a) FK as forms of capital embedded within CCW, with particular attention on aspirational and navigational capital, and (b) the complexities of racial microaggressions experienced by participants. This process highlights how this group of students accesses FK and CCW, and links these frameworks to connect and note the particular complexities of this highly visible group of students with invisible needs to their peers, staff, faculty, and institutional practices on community college campuses.

Intersecting Funds of Knowledge and Community Cultural Wealth via Critical Race Theory

Current theoretical and empirical scholarship has not fully explored how FK and CCW intersect. In fact, these two complement one another as we focus on previously incarcerated formerly gang-involved Students of Color in community colleges. While Yosso (2005) briefly linked funds of knowledge and CCW, she did not fully develop the connection between these frameworks. Therefore, to fill this void, the overarching bridge that holds these two frameworks together is further examined in this chapter by using CRT as the umbrella that unifies FK and CCW.

First, CRT allows for us to use its tenets to focus on the experiences of previously incarcerated and formerly gang-involved students as non-deficit forms of light in "dark spaces" encountered by this group—i.e., gangs, jail, and prison. In doing so, we explore the role of other social identities; challenge the dominant ideology and scholarship that focuses on race-specific marginalized group concepts; recognize the importance of legitimizing the personal stories and histories of previously incarcerated and formerly gang-involved People of Color; and ultimately push forward the commitment to social justice that stresses the importance of educational researchers to be committed to eliminating racism and other forms of oppression that exist within education. Second, Figure 4.1 couples FK and CCW carried by previously incarcerated, formerly gang-involved individuals to examine how this group of students experiences the prison to community college pipeline as part of their reintegration. Third, Figure 4.1 furthers the connection that both FK and CCW have to the experiences of racial microaggressions (RM) lived by this particular group of students on community college campuses. Last, Figure 4.1 illustrates using a CRT lens to analyze how these students experience racial microaggressions, and how these students draw on their FK and different forms of capital embedded in CCW to reintegrate into higher education.

The following two examples highlight the connection of these three bodies of theory and contextualizes Figure 4.1 by noting how the model plays out in the actual experiences of these students. For the previously incarcerated and formerly gang-involved men and women in this study, the FK activated within dark spaces were accessed through their experiences and CCW obtained in jail and prison, and through drug addiction and gang life. These FK and forms of capital embedded in CCW were profoundly critical as resources for survival under the circumstances experienced within those particular dark spaces. Importantly, however, the success in college of these students can also include the activation of

Critical Race Theory

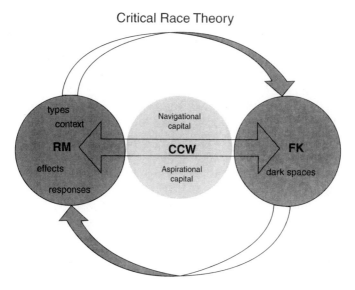

FIGURE 4.1   Prison to Community College Pipeline Reintegration Model

these FK and forms of capital as forms of light and hope from the dark spaces, and now positively impact their lives after prison and gangs, and specifically in their lives as college students.

Chris: None of that ever just crossed your mind, you know? What crossed your mind was gangbanging and drugs. That was it. That's what held me back. And the people I surrounded myself with, they didn't have no goals or dreams either. So, we're all just like, you know, in the same circle doing the same shit, and we wouldn't think outside of the box. All we're seeing was bullshit versions of what to do and get this money, and, oh, let's get on one. And, you know, that was it. Except now I use that shit to help me stay on track. I don't want that anymore. It keeps me humble.

Although this example notes what was the "norm" for this individual and his group of friends, it also highlights the internal conversations that happened while he occupied these dark spaces and that became sources of strength and forms of capital—as a means to transform, heal, and reintegrate. Ultimately, this combination fueled the activation of funds of knowledge from a different unit of analysis that served as light from dark spaces. Richard's comments support this notion:

Richard: I think that this time around, I honestly think it's different. I've said it so many times in the past, but it's different because now, the same mistakes

I've made, I have two of my daughters that I did not raise, but are in the same boat I am or I was. You know, my 17-year-old had just gotten off from doing two years, now she's back incarcerated. My other daughter, she's 20 years old and she ended up getting five years, five years of prison. So, I think that it's where I make that turnaround, where I said, "Damn, you know, I got to snap out of it because if I continue, then what kind of example am I doing for my girls?" I knew this since I was locked up. It came to me in a fuckin' cell.

The activation of FK in these dark spaces created a relevant connection to why these college students pushed forward despite the adversities and stress of being previously incarcerated and formerly gang-involved. The demands for this particular group of students not only included the demands that every college student experiences; it also included a deeper and complex transformative process. The exchange included identity, cultural negotiation, acceptance, probation and parole conditions, and modes of conduct that included cultural norms valued in prison and gang life that colleges do not exercise. These all serve as FK from a different unit of analysis—gangs, jail, prison. Essentially, these FK from dark spaces impact these students to continue to push forward. On the other hand, these can also include particular needs that are invisible to their college peers, staff, and faculty in higher education.

Often, "assaults" came in the form of racial microaggressions that were arguably invisible to faculty, staff, and other students alike. More importantly, this transformative process necessitated the activation of different forms of capital. Specifically, for this study, we note how this group of HBI participants accessed and activated aspirational, navigational, and familial capital as a means of reintegration and of adjusting to life as college students.

Funds of Knowledge as Forms of Capital

Contrary to the original FK study, the unit of analysis here is rooted in the family made through the gang and relationships made in prison. Although there are many conditioned forms of relationships within these new families for this group of students based on gang culture, these relationships often re-create FK and forms of capital that are later used in life after prison and gangs. Importantly, this study's college students accessed their FK and activated different forms of capital as part of their educational experiences that were created in dark spaces—i.e., gangs, jail, and prison.

Both the original FK study and the current study note that education is valued and needed to "succeed." Success in the current study means many different things. First, staying out of jail or prison is considered success. Some of the participants in this study have been in and out of jail and/or prison their entire lives from a very early age. Educational spaces have always been connected to negative and exclusionary experiences. Success for these students stemmed from changing the relationship that educational spaces hold. Success encompassed re-creating hope and goals, and slowly taking steps closer to changing the dynamics of learning within classrooms with teachers and other students. Success also meant that these students' self-assessment and identity would always be challenged and put to the test. This happened due to the FK and forms of capital embedded in CCW that informed these students' processes, from gang and prison, to community counterspaces, to college and classroom spaces.

Monique: I love going to school. I think education was my life raft in my life, you know? Like that was my savior because that was [a] life raft. I may have been drowning in life, and there comes education, and it just saved me.

Although there were marked differences in the types of labor histories and household activities between the families in the original FK study and this study's group of students, the educational ideologies remain the same. Education was important and valued by all. Ultimately, FK for this group of students were re-created by their new family, and the educational ideologies included education as hope for a better future. As one HBI participant explained:

Richard: When it's about me, they always encourage me to, you know, go to school, but I don't think they believe that I'm going to—that I could actually accomplish it. But school was always important to my parents for me. My homies also encouraged me too. They tell me that I'm gonna make it, cause I'm fuckin' smart.

The current study focuses on how different forms of capital are accessed from resources embedded in a different family—gangs and relationships in prison—as the unit of analysis. Although this change resulted in a different conception of family, it also highlights the significant similarities that stem from wanting to use education as an important goal for a better life. The difference between the two is significant. While the traditional family unit is not always stable and positive, gang and prison life are consistently dark spaces.

Xabi: When I was locked up in solitary confinement, you know, in my cell all alone, I used to imagine myself in college. I used to read books all the time that some of my homies locked up with me would tell me about. I read a lot. The time I had and the *clecha* [guidance] I got from the older homies helped me focus and get ready for the day that I would be a college student. I had the discipline, I just needed to work on my anger and attitude.

TABLE 4.2 Comparison Between FK of Homeboy Industries Students and the Original FK Study

	Original FK study	HBI Students FK
Labor and Family History	Ranching, farming, horse riding skills, animal management, construction, carpentry, masonry, automotive repair, manual labor	Unemployed, cash-paid work (under the table), drug sales, manual labor, automotive repair, delivery drivers, agricultural workers, garment workers, construction, carpentry
Household Activities	Religious: catechism, baptisms, Bible studies, moral knowledge/ ethics, childcare, cooking, budgets	Gang hang out, drug use, church outings, cooking, parties, survival knowledge
Educational Ideologies	School is important	School is important for career success

Importantly, although these spaces were "dark," this group of students also found light in those spaces. While this may be the case, oftentimes there are glimmers of hope that are introduced within these dark spaces that will resurface when an individual is ready for change. The FK chart in Table 4.2 illustrates the similarities and differences in the unit of analysis used in each study. Particularly, this chart highlights household activities and labor.

Community Cultural Wealth

Drawing from Yosso's (2005) definition of community cultural wealth, this study focused on aspirational, navigational, and familial capital to further examine how students used funds of knowledge and different forms of capital embedded within CCW accessed in dark spaces to navigate the reintegration process after prison, jail, and gang life. This process was significant for these students, as their experiences as college students connected the transformative process of being previously incarcerated and formerly gang-involved to college campuses and other educational spaces.

Navigational Capital

Yosso (2005) indicated, "Navigational capital refers to skills of maneuvering through social institutions" (p. 80). She highlighted the context of this maneuvering as happening through institutions that were not meant to include People of Color. Consequently, college campus practices were not equipped to receive the students in this study with the support systems to help them reintegrate and adjust to college life. Despite this, they still accessed navigational capital from cultural wealth learned in the spaces they had experienced—prison and gang life.

A clear example of this activation of funds of knowledge from dark spaces was highlighted by Xabi:

> People, just by their actions are . . . even the words especially if you're going to go and ask like . . . some of the teachers would be like, "Well, what are you doing here?" One time, I was there with my dude, right, on campus, and we were walking to class and, you know, he has tattoos on him and so as me. So, like, campus security came up to us. You know what I mean? There were all these people around, but then campus security came on to us and I was like, "Well, what was that all about?" You know what I mean? They were like, "Can we help you? What are you doing right here?" You know? I'm like, "What do you mean can you help me? I'm a student and he's my boyfriend taking me to class." They followed us to my class, then escorted him to his car. No words exchanged. Just the assumption that he was up to no good.

The following participant highlights this process by noting his connection to his experiences and how they resonate now as a college student.

Chris: I love learning. That's number one, and I love challenging the dominant groups of students. So, I love . . . this is the space where I already saw that I walk in and shut people's preconceived notions because I have a certain idea, like, because of what I look like. But then when I opened my mouth and I started participating, then it shadows on me. I knew this from the very beginning when I ran the streets. I'm a smart man and my homies would always come to me for leadership. I was a knucklehead but I was a smart one. I know how to handle myself because of what I've learned in prison and in the streets. I just got to learn more about writing essays and speaking without bad words.

Students in the sample not only accessed FK from dark spaces, but also activated different forms of capital embedded within CCW, and learned in these spaces to compensate for the lack of resources that specifically targeted their needs and that were available to them in community colleges. Often the activation of navigational capital in higher education for this group of students came through the recognition that they had resources that stemmed from the internal truth that they too mattered and had what it takes. An administrator at HBI supported this idea:

HBI Administrator 1: Definitely . . . you can see . . . there's an anxiety or maybe even PTSD that has to be shed, and that's a slow process as a student works towards understanding that they too can be a college student . . . like, how do other students perceive these students or how do teachers perceive these students, I think the most important thing [is] how the students perceive themselves. . . . But when you're conditioned to believe you're not going to go far with school, that's something that has to be talked about and has to be, I guess, there has to be a reconditioning done where the student looks at themselves and says, "I am a college student."

Importantly, this group of students learned tools to survive and thrive in community college. Not only did they activate different forms of capital embedded within their CCW and their FK to respond to the racial microaggressions they experienced, they also note the lack of training that higher education institutions have to support this particular group of students.

Conclusion

Higher education must accommodate the changing dynamics of the 21st century student. Diversity in higher education will continue to encompass myriad groups that include numerous intersecting combinations. As such, faculty, staff, and students must learn about the normative institutional practices that pose barriers for all students, including those who have previously been incarcerated and are former gang members. It is imperative that we discuss the harmful and demeaning effects that racial microaggressions impose on these students as they seek higher education as a way of reintegration.

This study, rooted in critical race theory, funds of knowledge, and community cultural wealth perspectives, has presented an alternative foundation for future empirical research and professional practices that incorporate previously incarcerated and former gang members as students within higher education institutions. CRT offers a counternarrative to seek inclusion of this otherwise marginalized student population. By acknowledging the embedded structural racist institutional practices along with individual enactments of racial microaggressions upon previously incarcerated and formerly gang-involved students within higher education, faculty, staff, and other students may better respond to the inclusion of other marginalized groups on campus. Significantly, future empirical research on this student population will require direct attention to how these two factors—prior incarceration and gang membership—present barriers that many higher education actors, policies, and practices cannot see, as they are specific to this group of students.

The reality of a racialized social structure remains for students seeking opportunities for educational advancement; it often hinders their access and success within higher education systems (Harper et al., 2009). Addressing educational barriers requires a commitment to social justice and social equity, and researchers often occupy a unique position and ability to advocate for students because they can highlight the lack of support, inclusion, and access to resources that address the needs of this student population.

Viewing these issues through a critical race theory lens allowed for a reflective understanding of how these students also purport an opportunity that is inclusive of respect, support, dignity, and sustainability of progression. This theoretical perspective pushed forward for dialogue, analysis, and empirical research that deconstruct the educational experiences of gang members in higher education with the purpose of furthering the research as well as the practices of students from marginalized groups. Ultimately, these findings push all higher education scholars to engage in transformational research and change that will allow for students who have been incarcerated and who have been gang-involved to access and redefine their own educational opportunities while reintegrating into the world.

Implications for Student Support Practice

Student services programs should be created to support students who have been incarcerated and who have been part of gang life on all college campuses. This would mitigate and address the invisibility of the needs of this group of students—needs that often go unnoticed. These services should include mental health services, academic support, financial aid, and motivational support groups that address the issues that these students contend with as they leave behind the gang and prison life. Perhaps colleges and universities can hire staff from Homeboy Industries to train and facilitate workshops for college faculty and employees. As one of the largest gang-intervention, rehabilitation, and re-entry programs in the country, Homeboy Industries has helped nurture into existence 46 similar programs in the United States as well as several outside of the country (Homeboy Industries, 2014). The goal is to create a national movement to address the lethal absence of hope among inner-city youth. Solidifying services through the implementation of lessons learned from the Global Homeboy Network, reconvening to share results, and advancing the movement are Homeboy's dreams for the coming years. Part of Homeboy's wish is to further broaden the impact of the service delivery model by establishing and building partnerships with peer organizations who can become a part of the national network (Homeboy Industries, 2014). Specifically, college staff and faculty should also receive training on how to work with previously incarcerated and formerly gang-involved students. Training on racial microaggressions and the effects that these have on students is needed for student services staff to provide more comprehensive services. With current federal and state funds allocated to community colleges, these trainings would provide an opportunity for staff, faculty, and administrators to better understand more about all their students.

In conclusion, CRT foregrounds race and racism, as well as challenges separate discourses on race, gender, and class by demonstrating how racism intersects with other forms of subordination on students. The impacts of racism and racial microaggressions on Students of Color cannot be ignored as they affect various social, academic, and psychosocial aspects of students' lives. The utilization of this theoretical framework sets a foundation to challenge the dominant racial ideology of oppression. Importantly, by exploring issues of power, class, ideology, and racism through examples of racial microaggressions, CCW and FK allow scholarship to connect and highlight the particular complexities of this highly visible group of students with invisible needs to their peers, staff, faculty, and institutional practices on community college campuses. These frameworks honor the lived experiences of these particular students. In doing that, we dignify people that are often negatively portrayed and ignored.

Note

1 Racial microaggressions are defined in this chapter as one form of systemic everyday racism used to keep those at the racial margins in their place. Racial microaggressions are verbal and non-verbal assaults directed toward People of Color, often carried out in subtle, automatic, or unconscious forms. They are layered assaults, based on a Person of Color's, race, gender, class, sexuality, language, immigration status, phenotype, accent, or surname. They are cumulative assaults that take a physiological, psychological, and academic toll on People of Color (Solorzano & Yosso, 2001).

References

American Civil Liberties Union. (2007). *Race & ethnicity in America: Turning a blind eye to injustice*. New York, NY: Author.

American Council on Education. (2011). *Minorities in higher education: Twenty-fourth status report*. Washington, DC: Young M. Kim.

Bahena, S., Cooc, N., Currie-Rubin, R., Kuttner, P., & Ng, M. (Eds.). (2012). *Disrupting the school-to-prison pipeline*. Cambridge, MA: Harvard Educational Press.

Boyle, G. (2010). *Tattoos on the heart: The power of boundless compassion*. New York, NY: Free Press.

Buenavista, T. L., Jayakumar, U. M., & Misa-Escalante, K. (2009). Contextualizing Asian American education through critical race theory: An example of U.S. Pilipino college student experiences. In S. D. Museus (Ed.), *Conducting research on Asian Americans in higher education* (pp. 69–81). New Directions for Institutional Research No. 142. San Francisco, CA: Jossey-Bass.

Chang, M., Altbach, P. G., & Lomotey, K. (2005). Race in higher education. In P. G. Altbach, R. O. Berdahl, & P. J. Gumport (Eds.), *American higher education in the twenty-first century: Social, political, and economic challenges* (2nd ed., pp. 517–556). Baltimore, MD: Johns Hopkins University Press.

Coffey, A. J., & Atkinson, P. A. (1996). *Making sense of qualitative data: Complementary research strategies*. Thousand Oaks, CA: Sage.

Garland, D. (2001). *The culture of control: Crime and social order in contemporary society*. Chicago, IL: University of Chicago Press.

Giraldo, L. G. (2016). *From incarceration to community college to work: Racial microaggressions and reintegration in the prison-to-school pipeline*. Doctoral dissertation. Retrieved from ProQuest Dissertations and Theses database (UMI No. 10016955)

Harper, S. R., Patton, L. D., & Wooden, O. S. (2009). Access and equity for African American students in higher education: A critical race historical analysis of policy efforts. *Journal of Higher Education, 80*(4), 389–414.

Homeboy Industries. (2014). Retrieved from www.homeboyindustries.org

Ladson-Billings, G., & Tate, W. F. (1995). Toward a critical race theory of education. *Teachers College Record, 97*(1), 47–68.

Moll, L. C., Amanti, C., Neff, D., & González, N. (1992). Funds of knowledge for teaching: Using a qualitative approach to connect homes and classrooms. *Theory Into Practice, 31*(2), 132–141.

Moll, L. C., & Greenberg, J. B. (1990). Creating zones of possibilities: Combining social contexts for instruction. In L. C. Moll (Ed.), *Vygotsky and education: Instructional implications and applications of sociohistorical psychology* (pp. 319–348). Cambridge: Cambridge University Press.

Pettit, B., & Western, B. (2004). Mass imprisonment and the life course: Race and class inequality in U.S. incarceration. *American Sociological Review, 69*(2), 151–169.

Rios-Aguilar, C., Kiyama, J. M., Gravitt, M., & Moll, L. C. (2011). Funds of knowledge for the poor and forms of capital for the rich? A capital approach to examining funds of knowledge. *Theory and Research in Education, 9*(2), 163–184. doi:10.1177/1477878511409776

Smith, C. (2009). Deconstructing the pipeline: Evaluating school-to-prison pipeline equal protection cases through a structural racism framework. *Fordham Urban Law Journal, 35*(5), 1009–1049.

Smith, W., Allen, W. R., & Danley, L. L. (2007). "Assume the position . . . You fit the description": Psychosocial experiences and racial battle fatigue among African American male college students. *American Behavioral Scientist, 51*(4), 551–578.

Solórzano, D. G. (1997). Images and words that wound: Critical race theory, racial stereotyping and teacher education. *Teacher Education Quarterly, 24*(3), 5–19.

Solórzano, D. G., & Delgado Bernal, D. (2001). Examining transformational resistance through a critical race and LatCrit theory framework: Chicana and Chicano students in an urban context. *Urban Education, 36*(3), 308–342.

Solórzano, D. G., & Yosso, T. J. (2000). Toward a critical race theory of Chicana and Chicano education. In C. Tejeda, C. Martinez, & Z. Leonardo (Eds.), *Charting new terrains of Chicana(o)/Latina(o) education* (pp. 35–65). Cresskill, NJ: Hampton Press.

Strauss, A., & Corbin, J. (1998). *Basics of qualitative research: Techniques and procedures for developing grounded theory* (2nd ed.). Thousand Oaks, CA: Sage.

Yosso, T. J. (2005). Whose culture has capital? A critical race theory discussion of community cultural wealth. *Race, Ethnicity, and Education, 8*(1), 69–91. doi:10.1080/1361332052000341006

Yosso, T. J., Smith, W. A., Ceja, M., & Solórzano, D. G. (2009). Critical race theory, racial microaggressions, and campus racial climate for Latina/o undergraduates. *Harvard Educational Review, 79*(4), 659–691.

Zipin, L. (2009). Dark funds of knowledge, deep funds of pedagogy: Exploring boundaries between lifeworlds and schools. *Discourse: Studies in the Cultural Politics of Education, 30*(3), 317–331. doi:10.1080/01596300903037044

5

LA LOTERÍA AS CREATIVE RESISTANCE

The Funds of Knowledge, Critical Pedagogy, and Critical Race Theory in Art Education

Luis-Genaro García

In this chapter, I draw on Darts' (2004) scholarship to introduce the notion of *creative resistance* as a practical form of using the arts as resistance in a high school setting (García, 2012, 2015). My perception of *creative resistance* has gradually developed from my teaching experiences in the school I once attended, my practice as an artist, and my community activism. The commitment to my community and its students has enabled me to draw from what scholars identify as the funds of knowledge (FK): students' historical and accumulated home-based knowledge and resources, which can help students navigate their environment, well-being, and/or social circumstances (Moll et al., 1992; Moll & Greenberg, 1990; González & Moll, 2002; González, Moll, & Amanti, 2005). By drawing from the home and cultural practices that students have, I use the game of La Lotería[1] in their learning spaces for the purpose of developing their critical consciousness for social transformation. Using the game of La Lotería as a pedagogy originated from a class project, where a student articulated her mother's babysitting occupation in relation to childcare between upper-class and working-class families. In the years that followed, I began to draw from the familial and occupational knowledge that exists in students' homes as a foundation; I made connections to critical pedagogy (CP) by using the cultural and socio-economic experiences of students to develop their socio-political awareness for their own social transformation (Freire, 1970; McLaren, 1994; Darder, 1995; Duncan-Andrade & Morell, 2008; Duncan-Andrade, 2006). I also included critical race theory (CRT) to examine issues of race, racism, and deficit models in educational theory, policy, and practice that are used to subordinate students of color (Solórzano, 1998; Solorzano & Delgado-Bernal 2001; Delgado Bernal, 2002; Yosso, 2005). This developed perception of creative resistance is where I connected concepts of the funds of knowledge, critical pedagogy, and CRT to challenge the academic barriers of marginalized students. This chapter presents the conceptual framework of creative resistance and its importance in marginalized schools with underfunded art programs. Before presenting the composition of this concept, I review art-education and education literature, along with their research limitations.

Limitations in Art Education

Research on the history of art education confirms that powerful elements in society have influenced and determined the purpose of the arts (Efland, 1990). More notably, Bourdieu (1986) identifies how similar dominant structures have maintained social reproduction and dominant mechanisms in society through different forms of capital, some of which include the arts. According to Efland (1990), these dominant structures have used suitable institutions to govern how the arts are appropriated in the social order through patronage, education, and censorship. Patronage, education, and censorship also serve the purpose of reproducing art-education appropriation in society. When considering how these three systems work within working-class populations, it is important to acknowledge the existing limitations in art education and the quality of art-education access that exists for students in marginalized schools. Despite having research showing the benefits art education has for students from low and high socio-economic status (SES) (Caterall, 2009; Caterall, Dumais, & Hampden, 2012; Woodworth, Gallagher, & Guha, 2007; Waldorf & Atwill, 2011), scholars have failed to recognize the socio-economic and academic disparities that contribute to the inequality of art education in working-class schools. We are made aware that art education has a significant influence on the academic aspirations of low- and high-SES students, but only in schools with rich art programs (Caterall, 2009; Caterall et al., 2012). To provide a specific example of this unequal appropriation in the education sector, I display the art courses offered at two high schools (identified by pseudonyms) in the Los Angeles Unified School District during the 2012–2013 school year. I offer data from this specific year because of its relevancy to the said literature (Caterall, 2009; Caterall et al., 2012; Parsad & Spiegelman, 2012; PCAH, 2011; Woodworth et al., 2007; Waldorf & Atwill, 2011). By displaying the average class size and the number of course offerings between Eastside High School (Figure 5.1), a Title I school in the heart of urban Los Angeles, and Marina High

EASTSIDE HIGH SCHOOL				COURSE LISTING							2012-2013	
Subject	Course	Course Code	Number of Schools'	Number of Classes	Number of Classes Meeting UC/CSU Entrance Requirements	Female Enrollment	Male Enrollment	Total Enrollment	Number of FTE Course Enrollment Teachers	Filtered Average Class Size	Average Class Size
Art	Ceramics (Beginning and Advanced)	2800	1	4	4	77	85	162	0.6	40.0	40.5
	Design	2801	1	2	2	40	37	77	0.3	38.0	38.5
	Drawing	2806	1	3	3	44	80	124	0.4	41.0	41.3
	Fundamentals of Art(secondary school standards)	2823	1	4	3	55	41	96	0.6	24.0	24.0
	Painting	2807	1	2	2	37	34	71	0.3	35.0	35.5
	Subject total for Art		1	15	14	253	277	530	2.2	35.0	35.3

FIGURE 5.1 Disproportionate Art Course Offerings in Los Angeles Unified School District–Eastside High School

MARINA HIGH SCHOOL   COURSE LISTING   2012-2013

Subject	Course	Course Code	Number of Schools*	Number of Classes	Number of Classes Meeting UC/CSU Entrance Requirements	Female Enrollment	Male Enrollment	Total Course Enrollment	Number of FTE Teachers	Filtered Average Class Size	Average Class Size
Art	AP Studio art: three dimensional	2876	1	1	1	1	3	4	0.2	4.0	4.0
	AP Studio art: two dimensional	2875	1	1	1	15	6	21	0.2	21.0	21.0
	Ceramics (Beginning and Advanced)	2800	1	9	9	107	84	191	1.0	21.0	21.2
	Cinematography/Artistic Videos (Begin or Adv)	2809	1	4	4	26	79	105	0.7	26.0	26.3
	Crafts	2802	1	2	0	29	31	60	0.3	30.0	30.0
	Drawing	2806	1	5	5	86	60	146	0.8	29.0	29.2
	Fundamentals of Art(secondary school standards)	2823	1	2	0	28	23	51	0.3	25.0	25.5
	Painting	2807	1	1	0	29	4	33	0.2	33.0	33.0
	Photography (Beginning or Advanced)	2805	1	7	7	90	72	162	0.9	23.0	23.1
	Subject total for Art		1	32	27	411	362	773	4.5	24.0	24.2

FIGURE 5.2 Disproportionate Art Course Offerings in Los Angeles Unified School District–Marina High School

School (Figure 5.2), a suburban school in one of the district's beach cities, we cannot ignore the disproportionate and unfit circumstances of art courses offered at Eastside High School.

By recognizing the way art education is structured within marginalized schools, art-education advocates can better understand how patronage, education, and censorship are systems controlled by the socially powerful. Waldorf (2011), for example, argues that community-based teaching artists, trained through district state standards, can provide rigorous instruction and learning experiences for students (p. 91). A problem with this approach is that community-based teaching artists, despite sometimes not being from the same community, are trained by the district's own standards, and may provide the students and communities they serve with irrelevant art practices. Researchers must acknowledge that art-education programs in historically underserved communities of color have maintained Westernized art perspectives through *banking education methods*[2] that do not acknowledge the histories or the cultural capital of marginalized students. For this reason, I present the concept of creative resistance as an art-based learning tool that draws from students' home knowledge, socio-political circumstances, and issues of race and racism to challenge the oppressive conditions that exist in their socio-economic and schooling environments (García, 2012, 2015). Creative resistance does not present a solution to art-education inequality; its purpose is to develop a student's ability to use their home knowledge through the arts as a form of resistance and social transformation.

Critical Perspectives in Art Education

Scholars have challenged traditional art education by using the arts as forms of resistance (Greene, 2007, 1994; Siqueiros, 1975; Cary, 1998; Kincheloe, 1991; Yokley, 1999; Tavin, 2002; Darts, 2004; Quinn, Ploof, & Hochtritt, 2011; García, 2012, 2015). Darts (2004) urges arts educators to move students beyond uncritical and superficial aesthetic understandings of art that fail to recognize the ideological struggles embedded within students' everyday visual experiences (p. 323). He identifies creative resistance as the attempt to transform the way meaning is produced in our society through art education. Drawing from his idea of creative resistance, I acknowledge that current art-education research fails to provide critical understandings of how students produce meaning of their environments through the arts. I also draw from scholarship that considers the arts to address issues of race, class, and gender to show the developing interdisciplinary methods of merging critical education and art education.

A more inclusive literature in art education considers addressing issues of race, class, and gender through the arts (Bell, 2010; Dewhurst, 2014; Beyerbach, 2011; Hanley, 2013; Quinn et al., 2011; Hutzel, 2012). Bell's (2010) research presents art-education methods that account for the role of race and racism and how they work within systemic structures. Bell's research shows the ways in which art education and counter-storytelling[3] can be used as a tool to examine and challenge issues of race and racism in education. However, Bell's research does not display the student perspectives that critical education scholars advocate for (Freire, 1970; Solórzano, 1998; Solorzano & Delgado-Bernal, 2001; Delgado Bernal, 1998, 2001, 2002; Yosso, 2005).

By adapting Freire's (1970) problem-posing methodology to the arts, students and myself have worked collaboratively on projects that challenge systemic inequalities through their cultural knowledge (García, 2012, 2015). Through this work, I expand on creative resistance through the experiences of students and pay attention to the ways they use the arts to analyze their socio-economic circumstances by drawing from their personal experiences. Drawing from my previous research, I draw on the developing definition of creative resistance as *practical forms of art, visual or performing, used by students, to challenge systemic-oppressive structures, actions, misconceptions, stereotypes, political agendas, or inequalities that diminish the development of a group of people or community* (García, 2015).

Resisting Traditional Art Education

Research on the history of art education argues that the arts have been a source of capital within social classes controlled by systems of patronage, education, and censorship (Efland, 1990). Both Bourdieu (1984, 1986) and Efland (1990) argue that pre-existing relationships within these systems have historically determined who is taught art and who is not. They acknowledge that socio-economic systems and structures continue to screen art and its benefits from specific marginalized populations (Bourdieu, 1984, 1986; Efland, 1990). Sociology scholars have also provided decades of evidence on the recurring inequalities that exist for students of color in schooling systems (Anyon, 2005; Kozol, 1991, 2005; Tierney & Colyar, 2006; Ochoa, 2013). Critical education scholars also recognize oppressive education methods presented to students of color and strategically challenge it by drawing from students' knowledge (Solorzano, 1989; Delgado Bernal, 2002; Duncan-Andrade & Morell, 2008; Freire, 1970; González et al., 2005; Solórzano, 1998; Solorzano & Delgado-Bernal, 2001; Yosso, 2005). For this reason, art education practitioners serving marginalized populations must consider challenging Eurocentric art instruction through critical pedagogical practices. In the case of my own classroom, I began using the game of La Lotería by drawing from the home knowledge and capital of my students in order to challenge their socioeconomic and academic limitations.

Overview of Frameworks

Funds of Knowledge

Getting to know student environments in depth within their own family homes gives educators the opportunity to understand, acknowledge, and adopt the practices that are shared in the homes of students and their families. By adopting the methods of teacher-researchers presented by González et al. (2005), art educators can use these bodies of knowledge in their own classroom curricula to acknowledge the history of their students, challenge dominant cultural practices, and generate student understanding of families' cultural and social capital. By adopting these bodies of knowledge and skills in art education, schools can provide opportunity for students to develop a critical consciousness through their own sources of knowledge and the visual arts.

Rather than taking the home-visit approach presented by González et al. (2005), I assign students to conduct their own family research. As their teacher, I cannot imagine going to the homes of the 240 students enrolled in my six periods. If I were to choose one of my classes for home visits, visiting the home of approximately 40 students would be an extremely strenuous task for an educator. For this reason, I consider taking the collaborative approach where students and myself are the producers of household knowledge. Students become the historians and knowledge producers of their own family by requiring them to interview their families on their occupational and migration history.

It is important to begin pursuing this approach in classrooms because many students do not know the histories of their own families. When I inquire about their family background, many do not know how their parents met, how they came to the U.S., or what cities their parents are from. The problem with this unrecognized family knowledge is that the histories of working-class families become lost as new generations of students acculturate or assimilate into a dominant culture that dismisses their own history (Valenzuela, 1999; Yosso, 2005). As an educator, I believe it to be unethical to ignore that students do not know their own history, especially if I continue to conceal their histories with layers of Eurocentric perspectives. Rather than continuing to marginalize them culturally and academically, I also believe that I can teach art through the mandated state/ Common Core standards by using the home knowledge of students. If these family histories are not being told at home or in our classrooms, then family knowledge is not passed on to the next generation of family members, and educators will continue to marginalize working-class populations. This is why I use the arts to unearth the repressed and unaccounted family knowledge of students' own histories.

Critical Pedagogy

If we are to meet the needs of working-class students, we must acknowledge the limiting socio-economic structures students live in, and co-create ways to transform those environments. Freire (1970) identifies a *pedagogy of the oppressed* as one that unveils the reality of oppression and commits itself to social transformation through the process of *Praxis*.[4] Once social transformation takes place, this pedagogy becomes a process of permanent liberation that challenges dominant culture through the process of action and reflection (p. 54). The struggle for liberation should start in the confines of the classroom, and be extended into the neighborhoods, streets, and home environments, where oppressive circumstances exist for students. Since the arts provide opportunities to build ideas and possibilities through imagination, the objective of the arts should be to build the consciousness of students through an imagination of possibilities—by creatively using their own cultural knowledge.

Although CP accounts for the production of knowledge between student and teacher as co-producers of knowledge, it does not consider the in-depth understanding of household knowledge production presented through the FK framework. FK understands the knowledge that exists within student households, communities, and schooling, and validates that knowledge within classroom practices. However, it does not recognize the need for political power or recognize the oppressive circumstances and systems that marginalize working-class students, families, and communities.

In order to bridge the elements of CP and FK together, I recognize that both frameworks account for the histories, community engagement, cultural practices, and student-teacher relationships to improve the academic outcomes of students. The framework of creative resistance therefore, draws from the knowledge that exists in student households through FK, to validate and transform the socio-economic limitations of students through CP, along with validating the stories and experiences of students through CRT tools; transformational resistance, counter-storytelling and community cultural wealth (Solórzano, 1989, 1998; Solorzano & Delgado-Bernal, 2001; Delgado-Bernal, 2002; Yosso, 2005).

Critical Race Theory

According to Solórzano (1998), a critical race theory in education challenges the dominant discourse on race and racism as they relate to education by examining how educational theory, policy, and practice are used to subordinate certain racial and ethnic groups (pg. 122). CRT in education scholars also recognizes the effects of race and racism in education by examining how schooling processes are used to subordinate students of color, and advocating for validating the stories of marginalized populations (Delgado-Bernal, 1998, 2001, 2002; Solorzano, 1998; Solorzano & Delgado-Bernal, 2001; Yosso, 2005; Yosso, Smith, Ceja, & Solórzano, 2009). Delgado-Bernal's (1997) framework on schooling resistance presents the forms of resistance students use in response to oppressive conditions in their academic settings. Among those, transformational resistance (Solorzano & Delgado-Bernal, 2001) refers to the acknowledging of one's oppressive conditions and structures of domination as motivation toward seeking social transformation.

Drawing on transformational resistance (Delgado-Bernal, 1997; Solorzano & Delgado-Bernal, 2001) within the context of art education, along with Yosso's counter-storytelling and community cultural wealth (2005), I continue to build on the framework of creative resistance. By drawing on the creative process as a tool of resistance through Yosso's (2005) counter-storytelling, students can reflect their lived experiences to raise critical consciousness about social and racial injustice (p. 10). Art-based counter-storytelling methods validate the living experiences of working-class students, and challenge art education that does not recognize the histories of marginalized students. Along with the concept of *community cultural wealth*[5] (Yosso, 2005), educators can strategically use student knowledge through the arts to develop their curricula and forms of transformational resistance against oppressive practices. In the following section, I explain how the framework of creative resistance is structured and how it can lead to the social transformation of underrepresented students when they use the arts, their own historical knowledge, and socio-economic struggles.

Creativity as Resistance

The Lotería Approach in Art Education

The game of La Lotería (Lottery) is a game that uses iconic images of people from various social classes and objects associated with everyday life. The point of the game is similar to bingo: to fill the player's card as directed by the dealer. Rather than using numbers, the game of La Lotería uses iconic images with a title and riddle. In his novel *Lotería*, Zambrano (2013) explains the rules of the game:

> There are fifty-four cards and each comes with a riddle, *un dicho*. There is a traditional set of riddles, but sometimes dealers create their own to trick the players. After the dealer "sings" the riddle the players cover the appropriate spots on their playing boards, their *tablas*, with either bottle caps, dried beans, or loose change.... You can win by filling a vertical line, horizontal, a diagonal; the four corners, the center squares, or blackout.
>
> *(Preface)*

According to Stavans (2003), during the Mexican Revolution, Don Clemente Jaques, the owner of an ammunition and canned goods business, attached Lotería boards to his products so that soldiers would pass the time during their service. The game gained popularity when soldiers returned home in search of the game, and Jaques began using his food label press to mass produce the game to meet the demand. Today, the game is distributed by Gallo Pasatiempos (Stavans, 2003, p. 33) and is played in the U.S. as well as other Latin American countries. Reflecting and drawing from the interest my students display when I bring this household cultural knowledge to my curriculum reminds me of Zambrano's (2013) novel, *Lotería*. In his novel, Zambrano tells the story of a young girl who uses the game of Lotería to cope with a broken family home. Each chapter uses a Lotería card to narrate a memory through the imagination of the main character. The novel reflects a resilient counter-story of the main character's economic, familial, and emotional hardships, which are experienced by many of the students in our classroom. Zambrano's novel is a reminder that the experiences our students have in our classrooms are sometimes the more settling spaces and environments they experience compared to their own homes.

The idea behind using the game of Lotería in the classroom is for students and myself to share the knowledge we have about playing the game. It also presents the opportunity for me to teach them about the history of the game, and how its images have maintained negative representations of race, class, and gender. I use the game as a methodological tool in the classroom to learn from and use their household and cultural knowledge as capital in their learning. Most importantly, I use the game of La Lotería with the purpose of meeting the following goals:

- To challenge the cultural stereotypes that exist in the original images of the game and continue to exist in society;
- To challenge gender roles that are portrayed in the game and those that continue to be reflected in society;
- To acknowledge the parental occupations of students by using them as iconic figures that resist negative imagery;
- To understand socio-economic class, based on their parental occupations;
- To acknowledge that the financial stability of their family is the foundation to the aspirations of students' academic future;
- To reciprocate and continue developing the understanding of students' environments, experiences, and history as they relate to their academic access; and
- To develop the creative resistance of students to achieve social transformation.

For a clearer understanding of this process, I provide a breakdown of my approach in the next section.

Because La Lotería is based on popular and cultural icons of Latin America, I try to connect them to the modern, everyday, household and personal experiences of students by drawing from their own family history. It also provides the opportunity to challenge the idea that "culture" is identified by the foods and diluted celebrations of particular ethnic groups (González et al., 2005). It allows students and myself to collaboratively use home knowledge to counter negative imagery through the capital they possess in their households.

To begin, I would like to clarify that I use the game of La Lotería as a foundational art project to set up a curriculum unit that draws from the familial history, occupational, household, and cultural knowledge of students. After completing the foundational project, students use the knowledge gained from the Lotería project as a source of reference to exploring, processing, understanding, and deconstructing issues of race, class, and gender, and developing ways of resisting their oppressive realities. I begin the semester by introducing students to the purpose of the class: as one that uses the arts to explore concepts of social class, race, and gender with the goal of developing an understanding of how particular structures in society limit their access to resources. The first unit of the class focuses on students learning about their family history and family knowledge. The first project asks students to fill out a family tree that identifies family members, their place of birth, and known occupations. Students must communicate with their parents (something I believe is much needed in our learning spaces) and take notes on their own family's labor history. The second part of the project requires students to create a visual family migration map that identifies each family member's place of birth, highest level of education, their known occupational knowledge, and route of migration (if any) they took to come to the United States. I explain to students that regardless of they or their parents being born in the U.S., someone in their family came to the U.S. at some point and must know who and how they got here. Each family member requires a profile image with a short description identifying the person, their work history, and their migration experience. Students include themselves as the final piece of this migration map, which ends with a reflection and discussion on the purpose of understanding their history, and their goals based on the experiences of their ancestors. Part 3 of this unit explores the concept of the cycle of poverty, identifies inequitable systems (education and legal) in society, and collaboratively develops an understanding (based on their own family labor history) of social hierarchy. The final part of this unit introduces students to the game of La Lotería, its history, and its own forms of negative imagery. This final part of the unit becomes a source of knowledge for the rest of the year. With an understanding of social class and occupational hierarchy, students explore how La Lotería's historical images have maintained misconceptions related to race, class, and gender in their own culture. It is through this project that students draw from the home and occupational capital that exists in their homes by re-creating their own Lotería card. This part of the project serves the purpose of challenging the negative imagery reflected in the game.

For example, one student recreated the image of "El Valiente" (the brave one). The original image of El Valiente (Figure 5.3) depicts a male figure in a stance that was described by students (during a class activity) as "Machista" (macho-like).

FIGURE 5.3 "El Valiente" Lotería Card from the Board Game by Don Clemente, Inc.

The image depicts him holding a poncho on one hand and a sickle with a bloody tip on the other. The student decided to redesign this image to challenge the idea that a person does not need a knife to be valiente (brave). The student explained, "In my eyes, my parent the mechanic is the valiente for the long hours he works, sometimes with no days off, to make sure we can pay the rent and have something to eat." He titled his piece *The Workingman* (Figure 5.4); according to him, "the working man is the tough guy and the only weapon he needs are his mechanic tools."

In this Lotería project, students use their parental occupations as icons of capital that need to be validated by educators, and most importantly by themselves.

FIGURE 5.4 Student-Developed Lotería Card

By becoming aware of the socio-economic capital that is tied to their parental occupations, they become critically conscious of their social circumstances by acknowledging and recognizing their sources of stability and financial support. This first introductory unit presents students with an understanding of why hierarchy exists, how it works, and how they can begin to resist and transform their socio-political circumstances. In the units that follow, students complete a number of projects based on their parental occupations as resources of knowledge. The projects range from creating a self-portrait, a remix of Tupac's "The Rose that Grew from Concrete," a stencil project, a visual counter-story on a tortilla, and a South Central *testimonio*.

How Creative Resistance Works

The framework of creative resistance is presented through the visual of *El Paraguas* (Figure 5.5) and justifies why this visual of an umbrella is the best fit for this framework. The structure of creative resistance is sustained by three primary components identified by the three primary colors: CP (red), FK (yellow), and CRT (blue). The word "*paraguas*" (umbrella) is itself a compound word created by "para" (stop) and "aguas" (water) that translates to "water-repellent." *El Paraguas* is also one of the original icons in the game of La Lotería—not one that carries negative connotations, but one that is useful to explain this framework. The purpose of using *El Paraguas* as the visual for the framework of creative resistance is to reflect how *El Paraguas* (the structure of creative resistance) serves the purpose of protecting individuals from "*aguas*." The term "aguas," in this case, not to be confused with "water," is a slang word in parts of Latin American equivalent to "watch out" or "heads up." For example, if a group of students is playing soccer at a park and they accidentally kick the ball towards a crowded area, it is courtesy for them to yell "aguas!" (watch out!) to warn the crowd of the incoming ball. Therefore, students can use the framework of creative resistance to protect themselves from the academic and limiting processes that they are prone to experience in their own environments.

   Through this visual, *El Paraguas* is used to show how CP, FK, and CRT are the frames that make up the whole umbrella of creative resistance. Because CP, FK, and CRT theories share similar elements, the figure of *El Paraguas* shows how each individual framework serves as a foundational component to creative resistance. Additionally, the visual displays a set of secondary colors that reflect where the primary components share similar theoretical elements. For example, CP (identified in red) has overlapping components of communication with FK (in yellow). The shared components between CP and FK include the use of dialogue from CP and household communication from FK. Student-teacher relationships in CP are also forms of networks that are similar to community networks in FK. The process of Praxis, which is a practice of Action-and-Reflection in CP, is similar to the household abilities, practices, and

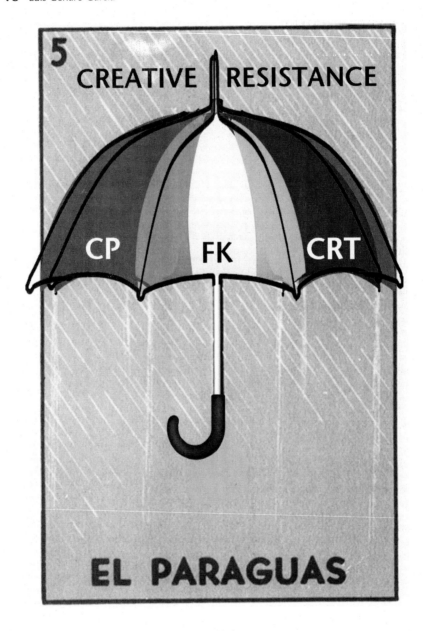

FIGURE 5.5 Creative Resistance Framework

skills reflected in FK. In color theory, when two primary colors are mixed (i.e. red and yellow), they create a secondary color (i.e. orange). For this reason, the overlapping areas between CP and FK are displayed through the color orange. FK also has elements similar to those found in CRT. FK and CRT are similar through the community networks as tools of navigation, which are presented in FK, and community cultural wealth, which is used as navigational capital. It also shows a similarity between the use of household communication in FK and the counter-stories, Chicana/Latina epistemologies, presented in CRT. The use of household abilities, practices, and skills in FK is also similar to pedagogies of the home, which draws from transformational resistance (Delgado-Bernal, 1997; Solorzano & Delgado-Bernal, 2001). The overlapping areas of these yellow and blue frameworks are therefore identified in green. Lastly, to display that both CP and CRT share components of social justice and forms of transformation, an overlapping section is identified through the color violet. As I stated in the previous section, although CP and CRT hold their own unique frameworks, they do share the process of resistance for social transformation, as well as a commitment to challenging class oppression.

Discussion

As a student, I played the game of Lotería in my Spanish course, and it gave me a sense of relevance despite not feeling connected to the type of Spanish I was being taught in class. As an educator, I've seen the great interest the game of Lotería provides students in my classroom and have seen the immediate relevance it gives the most emotionally conflicted and disadvantaged students in my classes. Art educators cannot continue to marginalize and bury the knowledge that exists in students' homes by continuing to teach through Westernized or irrelevant art perspectives.

In providing a much-needed narrative from students of color in art education, I offer these two contributions. First, together with students, we co-constructed the critical approach of La Lotería; using their knowledge, we were able to create a consciousness that provided a culturally relevant means of resistance to the realities of their environments. That is, students use critical education and the arts to understand and articulate their oppressive realities, informed by intersections of race, class, and gender. Second, I introduce the conceptual framework of creative resistance that brings together and extends the theories of critical pedagogy, funds of knowledge, and critical race theory. As demonstrated, the framework is represented visually through *El Paraguas* (Figure 5.5). Creative resistance, reflected through the image of the paraguas, can be used as a tool for protecting the self from the toxic surroundings and oppression present in students' multiple environments, particularly those found in academic spaces.

Suggestions for Educators

Before suggesting what steps to take towards an art-based pedagogical approach in underfunded schools, I would like to reassure that I do not want to direct practitioners with a how-to, step-by-step process that reflects a banking model approach. I do want to suggest that educators find a way to establish consistent programs that will enable students and educators to develop long-term and trusting relationships. Despite having a college and career readiness initiative through the A–G subject requirements, the Los Angeles Unified School District requires students to take only one year of art. This is a problem in underfunded schools, because one year of art does not provide students with courses beyond introductory levels. In order to establish a consistent program that prepares students to challenge their oppressive circumstances through the arts, I requested administrators and counselors to develop cohorts of students interested in developing their artistic abilities through critical perspectives. This is not necessarily an art program that prepares students to get into art schools, but one that uses art that encourages students to pursue higher education and prepares them to challenge their oppressive circumstances.

An advantage that has made this method accessible in the classroom was my upbringing in the same social and cultural demographics of my students. It has made it much easier for students and parents to trust me, knowing that I came from the same community. Even if educators do not share the cultural or demographic backgrounds of their students, they can begin familiarizing themselves with critical education frameworks, and develop trust with their students by getting to know them outside of their learning spaces. I suggest that educators begin using concepts from critical pedagogy, funds of knowledge, and critical race theory (not necessarily in that order), and develop their curricula conceptually. More notably, educators should ally themselves with other educators who are committed to social justice. Educators should understand that critical frameworks and methodologies will not be presented through their schools' professional development; this is something that educators must hold themselves accountable to if they want the best outcome for their students. Before developing this idea of creative resistance, I became familiar with critical pedagogy scholars (Freire, 1970; McLaren, 1994; Duncan-Andrade & Morell, 2008) in order to draw from student knowledge and focus on developing their political awareness. It was during my doctoral program that I began drawing from funds of knowledge (González, Moll, & Amanti, 2005) and critical race theory (Delgado-Bernal, 1998, 2001, 2002; Yosso, 2005) to support my art-based methodology. I do want to point out that this framework was not something that I developed from one day to the next, but a combination of my personal and professional experiences (García, 2012, 2015). This has been my own creative resistance, developed through my own conditions that I use to challenge the inequality that exists for students of color. Although I provide only one example of the Lotería approach, this chapter introduces the origins and foundations of creative resistance. Future research will provide student testimonials and detailed work samples of student learning experiences inside and out of the classroom and the influence it has on pursuing a higher education.

Conclusion

This is a call to art educators and social justice advocates in education to learn from the home and community knowledge our students possess. At a time when openly racist government representatives are threatening the nation, this is the most appropriate moment to develop the resistance of students as they navigate social, economic, and political challenges. Additionally, we are reminded by Rios-Aguilar and Kiyama (2012) that students in marginalized communities have the most disproportionate opportunities to access higher education. If we are not preparing students to navigate or challenge the limiting circumstances in society by drawing from their funds of knowledge, then we are providing a disservice to the students in our most underserved schools. In this chapter, I briefly display how student aspirations and appreciation are influenced by their parents' occupational knowledge. This is important for the work on funds of knowledge because it expands the evidence provided by Kiyama (2010), demonstrating that funds of knowledge influence students' aspirations of going to college through art education practices. I do not make an argument to provide more funding for art education programs; such an agenda is useless if students cannot imagine possibilities to their circumstances or have the knowledge to transform them. Therefore, art programs in marginalized neighborhoods should consider developing the social consciousness of students by drawing from their funds of knowledge to develop the means, tools, consciousness, and imagination to create their own social change and transformation.

Notes

1 An iconic game, similar to bingo, used as a cultural practice in Latino households. Rather than using numbers to fill a player's game board, La Lotería uses imagery of people from various social classes and everyday life objects.
2 Freire (1993) identifies banking education as the process in which educators narrate information to student receptors. He describes education as the act of depositing information that students memorize, use, and repeat (p. 72). Through this process, there is no interaction or dialogue between the teacher and student.
3 Yosso (2005) identifies counter-storytelling as a method of recounting the experiences and perspectives of racially and socially marginalized people that allows the people telling the story to challenge the dominant perspectives that exclude and dismiss the first-hand experiences of marginalized communities (p. 10).
4 Freire (1970) identifies Praxis as the process of action-and-reflection. It is a component of true liberation that cannot be limited to intellectualism but must involve action; nor can it be limited to mere activism, but must include serious reflection. It is the process of acting toward liberation and reflecting on the action for a sustainable and liberating Independence.
5 *Community cultural wealth* encompasses six forms of capital—aspirational, navigational, social, linguistic, familial, and resistant capital—that acknowledge the cultural capital of working-class families of color.

References

Anyon, J. (2005). *Radical possibilities: Public policy, urban education, and a new social movement*. New York, NY: Routledge.

Bell, L. A. (2010). *Storytelling for social justice: Connecting narrative and the arts in antiracist teaching*. New York, NY: Routledge.

Beyerbach, B., & Davis, R. D. (2011). *Activist art in social justice pedagogy: Engaging students in global issues through the arts*. New York, NY: P. Lang.

Bourdieu, P. (1984). *Distinction: A social critique of the judgment of taste*. Translated by R. Nice. Cambridge, MA: Harvard University Press.

Bourdieu, P. (1986). Forms of capital. In J. G. Richardson (Ed.), *Handbook of theory and research for the sociology of education*. New York, NY: Greenwood.

Cary, R. (1998). *Critical art pedagogy: Foundations for postmodern art education*. New York, NY: Garland Publishing Inc.

Caterall, J. S. (2009). *Doing well and doing good by doing Art: A 12-year longitudinal study of arts education—Effects on the achievements and values of young adults*. Los Angeles, CA: I-Group Books.

Caterall, J. S., Dumais, S. A., & Hampden-Thompson, G. (2012). *The arts and achievement in at-risk youth: Findings from four longitudinal studies*. Washington, DC: National Endowment for the Arts.

Darder, A. (1995). Bicultural identity and the development of voice: Twin issues in the struggle for cultural and linguistic democracy. In J. Frederickson (Ed.), *Reclaiming our voices: Bilingual education critical pedagogy and praxis* (pp. 36–52). Covina, CA: California Association of Bilingual Education, CABE Publishing.

Darts, D. (2004). Visual culture jam: Art pedagogy and creative resistance. *Studies in Art Education, 45*(4), 313–327.

Delgado Bernal, D. (1997). *Chicana school resistance and grassroots leadership: Providing an alternative history of the 1968 East Los Angeles blowouts*. Unpublished doctoral dissertation, University of California, Los Angeles.

Delgado Bernal, D. (1998). Using a Chicana feminist epistemology in educational research. *Harvard Educational Review, 68*(4), 555–582.

Delgado Bernal, D. (2001). Learning and living pedagogies of the home: Mestiza consciousness of Chicana students. *International Journal of Qualitative Studies in Education, 14*(3), 623–639.

Delgado Bernal, D. (2002). Critical race theory, Latino critical theory, and critical raced-gendered epistemologies: Recognizing students of color as holders and creators of knowledge. *Qualitative Inquiry, 8*(1), 105–126.

Dewhurst, M. (2014). *Social justice art: A framework for activist art pedagogy*. Cambridge, MA: Harvard Education Press.

Duncan-Andrade, J. (2006). Utilizing cariño in the development of research methodologies. In J. Kincheloe, P. Anderson, K. Rose, D. Griffith, & K. Hayes (Eds.), *Urban education: An encyclopedia* (pp. 451–486). Westport, CT: Greenwood Publishing.

Duncan-Andrade, J., & Morell, E. (2008). *The art of critical pedagogy: Possibilities for moving from theory to practice in urban schools*. New York, NY: Peter Lang.

Efland, A. D. (1990). *History of art education: Intellectual and social currents in teaching the visual arts*. New York, NY: Teachers College Press.

Freire, P. (1970). *Pedagogy of the oppressed* (1st ed.). New York, NY: Continuum.

Freire, P. (1993). *Pedagogy of the oppressed* (2nd ed.). New York, NY: Continuum.

García, L-G. (2012). Making cultura count inside and out of the classroom: Public art & critical pedagogy in south central Los Angeles. *Journal of Curriculum and Pedagogy, 9*(2), 104–114.

García, L-G. (2015). Empowering students through creative resistance: Art-based critical pedagogy in the immigrant experience. *Diálogo, an Interdisciplinary Studies Journal, 18*(2). Center for Latino Research at De Paul University.

González, N., & Moll, L. (2002). Cruzando el puente: Building bridges to funds of knowledge. *Journal of Educational Policy, 16*(4), 623–641.

González, N., Moll, L. C., & Amanti, C. (2005). *Funds of knowledge: Theorizing practices in households, communities, and classrooms.* Mahwah, NJ: Erlbaum.

Greene, M. (1995). *Releasing the imagination: Essay on education, the arts, and social change.* San Francisco, CA: Jossey-Bass.

Greene, M. (2007). Imagination and the healing arts. [Monograph]. Retrieved from http://www.maxinegreene.org/pdf/articles/downloader.php?file=imagination_ha.pdf

Hutzel, K. (2012). A possibility of togetherness: Collaborative art learning for urban education. In K. Hutzel, F. M. C. Bastos, & K. Cosier (Eds.), *Transforming city schools through art: Approaches to meaningful K–12 learning* (pp. 95–102). New York, NY: Teachers College Press.

Kincheloe, J. (1991). *Teachers as researchers: Qualitative inquiry as a path to empowerment.* London: Falmer.

Kiyama, J. M. (2010). College aspirations and limitations: The role of educational ideologies and funds of knowledge in Mexican American families. *American Educational Research Journal, 47*(2), 330–356.

Kozol, J. (1991). *Savage inequalities: Children in America's schools.* New York, NY: Crown Publishers.

Kozol, J. (2005). *The shame of the nation: The restoration of apartheid schooling in America.* New York, NY: Three Rivers Press.

McLaren, P. (1994). *Life in schools: An introduction to critical pedagogy in the foundations of education.* New York, NY: Longman.

Moll, L. C., Amanti, C., Neff, D., & González, N. (1992). Funds of knowledge for teaching: Using a qualitative approach to connect homes and classrooms. *Theory Into Practice, 31*(2), 132–141.

Moll, L. C., & Greenberg, J. B. (1990). Creating zones of possibilities: Combining social contexts for instruction. In L. C. Moll (Ed.), *Vygotsky and education: Instructional implications and applications of sociohistorical psychology* (pp. 319–348). Cambridge: Cambridge University Press.

Ochoa, G. L. (2013). *Academic profiling: Latinos, Asian Americans, and the achievement gap.* Minneapolis, MN: University of Minnesota Press.

Parsad, B., & Spiegelman, M. (2012). *Arts education in public elementary and secondary schools: 1999–2000 and 2009–10* (NCES 2012–014). Washington, DC: National Center for Education Statistics, Institute of Education Sciences, U.S. Department of Education.

President's Committee on the Arts and the Humanities. (2011). *Reinvesting in arts education: Winning America's future through creative schools.* Washington, DC: President's Committee on the Arts and the Humanities. Retrieved from www.pcah.gov

Quinn, T., Ploof, J., & Hochtritt, L. (2011). *Art and social justice education: Culture as commons.* New York, NY: Routledge.

Rios-Aguilar, C., & Kiyama, J. M. (2012). Funds of knowledge: A proposed approach to study Latina/o students' transition to college. *Journal of Latinos and Education, 11*(1), 2–16.

Siqueiros, D. (1975). *Art & revolution*. London, UK: Lawrence and Wishart.

Solórzano, D. G. (1989). Teaching and social change: Reflections on a Freirean approach in a college classroom. *Teaching Sociology, 17*(2), 218–225.

Solórzano, D. G. (1998). Critical race theory, race and gender microaggressions, and the experience of Chicana and Chicano scholars. *International Journal of Qualitative Studies in Education, 11*(1), 121–136.

Solórzano, D. G., & Delgado Bernal, D. (2001). Examining transformational resistance through a critical race and LatCrit theory framework: Chicana and Chicano students in an urban context. *Urban Education, 36*(3), 308–342.

Stavans, I. (2003). ¡Lotería! or the ritual of chance. *AGNI, 58*, 30–35.

Stone Hanley, M. (Ed.). (2013). *Culturally relevant arts education for social justice: A way out of no way*. New York, NY: Routledge.

Tavin, K. (2002). Engaging advertisements: Looking for meaning in and through art education. *Visual Arts Researcher, 28*(2), 38–47.

Tierney, W. G., & Colyar, J. E. (2006). *Urban high school students and the challenge of access: Many routes, difficult paths*. New York, NY: Peter Lang.

Valenzuela, A. (1999). *Subtractive schooling: U.S.-Mexican youth and the politics of caring*. New York, NY: SUNY Press.

Waldorf, L., & Atwill, K. (2011, January 1–10). *Arts for all school arts survey: Measuring quality, access and equity in arts education*. Arts for All.

Woodworth, K. R., Gallagher, H. A., & Guha, R. (2007). *An unfinished canvas. Arts education in California: Taking stock of policies and practices. Summary report*. Menlo Park, CA: SRI International.

Yokley, S. H. (1999). Embracing a critical pedagogy in art education. *Art Education, 52*(5), 18–24.

Yosso, T. J. (2005). Whose culture has capital? A critical race theory discussion of community cultural wealth. *Race, Ethnicity, and Education, 8*(1), 69–91. doi:10.1080/1361332052000341006

Yosso, T. J., Smith, W. A., Ceja, M., & Solórzano, D. G. (2009). Critical race theory, racial microaggressions, and campus racial climate for Latina/o undergraduates. *Harvard Educational Review, 79*(4), 659–691.

Zambrano, M. A. (2013). *Lotería: A novel*. New York, NY: Harper Collins.

PART 2

College Access and Persistence

6

COLLEGE ASPIRATIONS AND LIMITATIONS

The Role of Educational Ideologies and Funds of Knowledge in Mexican American Families[i]

Judy Marquez Kiyama

Under-represented students continue to struggle with a myriad of social and educational inequities in their pursuit of higher education. Their under-representation in colleges and universities has been influenced not by a lack of academic ability (Gonzalez, Stone, & Jovel, 2003), but by rising costs of college, increased standards in admissions criteria, and inadequate secondary education preparation (Auerbach, 2004; Valenzuela, 1999).

Chapa and De La Rosa (2004) state that Mexicans[1] have the lowest educational attainment compared to other Latino sub-groups including the lowest high school completion rates at 26.7%. Despite the dismal statistics, Mexicans hold education as an important value and have positive educational aspirations.[2] However, negative educational myths about this group continue to exist. Often parents who are not engaged in traditional involvement roles are perceived as unengaged in their students' "educational lives" (Lopez, 2001, p. 417). Quite conversely, Mexicans are a literate population, in English and especially in Spanish (Vélez-Ibáñez & Greenberg, 1992), have passed on strong educational values despite having fought through years of educational systems subordinating their culture (Valenzuela, 1999; Vélez-Ibáñez, 1996) and instill these educational values and agency through life lessons (Lopez, 2001). This deficit view stems from the concept of "familial deficits" which argues that Mexican Americans do not hold education in high value, thus leading to inadequate familial socialization for academic competence and contributing to school failure for their children (Valencia & Black, 2002, p. 83).

As research and practice shift, and this deficit view is challenged, educators are increasingly attempting to incorporate parents in various educational opportunities (Lopez, 2001). Evidence indicates that parents have already shaped the educational aspirations of their children during K–6 grades (Goldenberg, Gallimore,

Reese, & Garnier, 2001). Likewise, college outreach literature states that outreach initiatives should begin during elementary school as students are forming their college aspirations (Auerbach, 2004; Tierney, Colyar, & Corwin, 2003). Finally, rather than attempting to involve parents in traditional ways, research suggests identifying the ways parents are already involved, specifically tapping into families' funds of knowledge (González et al., 2005; Lopez, 2001).

In an effort to challenge the literature on familial deficits, the intent of this research is to understand families from a different model, that of funds of knowledge. In doing so, this study will highlight the educational ideologies[3] of families to better understand the development of educational philosophies, processes, and aspirations.

While funds of knowledge has not been used to study the connection between values and resources in the home with college access, studies do show the development of enhanced literacy (Rubinstein-Ávila, 2004), enhanced mathematical skills (Knobel, 2001) and overall student confidence (Vélez-Ibáñez, 1996). I argue that when funds of knowledge are examined through the lens of college culture and access, this framework can be useful in understanding the development of families' educational ideologies and aspirations.

Utilizing the theoretical framework of funds of knowledge as well as social and cultural capital, the following research questions are addressed: What factors influence the development of families' educational ideologies? How might educational ideologies influence future college access?

Educational Ideologies and Aspirations of Mexican Families

The misguided educational beliefs about Latino parents discount their views and diminish their value (Lott, 2001). Valencia and Black (2002) deconstruct these deficit thoughts and present evidence of the value of education through the historical and contemporary struggle for equal educational opportunity and the involvement of parents as illustrated in scholarly literature. Commitment to education is also illustrated in non-mainstream forms of teaching, from *consejos* (advice-giving narratives) (Delgado-Gaitan, 1994; Lopez, 2001) and counternarratives used to contest family practices viewed as problematic (Villenas, 2001), to the use of funds of knowledge (Vélez-Ibáñez, 1996). Involvement is demonstrated by highlighting parents' active engagement and agency; in some cases, parents have begun demanding to be more involved, holding schools accountable (Delgado-Gaitan, 1993; Lopez, 2001).

Lopez (2001) notes that oftentimes families are already involved in educational processes, but may not be in traditionally recognized ways. Delgado-Gaitan (1992) highlights Mexican American families where both parents and children are active agents of their educational environments; parents transmitted positive educational values to their children and children transmitted knowledge in return to parents.

It is evident that while Mexicans continue to be under-represented in institutions of higher education, their families do value education. As demonstrated, the transmission of sociocultural values is an important form of educational involvement (Lopez, 2001). Through the findings that follow, I intend to demonstrate that the transmission of sociocultural values also acts as an important means of establishing positive educational ideologies, specifically about college-going processes.

Theoretical Framework

This study draws from three theoretical frameworks. The primary framework is funds of knowledge (González, Moll, & Amanti, 2005), with social capital (Bourdieu, 1973, 1977; Stanton-Salazar, 2001) and cultural capital (Bourdieu & Passeron, 1977) serving as supplemental frameworks. I draw from the constructs found within each framework rather than operating within the strict parameters of one particular theory.

Funds of Knowledge

The framework of funds of knowledge refers to the bodies of knowledge and skills in a household that have accumulated over time (Moll, Amanti, Neff, & González, 1992). Funds of knowledge is based on the foundation that people are competent and have experiential knowledge that is valuable (González, Moll, & Amanti, 2005). Economic and political forces shaped the nature of binational households and families across the U.S./Mexico border. These forces contributed to the transformations of cultural and behavioral practices termed *funds of knowledge* (Vélez-Ibáñez & Greenberg, 2005). Defining funds of knowledge within families requires an understanding of strategic bodies of information that households utilize in their daily activities and need for their survival and well-being.

Funds of knowledge are found both within households and within the cluster networks of the community where children play and associate (Vélez-Ibáñez & Greenberg, 2005). When funds of knowledge are fully understood and properly utilized, they facilitate a powerful way to represent communities in terms of their inherent resources and create opportunities to use those resources for classroom teaching (González, Moll, & Amanti, 2005). This view of families is different from the accepted perceptions of cultural and intellectual deficiencies.

Cultural and Social Capital

Originally presented as a theoretical hypothesis to explain the unequal academic achievement of children in different social classes (Bourdieu, 1986), cultural capital is summarized as "high status cultural signals used in cultural and social selection" and is used to analyze "how culture and education contribute to social reproduction" (Lamont & Lareau, 1988, p. 153). Cultural capital is used both to address various cultural forms, competencies, and knowledge that certain individuals possess and to address the systemic perpetuation of power and privilege (McDonough, 1997; Tierney, 2002).

Social capital is described as the aggregate of resources that are linked to possession of a network or membership in a group which provides its members with collectively-owned capital (Bourdieu, 1986). I draw from Stanton-Salazar's (2001) definition of social capital which highlights these relationships among people and the properties within them that "when activated, enable them to accomplish their goals or to empower themselves in some meaningful way" (p. 265). The dimensions of social capital—norms, networks, and obligations, highlight aspects of the relational investments, standards and information transfer created when social capital is activated. This is similar to the ideas of exchange relations (Vélez-Ibáñez, 1996) developed in the transmission of funds of knowledge.

Although funds of knowledge is the primary framework utilized in this study, there are commonalities with cultural and social capital. One key commonality is that all three forms can be transmitted. Although there are differences in how each is transmitted and the context of the transmission process, each can be passed on to others. Secondly, all three forms can be converted. For example, cultural capital can be converted into economic capital and academic gains, social capital can be converted into economic capital and institutionalized gains (Bourdieu, 1986), and funds of knowledge can be converted (if valued and recognized) into social and cultural capital. There are also commonalities in how each form measures and defines its properties.

When considering funds of knowledge and social capital, both can be accumulated and membership in a network can translate into future benefits for the members. Funds of knowledge and cultural capital share a common perspective in how educational knowledge and culture is valued. Both frameworks assert that certain individuals and their knowledge are not valued because they do not belong to the dominant culture (Rios-Aguilar, Kiyama, Gravitt, & Moll, 2011). I acknowledge a warning that Lubienski (2003) provides. She shares that funds of knowledge, and specifically cultural capital, are being used synonymously and doing so avoids differentials in power and resources held by various groups. She aptly points out that although both funds of knowledge and cultural capital have value, funds of knowledge is not cultural capital because under original definitions of Bourdieu, its worth is not such that it would lead to a place in privileged social groups.

I include social and cultural capital as supplemental frameworks because they provided a way to understand concepts such as social networks, reciprocity, cultural signals, perpetuation of social class placement, and conversion. I also include these frameworks to better understand why funds of knowledge "have or have not translated into better educational opportunities and outcomes for under-represented students" (Rios-Aguilar et al., 2011, p. 167). Finally, utilizing these complementing frameworks provides an opportunity to look beyond a functionalist perspective that privileges the dominant class and addresses power structures within the system by challenging those inequities (Rios-Aguilar et al., 2011).

Methodology

The data represented in this article are drawn from a larger study examining the funds of knowledge present in Mexican American families and how those funds of knowledge contribute to the development of educational ideologies within their family unit. The study was conducted at a large research university located in the Southwest and included two phases of data collection. The institution sponsors the Parent Outreach Program[4], which provides parents of K–5 students information about high school and college as a way to prepare children for academic success.

Site and Sample Population

During the time this study was conducted, the Parent Outreach Program served about 85 families a year, approximately 40% of whom were primarily English speaking and 60% of whom were primarily Spanish speaking. The majority of parents identified as Hispanic. The Parent Outreach Program provided the opportunity to discuss issues of college access and choice with families who already indicated positive educational aspirations for their children as evidenced by their program participation. Thus, the program provided access to a sample that was then purposefully assembled based on criterion measures which ensured that each case met some criterion (Creswell, 2007).

The sample selected for both phases of this study consisted of Mexican American, English speaking families. Families are defined by the parent(s), guardian(s), children, and extended family that live in the household or frequently visit, including grandparents, aunts, uncles and cousins. Findings from this study are not representative of all families participating in the Parent Outreach Program and I recognize that the stories of the Spanish speaking families represent valuable insight not shared here. The final sample was constructed to ensure variation of family units (i.e., single-parent homes, multiple generation homes, and number of children in the household). This was done in an effort to assemble a sample that was more reflective of the diverse nature of families.

Data Collection and Analysis

The initial data collection phase originated from interviews with 27 parents during the first year of the program (spring 2004). Semi-structured, pre- and post-program interviews were conducted with each set of parents. The interview questions focused on their expectations for the program, educational values and ideologies, social and cultural capital, and program outcomes. During analysis of these interviews discussions around families' funds of knowledge ensued. Our team was interested in exploring not only the programmatic expectations and educational values of parents, but how daily home practices shaped those expectations and values. Thus, this first phase of data collection provided the basis from which the second round of data collection grew.

The second phase of data collection and primary data source, multiple-case studies were conducted with six families during the spring 2007 program. In this phase, family units represented the cases and served as the objects of analysis. The choice of a multiple-case study design is advantageous as multiple-case studies have been regarded as producing compelling data because of "replication logic" (Yin, 2003, p. 47). The funds of knowledge framework was a guiding factor in choosing case studies for this design. Funds of knowledge provide a rich framework that allows for similar patterns to emerge across several cases (a literal replication) (Yin, 2003, p. 48). Therefore, multiple-case studies guided by a rich framework become helpful in informing new cases drawing from the same framework.

The second phase of data collection included 12 semi-structured pre- and post-program interviews combined with approximately 20 open-ended oral history interviews with six families (a total of five to six interviews with each family). The goal of the interviews was two-fold: to gather data and to create the relational aspect of the research, a critical element in understanding participants' perspectives when employing an ethnographic approach to the case study (Mertens, 1998).

The protocol utilized for the pre- and post-program interviews was consistent with that of the initial phase of data collection. Oral history interviews were conducted approximately three to four times with each family while the program was in session and occurred over the course of nine months. Conducting oral histories allowed participants to remember the past and link it to the present (Mertens, 1998) and allowed me to partially mimic the original funds of knowledge research conducted by González, Moll, and Amanti (2005). The guiding oral history questions for the current study were informed by the protocol used in the original funds of knowledge study. These interviews consisted of questions about family history, labor history, routine household practices, and child-rearing philosophies. Finally, conducting oral histories allowed for a deeper understanding of the social history of families' households and how knowledge is taught and received in their households. In addition to loosely structured interviews, the data collected for oral histories included unstructured observations, attendance at family events, conversations, and audio recordings. Understanding the context of where families live is important as exchange relations often take place within the social networks in the community (González, Moll, & Amanti, 2005).

A list of informal codes using open coding was developed based on an initial read of the transcripts. This open coding allowed me to add to a pre-existing list of codes that was originally informed by the study's theoretical framework. Coding involved both deductive and inductive processes and led to axial coding where specific categories were developed (Creswell, 2007). Grouping data into categories allowed me to establish themes across cases (Creswell, 2007). Specifically, educational ideologies as a theme consisted not only of educational aspirations for families, but where the information came from and the factors or experiences that shaped those ideologies. Codes were established for ideologies that both helped and limited the children. Finally, I also coded for examples that illustrated how successful ideologies were measured.

Trustworthiness

Member-Checking and Transcript Review

I offered study participants the opportunity to read over their interview transcripts. This allowed for them to make corrections, add new information, verify findings, and critique specific questions if they did not feel the questions were appropriate (Creswell, 2007). All but two families chose to read over the transcripts. Of those that did read over the transcripts, verifications rather than corrections were offered.

Peer Debriefing

To reduce bias in analysis, I debriefed (Creswell, 2007) with members of the College of Education/Parent Outreach Program research team and a colleague whose research is in a similar field, to review findings from the interviews. Peer review helped to verify patterns and themes and offered a critical perspective on the nature of the questions. The peer review process also aided in the interpretation of data. Finally, these meetings and presentations of my work also helped me to process many of the limitations that had not yet been considered.

Researcher's Voice

There are multiple tensions found within this paper [chapter]. These tensions are highlighted in the ways in which college limitations are placed upon families by programs and institutions and by the limitations developed within families. I experience great tension because of my own identity as a first-generation, Mexican American from a working-class background similar to families in this study. My identity allowed me to connect with families while at the same time distancing me from them because I have another identity of academic layered upon it. I believe it is important to highlight the rich educational values and lessons found within our families. However, I also believe it is important to represent the complexities of our experiences and the consequences that result from those complexities. Therefore, in presenting the findings and implications that follow, I attempt to present *both* the successes among families and the complex limitations that sometimes challenge a smooth transition into college-going opportunities for their children.

Findings and Discussion

It was evident in this study, as it is also supported in the literature (Delgado-Gaitan, 1992; Lopez, 2001; Valencia & Black, 2002; Villenas, 2001; Zarate, 2007), that Mexican parents placed a high value on education. This study presents additional evidence that families form educational ideologies in a variety of ways and many times, those ideologies serve as positive influences. Equally relevant and evident are the realistic tensions surrounding the families' circumstances, resulting in limiting educational ideologies.

A number of factors influence the development of families' educational ideologies. College artifacts and symbols are explored in greater detail, as is the role of social networks. The college process, including choice and preparation, was constructed in non-traditional ways and often included an incomplete understanding of the process. While the Parent Outreach Program did not change the value placed on education, it did allow families to see college as a more realistic option and provided families with concrete information. Thoughts about educational choices were often found at two ends of the spectrum. Either families' college knowledge was limited to the local institutions or they wanted their children to attend the most prestigious institutions. A few exceptions emerged where parents developed their college-choice ideologies based on a particular experience. Those examples will be highlighted in the next few pages.

Sources of College Information: Social Networks, Cultural Symbols

Social Networks

Children often first learn about college from their parents. Although characterized as first-generation college families, the families in this study constructed conceptions of college from social and familial networks, and specifically by personal experience or family members who had attempted college. In both social capital and funds of knowledge, social networks are considered the means by which information is channeled from one member to another. It is clear that these networks facilitated higher levels of accomplishment and empowerment that may not have been possible without them (Stanton-Salazar, 2001). Networks served as information channels and highlighted relationships built on trust that allowed for exchange of support and resources (Stanton-Salazar, 2001).

For example, a mother of two young boys was accepted to the local university after graduating from high school and explained,

> It was overwhelming to me the thought of it, and just money wise. I went to [the local community college] and then from there to a medical institute.

I didn't even know where the university was when I graduated [high school].

(Elsa[5], occupation unknown, sons ages 10, 6, 2004)

Elsa explained that her family was just happy that she had graduated high school and did not even realize there was college after high school. While education was a central value to this family, their conceptions of college were influenced by Elsa's past experiences of feeling overwhelmed which served as a limiting factor in their development of college-going ideologies. This sentiment is consistent with parents in Auerbach's (2007) study whose disappointing educational experiences led them to be cautious about future opportunities.

However, social networks also served as informational resources and provided families with concrete examples toward which they were able to aspire. This supports research by Delgado-Gaitan (1992) who found that social networks facilitated an important exchange about schooling issues. In the current study, one family had a niece attending San Jose State University and through her, the family became aware of different institutions and had someone in college to whom they could ask college related questions.

The great thing about it is this generation—not [my daughter's] generation but the generation before her—my nieces—they are going to college. Casandra is in her third year now. So hopefully when [my daughter] starts showing interest, Casandra will be there to answer questions she might have and stuff. You know truly and honestly, Judy, if nothing else I want my girls to go to school and just experience life.

(Janice, insurance biller, daughters ages 14, 12, 5, 2007)

These experiences support research that encourages researchers and practitioners to acknowledge the "rich, varied, and positive experiences regarding the importance of education" (Saracho & Martinez-Hancock, 2004, p. 258). These examples acknowledge the families' experiences in higher education and how those experiences shaped their college ideologies.

A grandfather who participated in the first year of the Parent Outreach Program had extensive experience at the local university in his role as a vending machine repair man. He had this to offer, "I spend a lot of time there. We handle all the snack machines on campus. I'm down there quite often." To which his wife laughed and responded, "See if you got a complaint, you got the number you can call him." During our post-program interview the grandfather's on-campus experience was again mentioned:

Grandfather: Uh, well actually knowing what departments are at the [university], really. I mean I spend a lot of time down there and there's a lot of stuff that I wasn't aware of. And knowing where a lot of this stuff is now and knowing who you can actually go and ask for.

JMK: Were you guys able to go on the tour the day that they had it?

Grandfather: My wife did. I work down there quite a bit, with my business so I've been there. Like I told [the director], I could probably take you places she's never been. But that was just between us.

(Rogelio, vending machine repair man, grandchildren ages 11, 9, 7, 2004)

Our conversations highlight a number of interesting themes. His experience, although not a traditional university position, provided the grandfather with an understanding of the campus. He knew how to successfully navigate the physical campus. The grandfather's role as a vending machine repair man illustrated funds of knowledge in various forms. His expertise in maintenance and repair fit the funds of knowledge framework as it demonstrated knowledge that could be taught within a family unit. It is understood that his role took place on a university campus, extending funds of knowledge beyond the household and creating opportunities for his family to learn about an important educational setting. Yet, despite this knowledge there is a negative perception about his role. His wife mentioned contacting him when complaints arise; in a subtle way she is highlighting the stereotypical characteristics of a service professional's role typically held by people of color and twice as likely held by Latinos (Chapa & De La Rosa, 2004); lacking in professional expertise; and available to serve the needs and complaints of the dominant group. However, I argue that this grandfather's knowledge of the physical campus is quite valuable. Not only might this grandfather extend this knowledge to his family and introduce them to the educational setting, but the Parent Outreach Program could have expanded upon that knowledge to help him and other parents navigate campus. As previously expressed, he said that he could show us places on campus most people would not know about. Why not encourage the grandfather to do so? Such an act validates his role, builds confidence in his knowledge, and provides a concrete example of household expertise to other parents. Incorporating parents into leadership roles provides a sense of ownership, and can result in long-term maintenance of college-knowledge within the community (Downs et al., 2008).

Unfortunately, the link between knowledge of the physical campus and the translation into concrete college knowledge was not present. Although this grandfather did not know *how* to make college a reality he did know *where* to make college a reality. For some parents, the physical campus itself serves as a barrier, accessible to only a select few. In this particular case, the grandfather already had access to the physical campus; however, I am uncertain whether he realized the access he was granted.

Building social capital among networks of educators, families, and communities provides positive outcomes. These outcomes are realized in the form of increased parental support and improved understanding of children's needs (Auerbach, 2007). Social networks associated with educational experiences can also provide an improved understanding of the educational system and concrete aspirations about future college attainment. However, if social networks are associated with negative educational experiences like a difficult transition from high school, taking college courses and not finishing, one can also pass on ideologies surrounded by misinformation, fear, and lack of understanding.

Academic Cultural Symbols

Symbols around the culture of education shaped the ways in which families organized their thoughts about college-going realities. One of the most telling examples of how cultural symbols shape educational ideologies is found in the following example, "the University of Michigan Story." I began the topic of college-choice by asking this father where he hoped his daughters would go to college.

Father: My oldest one's already talking about Michigan. . . . She's had it, like, the last three years.
JMK: So how did she find out about Michigan?
Father: Play Station and me watching college football . . . because everybody just knows, oh, [the local university] because of commercials, the news and everything. But it's true, if you watch sports on the weekends, of another school, it's like wow. Because you know, during the games, they give—
JMK: Right. They show little clips of the school.
Father: This is what you're going to get at this school. And when she saw Michigan—first, the colors. Boom. But then I showed her, look at the marching band because she's like me, "Oh, wow." And then, she goes, "Let's look up Michigan," . . . she just saw it and was just like, "I want to go to that school."

(Will, Army veteran and student, daughters ages 11, 9, 2007)

A couple of minutes into this conversation Will's daughter began playing the University of Michigan fight song on her band instrument. Will interrupted the conversation to explain what I was hearing. During a football game his daughter had asked the name of the University of Michigan fight song. She realized it was in her band songbook and began practicing the first four bars.

It was encouraging to see that this father and daughter created high college aspirations. However, in all of my conversations with Will, he very rarely mentioned the steps necessary to achieve such aspirations. Will's example highlights aspirations and a limitation: high value for education and knowledge about particular pieces of the college process, but missing certain components of how to get there. This is not uncommon of first-generation college students as they often have less access to information about postsecondary education (Lundberg, Schreiner, Hovaguimian, & Miller, 2007). However, families in this study are already creating supportive aspirations in the pursuit of higher education.

The example in this section illustrated a father tapping into his own funds of knowledge and love of sports. He took the time to use the Internet to introduce his daughter to the campus and the fight song. This allowed her to connect an abstract idea about college with a concrete act of creating a college sound. Funds of knowledge were successfully transferred from the father to the daughter and she incorporated that knowledge into her own educational ideologies about a particular institution. As evidenced, college ideologies do not follow a traditional pattern and do not fit into established literature about college-choice processes (Hossler & Gallagher; 1987).

College Aspirations and Limitations

Barriers to College Attendance: Finances and Choice

All of the parents in the outreach program anticipated that their children would pursue a college education. However, aspirations were sometimes entangled with misconceptions about the process. When asked if there was anything that might stop their child from attending college, many parents cited finances. While parents gained an increased understanding of the costs of college through the Parent Outreach Program, they did not have a complete understanding of the financial assistance available and some left the program wanting more information about navigating the financial-aid application process. Although parents felt that finances might serve as barriers, they offered examples of sacrifice as to how they would compensate for those financial hurdles. One mother explained, "I've already decided that if I have to move back into a one-bedroom apartment, that's what I'll do." Another father stated that he was willing to scrub toilets on campus if it meant his sons would receive a tuition waiver. Parents' concerns about financing college provides outreach programs opportunities to have in depth discussions beyond the costs of college and into the financial-aid application process and requirements for maintaining aid.

Conflicts between aspirations and limitations were also present. These conflicts manifested around where students should attend college. Most parents in the study associated college either with the university that sponsored the outreach program or elite institutions.

Not only were some college aspirations limited to local institutions and Ivy League universities, but their knowledge of these Ivy League programs was of name only. Torres and Hernandez (2007) described this conflict as support "provided for education, but not for changing the status quo within the family" (p. 570). This is associated with families' uneasiness with leaving home and enrolling in a college or university of which they know little to nothing about. These examples illustrate the complexity of families' aspirations about where their children should attend college. Staying close to or living at home represents a cultural strength of these families and provides the opportunity for their children to continue to draw upon family and community resources while in school. It also represents the fear that mothers might have in losing the closeness with their children as they contemplate moving away (Auerbach, 2007). The complexity of this issue is developed in the following conversation with Danielle:

JMK: Do you have a preference about where they should go to school?
Mother: There's nothing wrong with the [local U] so I prefer that.
JMK: If they were to get a scholarship out of state—
Mother: I would really be scared. I would be scared because you can't protect your kid when they are so far away, but I would rather for them to go cause I don't want kids that depend on mommy for everything. So if they wanted to, it would break my heart but I want them to learn. I want them to live on their own and not regret—I wish I did this, you know.

(Danielle, corrections officer, children ages 7 and 6, 2007)

The Parent Outreach Program was successful in establishing a college connection for families in the program. The connection to the local university was key in the creation of their college path as families felt secure with and formed positive perceptions of the local university. Families left the program with a strong loyalty to the sponsoring university and knowledge of the local community college, however, they had limited knowledge about other educational options.

Symbols as Potential Limiting Factors

It is clear that cultural symbols are influential factors in shaping educational ideologies. One final symbol came to signify the Parent Outreach Program and was intended to serve as a resource and physical guide for parents. The following examples center on the "Red Book," a notebook given to parents during the Parent Outreach Program containing college tips, handouts, websites, and various university resources. Responses referencing the notebook were typically shared during questions about the content of the information parents received during the program and about how parents would find future college information. One mother indicated that the notebook served as a refresher, "I think the red book was pretty helpful. I read it every time I needed to refresh my memory on things." She also understood that if she needed future college information she could visit any of the websites listed, "plus I would go back to the red book if it could help me. I know there are a lot of resources in there as far as websites that I could go to." This book represented their successful experience in the outreach program and a primary source of college information. As one mother mentioned, "I have it all written down in my notes, everything. It was great that we had that notebook to keep up with the . . . if we ever have to go back to it it's there." A grandfather explained to me,

> And I don't know where my wife has the notebook because I could bring some of that stuff up, but I don't know where she has the notebook. It may be in her satchel, she carries it around with her all the time.
>
> *(Rogelio, vending machine repair man, grandchildren ages 11, 9, 7, 2004)*

The "Red Book" served as a means to organize all of the important documents and information presented during the program. In carrying the book around, college information became a part of families' daily lives, a resource readily available. While it is concerning that family members might rely solely on the book and the people and information listed in the book, it also provides parents with the opportunity to obtain additional information on their own, thus enacting their agency. Families did not talk about how they might build upon the concepts within the book. However, I believe that this book provided an outline from which families can begin constructing a college plan. Rather than becoming a symbol that turns into a source of misinformation, the Red Book may represent the basis of expanding college knowledge and the beginnings of a collegiate social network.

Conclusion and Implications

The educational ideologies outlined here highlight the ways in which ideologies, particularly around college-going processes were formed. College information came from social networks and from academic symbols that were part of families' everyday lives. Ideologies manifested as both helpful and hurtful. Despite the educational limitations in families the sense of college being a realistic goal was present.

This study is significant for several reasons as it extends our understanding of the college aspiration and college-choice process for Mexican American students. The examples presented in this paper [chapter] exemplify what Valenzuela (1999) characterizes as *educación*, a notion that highlights the role of family in creating a sense of "moral, social, and personal responsibility and serves as the foundation for all other learning" (p. 23). As illustrated, families' embodiment of *educación* respected formal education and demonstrated the importance of reciprocal social relations. Thus, *educación* complements the funds of knowledge framework. Findings from this study also extend the discussion on funds of knowledge beyond traditional K–12 literature as this study represents one of the first that utilizes this framework when studying issues of college access. Likewise, outreach literature is also extended, as the findings from the study present new opportunities for engaging family members in culturally relevant ways. Finally, the use of funds of knowledge with cultural and social capital illustrate the importance of considering a theoretical overlap especially when understanding social relationships, networks, and issues of access and power.

Reframing Deficits

As researchers, we continue to recommend that parents be incorporated into students' educational experiences. As practitioners, we continue to seek ways to involve parents. However, I assert that we must step back from this process and dismantle the deficit perspective. Otherwise, we will overlook the inherent resources that are already present in these families. We must begin to understand families from a more balanced perspective. Yes, they value education and yes, they want their children to attend college. However, these aspirations are complex and sometimes incomplete as steps required to achieve these goals can be misunderstood or unknown. On the flip side, we must also consider how K–12 teachers and administrators, outreach programs, policy makers, actors within higher education, and the relevant literature might also serve as limiting factors. It is naïve to assume that there are not limiting factors present in families. However, it is equally naïve to assume that various educational actors do not play a role in perpetuating those limitations and deficits. By adopting a more critical view of the role that organizations play, and by developing a more complete understanding of the inherent resources present in underrepresented families, perhaps larger gains can be made in the college-going rates for these students.

Programmatic Recommendations

Despite many recommendations to incorporate parents in school systems and outreach programs, there is a gap in the practical application, as well as in the literature illustrating programs that utilize comprehensive methods of incorporating parents. I acknowledge the constraints that outreach programs face. Outreach programs are continually asked to serve larger numbers with less budget and personnel. These programs operate with the dual challenge of decreasing resources and maintaining legitimacy by increasing access for populations that do not have high college-going rates.

Findings from this study present an opportunity to build on the work that outreach programs are already doing. These recommendations are not meant to serve as *the* solution for successfully incorporating families into outreach programs; however, they can be used to expand on the notion of cultural integrity and further incorporate families from a non-deficit perspective.

Outreach programs should help parents utilize their extensive social networks as a means of practicing and activating social capital. It is also evident that families possessed considerable information regarding college-going processes. Encouraging family members to share and build on that information during outreach program sessions is critical. Doing so would also build family members' confidence when seeking new information or resources. To keep materials relevant for family members, outreach programs might offer structured and continuous follow-up with former participants, if parents are expected to continue to incorporate new information, strategies, and college conversations into their daily activities. By offering continuous follow-up, outreach programs have the opportunity to address the persistence rates of under-represented students once they begin college. These recommendations represent an opportunity to utilize funds of knowledge in a new, untapped way and provide a contribution to the effort of affecting change in the structure of education.

Future Research

Many questions remained unanswered. The interviews with study participants were conducted during their time in a university outreach program. Participants have not been followed up with to determine where their children are on the collegiate path. Future research should examine how and if those funds of knowledge are being converted into concrete educational opportunities for children throughout K–12 and into and out of their college experiences. Future research should also examine how educational ideologies shift over time based on experiences, outreach initiatives, and familial funds of knowledge.

This research represents one of the first studies to utilize funds of knowledge to understand families and outreach programs in higher education. Additional research is necessary to understand the utility of funds of knowledge in access and outreach programs and in under-represented families while in college, not only on the path to college. Finally, it would be beneficial in the future to examine family aspirations and student aspirations separately to better understand how and if college aspirations from family members are transferred and develop into college aspirations for their youth.

Conclusion

One of the most difficult challenges that we experience as educators and researchers is to understand the realities behind what is often perceived to be a lack of involvement or lack of interest among low income and underrepresented families. It is important to study and represent families from an asset-based perspective. However, it is challenging to allow the limiting factors to also be exposed. Lack of information does not mean lack of interest; it also does not mean lack of value of education. In fact, the families in this study not only had strong educational values, rich ideologies about education, but also important pieces of educational information that just needed to be woven together. It is our role as educators, practitioners and researchers to ensure that happens.

Notes

i This chapter represents a shortened reprint of the article: Kiyama, J. M. (2010). College aspirations and limitations: The role of educational ideologies and funds of knowledge in Mexican American families. *American Educational Research Journal, 47*(2), 330–356. Copyright © [2010]. Reprinted by permission of SAGE Publications.
1 The terminology used for persons of Latin American origin is sensitive. For the sake of clarity, I refer to study participants as Mexican American, as families represented those of Mexican heritage born in the United States. In doing so, I highlight experiences specific to Mexican Americans, further illustrating the diversity within the larger Mexican sub-group. Literature referencing Mexicans often includes both Mexican immigrants and Mexican Americans. In 2000, the Mexican sub-group made up about 58 percent of the total Latinos in the United States (Chapa & De La Rosa, 2004). When referencing literature, the terms *Hispanic* and *Latino* are used interchangeably. I have not substituted those terms for any other descriptor so that the integrity of the literature being referenced will be maintained.
2 I draw upon a definition of educational aspirations developed by Quaglia and Cobb (1996), summarized as, "a student's ability to identify and set goals for the future, while being inspired in the present to work toward those goals" (p. 130).
3 Ideologies refer to an integrated or comprehensive set of ideas or perspectives. I look specifically at educational ideologies, comprehensive perspectives about education and the college-going process. In developing this working definition of educational ideologies, I draw from sociological research on ideologies that look primarily at the nature and the extent of the distribution of particular ideas (Cheal, 1979).
4 In order to maintain anonymity, "Parent Outreach Program" is a pseudonym. This program is coordinated through the University's outreach office and represents a collaborative relationship between the University and a local school district. All of the elementary schools within the district participate in the Parent Outreach Program.
5 The names of all participants, their family members, and any local identifiers [have] been changed in order to maintain anonymity.

References

Auerbach, S. (2004). Engaging Latino parents in supporting college pathways: Lessons from a college access program. *Journal of Hispanic Higher Education, 3*(2), 125–145.

Auerbach, S. (2007). From moral supporters to struggling advocates: Reconceptualizing parent roles in education through the experience of working-class families of color. *Urban Education, 42*(3), 250–283.

Bourdieu, P. (1973). Cultural reproduction and social reproduction. In R. Brown (Ed.), *Knowledge, education and cultural change* (pp. 71–112). London, UK: Tavistock Publications Limited.

Bourdieu, P. (1977). Cultural reproduction and social reproduction. In J. Karabel & A. H. Halsey (Eds.), *Power and ideology in education* (pp. 487–511). New York: Oxford University Press.

Bourdieu, P. (1986). Forms of capital. In J. G. Richardson (Ed.), *Handbook of theory and research for the sociology of education*. New York: Greenwood.

Bourdieu, P., & Passeron, J. C. (1977). *Reproduction in education, society, and culture*. Beverly Hills, CA: Sage.

Chapa, J., & De La Rosa, B. (2004). Latino population growth, socioeconomic and demographic characteristics, and implications for educational attainment. *Education and Urban Society, 36*(2), 130–149.

Cheal, D. J. (1979). Hegemony, ideology, and contradictory consciousness. *The Sociological Quarterly, 20*, 109–117. doi:10.1111/j.1533–8525.1979.tb02188.x

Creswell, J. W. (2007). *Qualitative inquiry & research design: Choosing among five approaches*. Thousand Oaks, CA: Sage Publications.

Delgado-Gaitan, C. (1992). School matters in the Mexican-American home: Socializing children to education. *American Educational Research Journal, 29*(3), 495–513.

Delgado-Gaitan, C. (1993). Researching change and changing the researcher. *Harvard Educational Review, 63*(4), 389–411.

Delgado-Gaitan, C. (1994). Consejos: The power of cultural narratives. *Anthropology & Education Quarterly, 25*(3), 298–316.

Downs, A., Martin, J., Fossum, M., Martinez, S., Solorio, M., & Martinez, H. (2008). Parents teaching parents: A career and college knowledge program for Latino families. *Journal of Latinos and Education, 7*(3), 227–240.

Goldenberg, C., Gallimore, R., Reese, L., & Garnier, H. (2001). Cause or effect? A longitudinal study of immigrant Latino parents' aspirations and expectations, and their children's school performance. *American Educational Research Journal, 38*(3), 547–582.

Gonzalez, K. P., Stone, C., & Jovel, J. E. (2003). Examining the role of social capital in access to college for Latinas: Toward a college opportunity framework. *Journal of Hispanic Higher Education, 2*(1), 146–170.

González, N., Moll, L. C., & Amanti, C. (2005). *Funds of knowledge: Theorizing practices in households, communities, and classrooms*. Mahwah, NJ: Erlbaum.

Hossler, D., & Gallagher, K. S. (1987). Studying student college choice: A three-phase model and the implications for policy makers. *College and University, 2*(3), 207–221.

Knobel, M. (2001). "I'm not a pencil man": How one student challenges our notions of literacy "failure" in school. *Journal of Adolescent & Adult Literacy, 44*(5), 404–414.

Lamont, M., & Lareau, A. (1988). Cultural capital: Allusions, gaps and glissandos in recent theoretical developments. *Sociological Theory, 6*, 153–168. doi:10.2307/202113

Lopez, G. (2001). The value of hard work: Lessons on parent involvement from an (im) migrant household. *Harvard Educational Review, 71*(3), 416–437.

Lott, B. (2001, August). *Recognizing and welcoming the standpoint of low-income parents in the public schools*. Presented at the Annual Conference of the American Psychological Association, 109th, San Francisco, CA.

Lubienski, S. T. (2003). Celebrating diversity and denying disparities: A critical assessment. *Educational Researcher, 32*, 30–38. doi:10.3102/0013189x032008030

Lundberg, C. A., Schreiner, L. A., Hovaguimian, K. D., & Miller, S. S. (2007). First-generation status and student race/ethnicity as distinct predictors of student involvement and learning. *NASPA Journal, 44*(1), 57–83.

McDonough, P. (1997). *Choosing colleges: How social class and schools structure opportunity*. Albany, NY: State University of New York Press.

Mertens, D. M. (1998). *Research methods in education and psychology: Integrating diversity with quantitative and qualitative approaches*. Thousand Oaks, CA: Sage Publications.

Moll, L. C., Amanti, C., Neff, D., & González, N. (1992). Funds of knowledge for teaching: Using a qualitative approach to connect homes and classrooms. *Theory Into Practice, 31*(2), 132–141.

Quaglia, R. J., & Cobb, C. D. (1996). Toward a theory of student aspirations. *Journal of Research in Rural Education, 12*(3), 127–132.

Rios-Aguilar, C., Kiyama, J. M., Gravitt, M., & Moll, L. C. (2011). Funds of knowledge for the poor and forms of capital for the rich? A capital approach to examining funds of knowledge. *Theory and Research in Education, 9*(2), 163–184.

Rubinstein-Ávila, E. (2004). Conversing with Miguel: An adolescent English language learner struggling with later literacy development. *Journal of Adolescent & Adult Literacy, 47*(4), 290–301.

Saracho, O. N., & Martinez-Hancock, F. (2004). The culture of Mexican-Americans: It's importance for early educators. *Journal of Hispanic Higher Education, 3*(3), 254–269.

Stanton-Salazar, R. D. (2001). *Manufacturing hope and despair: The school and kin networks of U.S. Mexican Youth.* New York: NY: Teachers College Press.

Tierney, W. G. (2002). Parents and families in precollege preparation: The lack of connection between research and practice. *Educational Policy, 16*(4), 588–606.

Tierney, W. G., Colyar, J. E., & Corwin, Z. B. (2003). *Preparing for college: Building expectations, changing realities* (pp. 1–21). Los Angeles, CA: Center for Higher Education Policy Analysis, University of Southern California.

Torres, V., & Hernandez, E. (2007). The influence of ethnic identity on self-authorship: A longitudinal study of Latino/a college students. *Journal of College Student Development, 48*(5), 558–573.

Valencia, R. R., & Black, M. S. (2002). "Mexican Americans don't value education!"—On the basis of myth, mythmaking, and debunking. *Journal of Latinos and Education, 1*(2), 81–103.

Valenzuela, A. (1999). *Subtractive schooling: U.S.-Mexican youth and the politics of caring.* New York, NY: SUNY Press.

Vélez-Ibáñez, C. (1996). *Border visions: Mexican cultures of the Southwest United States.* Tucson, AZ: The University of Arizona Press.

Vélez-Ibáñez, C., & Greenberg, J. (1992). Formation and transformation of funds of knowledge among U.S.-Mexican households. *Anthropology & Education Quarterly, 23*(4), 313–335.

Vélez-Ibáñez, C., & Greenberg, J. (2005). Formation and transformation of funds of knowledge. In N. González, L. C. Moll, & C. Amanti (Eds.), *Funds of knowledge: Theorizing practices in households, communities, and classrooms* (pp. 47–70). Mahwah, NJ: Lawrence Erlbaum Associates.

Villenas, S. (2001). Latina mothers and small-town racisms: Creating narratives of dignity and moral education in North Carolina. *Anthropology & Education Quarterly, 32*(1), 3–28.

Yin, R. K. (2003). Case study research: Design and methods (3rd ed.). In L. Bickman & D. J. Rog (Eds.), *Applied social research methods series.* Thousand Oaks, CA: Sage Publications.

Zarate, M. E. (2007). *Understanding Latino parental involvement in education. Perceptions, expectations, and recommendations* (pp. 1–18). Report by the Tomás Rivera Policy Institute.

7

A FAMILY AFFAIR

Examining College-Going Among Sub-Saharan African Immigrants in the U.S. Through a Funds of Knowledge Lens

Chrystal A. George Mwangi

Sub-Saharan African immigrants, originating from African countries that lie south of the Sahara Desert, are one of the fastest growing immigrant populations in the United States, increasing by almost 100 percent into the 21st century (Hernandez, 2012). The U.S. is estimated to receive the largest number of immigrants from sub-Saharan Africa, and according to the Migration Policy Institute, "if the trends of the past decade continue, by 2020 Africa will likely replace the Caribbean as the major source region for the U.S. Black immigrant population" (Capps, McCabe, & Fix, 2011, p. 3). While nearly 40 percent of African immigrant adults in the U.S. possess a college degree (Hernandez, 2012), there is limited research addressing their postsecondary aspirations and college access strategies. Furthermore, approximately 80 percent of children in sub-Saharan African families in the U.S. are second generation (U.S.-born) (Thomas, 2010), and these children are increasingly entering the U.S. education pipeline and seeking access to college. However, only a few researchers have explored the educational experiences of the children of African immigrants (e.g., Awokoya, 2012), and to date, none have examined how these families communicate about academic expectations and college-going.

This study addresses these gaps by exploring the postsecondary aspirations, expectations, and access strategies of sub-Saharan African immigrant multigenerational families. I investigated the research question: What pre-existing familial and/or community-based resources, knowledge, and skills do sub-Saharan African immigrant families draw upon for engaging in college preparation? Specifically, I use the concept of funds of knowledge to explore this question within a familial context and consider how family/community relations and engagement impact academic motivation for African immigrants. While funds of knowledge is typically used to examine the experiences of Latinos, the framework's emphasis on family and community knowledge, immigrant experiences and adjustment, and learning in the home (Moll, Amanti, Neff, & González, 1992; Vélez-Ibáñez & Greenberg, 1992) provides a relevant lens for this study.

Unlike other immigrant groups, ethnicity is often overlooked for African immigrants, particularly after the first generation, and data are rarely disaggregated for Black students relating to ethnicity, nativity, and generational status (George Mwangi, 2014; Kasinitz, Waters, Mollenkopf, & Holdaway, 2008). However, as the African immigrant population continues to grow and create roots in the U.S., it is important to learn whether the educational achievement experienced among new arrivals will continue over subsequent generations.

Theoretical Perspectives

There is not a body of higher education literature on the college access and choice of African immigrants in the United States. Therefore, I consulted literature more broadly on the role of family in college access and choice, as well as the college-going process of other immigrant populations. Much of this research focuses on the role of parental encouragement and involvement, and the impact of structural factors (e.g., parental income, education level). For example, researchers conclude that while parents play a critical role in college choice, support is hindered or enhanced by structural factors, which create inequities for students in navigating the process (Cabrera & La Nasa, 2000; Perna, 2006; Rowan-Kenyon, Bell, & Perna, 2008). While structural factors impact college access for students generally, immigrants/children of immigrants experience differences in the process of educational attainment as compared to native peers or traditional models of college choice (Baum & Flores, 2011; Griffin, del Pilar, McIntosh, & Griffin, 2012; Kiyama, 2010, 2011; Portes & Fernandez-Kelly, 2008). Furthermore, although there is acknowledgement of diverse family structures and support in college access/choice research, the research frameworks, samples, and analyses used in this scholarship do not always reflect this diversity (Knight, Norton, Bentley, & Dixon, 2004; Tierney & Auerbach, 2005; Yosso, 2005).

I chose to use a family-centered model because research about African immigrants often finds this population to have a family/community-centric worldview (see Arthur, 2000, 2008, 2010; Nyang, 2011; Swigart, 2001). Specifically, I selected funds of knowledge, which focuses on households' labor history, social interactions, educational experiences, language use, and daily activities (Moll et al., 1992). The framework aligns with my study's focus on family because it fully incorporates familial and community background into the educational experience. It also integrates the traditional and nontraditional knowledge and resources families use to define and navigate U.S. education processes such as college preparation.

Funds of knowledge can reframe the role of family in higher education by centering families as the unit of analysis (Rios-Aguilar, 2010; Rios-Aguilar & Kiyama, 2012). While studies often identify funds as a set of resources, it is also important to understand "how, when, and by whom funds of knowledge are negotiated, activated, and expanded upon" (Rios-Aguilar & Kiyama, 2012, p. 13). There are uncertainties in how funds of knowledge are developed and operationalized. Thus, while I define funds of knowledge in this study as the accumulated strategies, networks, and forms of knowledge embedded in the life experiences, cultural practices, and daily routines of families, I place emphasis on how funds of knowledge are transmitted by families and engaged by students within the college-going process. Furthermore, Rios-Aguilar and Kiyama (2012) suggest, "it is important for the development and understanding of funds of knowledge to also include other subgroups of Latina/o students and other ethnic minority, immigrant, and low-income families" (p. 13). I expand the application of this model to African immigrant families engaged in college preparation, highlighting the role familial and cultural factors play in establishing educational aspirations and achievement (Kiyama, 2010).

Methods

I use an ethnographic multi-case study design, which combines case study techniques with ethnographic interpretation (Simons, 2009) to give "a sociocultural analysis and interpretation of the unit of study" (Merriam, 1988, p. 23). Each case is defined as a family and individuals as embedded units within each case. In this study, families were identified as cases because of my interest in exploring and interpreting the contextual conditions critical to the family unit as they engaged in the college-going process. While much of college-choice literature emphasizes the individual student, defining students as cases was not appropriate given my focus on the transfer of funds of knowledge within families and how families together navigate college choice. Defining the family unit[1] as a case is also more culturally relevant to understanding the college-going process of African immigrants, as this population often possesses a familial/community-centered worldview (Arthur, 2000, 2008, 2010; Nyang, 2011; Swigart, 2001).

I use some ethnographic techniques, such as participant observation and directive and nondirective interviewing; however, ethnographic case studies are not limited by the data collection and analysis techniques found in traditional ethnography and can be conducted in familiar or unfamiliar cultures (Simons, 2009). I use an ethnographic approach to case study because of my emphasis on cultural transmission, via funds of knowledge, within families as part of college-going. I used the concept of culture on multiple levels to inform the research, including the use of ethnographic methods, development of research questions and framework (funds of knowledge), and as a theme to guide data analysis.

Research Sample

I bounded this study to the population of Black sub-Saharan African immigrants in the Washington DC metropolitan area. This area is the second-largest U.S. destination for African immigrants (11.3 percent) (Terrazas, 2009). Recruitment was conducted through community organizations that work with African immigrants and snowball sampling (Merriam, 2009; Small, 2009). Families selected had to meet certain criteria:

1. All members of the immediate family must be Black sub-Saharan African immigrants from an Anglophone country and voluntary immigrants (e.g., not refugees or asylees).
2. Parent(s) are first-generation (immigrants to the U.S., born abroad) and at least one of their children was born abroad, but immigrated to the U.S. before age 12 or was a U.S.-born child.
3. The child is a college-going individual, in grades 7–12 with the intent of college enrollment.

The participants are a purposeful sample of nine families (30 individuals). Families originate from Nigeria, Kenya, Cameroon, and Ghana. All have immigration histories reflecting a move to the U.S. for career or educational advancement. Table 7.1 provides a demographic summary of the families. Ten college-going children across the families participated. Table 7.2 provides a demographic summary of these participants.

Data Collection

I utilized semi-structured interviews and participant observation to engage in three data collection sessions with each family. During each session, I conducted an interview with the family together as a group and conducted 1:1 interviews with individual family members. I started with the family group interview to explore the "family conversational voice" (Beitin, 2007, p. 50) that emerges when families have social exchange and can construct meaning together. After the group interview, I conducted individual interviews with the college-going student, parent(s), and other participating family members to provide them the opportunity to describe their experiences privately and in more detail. Individual interviews lasted 45 to 60 minutes each, and family group interviews lasted 60 to 90 minutes each. The first session focused on gathering data about the family such as family history, culture, dynamics, and educational experiences. The second and third sessions focused on the families' college-going process. Over the course of the study, I spent 10 to 21 hours interviewing each family.

During each session, I spent 30 minutes to two hours with the families outside of the formal interview time engaging in conversation and building rapport. This

TABLE 7.1 Demographic Summary of Households

Family Pseudonym	Origin	Pseudonym (Age)	Relation to College- Going Child	Level of Education Attained	Years in the U.S.
Enemari Family	Nigeria	Adakole (48)	Father	Masters	21
		Owole (47)	Mother	High School	12
		Simon (23)	Brother	High School	12
		Nehemiah (21)	Brother	High School	12
		Helen (18)	Sister	High School	12
		David (18)	Brother	High School	12
Obi Family	Nigeria	Esther (62)	Grandmother	Middle School	11
		Ruth (36)	Mother	Masters	18
Magimbi Family	Kenya	Gatwiri (36)	Mother	Masters	18
Amolo Family	Kenya	Atieno (44)	Mother	Masters	14
		Kenneth (46)	Stepfather	Bachelor	28
		Sara (18)	Sister	High School	14
		Imani (7)	Half Brother	1st Grade	U.S.-born
Fatoki Family	Nigeria	Minnie (40)	Mother	Associate	20
		Breaker (46)	Father	Bachelor	29
		Will (10)	Brother	4th Grade	U.S.-born
		Chelsea (22)	Half Sister	Bachelor	U.S.-born
Mbai Family	Kenya	Raz (38)	Mother	Associate	13
Osei Family	Ghana	Karen (39)	Mother	Bachelor	21
Blomo Family	Cameroon	TeeJay (42)	Mother	Bachelor	15
		Ben (45)	Father	Bachelor	15
		Sheila (25)	Sister	Bachelor	15
		Pam (70)	Grandmother	High School	5
Nyom Family	Cameroon	Judy (52)	Mother	Bachelor	22
		Ron (55)	Father	Masters	24
		Daniel (10)	Brother	4th Grade	U.S.-born

TABLE 7.2 Demographic Summary of College-Going Participants

Family Pseudonym	Pseudonym	Gender	Country of Birth	Age	Grade
Enemari Family	Agaba	Male	United States	13	7th
Obi Family	Priscilla	Female	United States	15	10th
Magimbi Family	Olaf	Male	Kenya (immigrated at age six)	16	11th
Amolo Family	Hannah	Female	Kenya (immigrated at age seven)	17	12th
Fatoki Family	Kate	Female	United States	16	11th
Mbai Family	Rem	Male	Kenya (immigrated at age five)	16	12th
Osei Family	Victor	Male	United States	18	12th
Blomo Family	Mary	Female	Cameroon (immigrated at age two)	17	10th
	Victoria	Female	United States	14	8th
Nyom Family	Andi	Female	United States	16	11th

included when I first arrived in the home, engaging in conversation in-between individual interviews, and after the conclusion of formal interviews. My observations focused on how the families interact with each other (family dynamics and communication), insights participants made about education/college going, and the interview space (home) and how the space is used in the college-going process. To document this engagement and other insights gathered, I conducted participant observation throughout data collection. I recorded field notes using Schatzman and Strauss' technique (Emerson, Fretz, & Shaw, 2001) to document observations.

Data Analysis

I used Merriam's (2009) constant comparative method of case study analysis, which was completed in several iterative stages beginning with data management and preliminary analysis. NVIVO 10 software was utilized to organize and manage all data as a case study database (Merriam, 2009). This study followed a multiple-case study analysis in which the data are first examined case by case through thematic analysis (Merriam, 2009; Stake, 1995). I treated each family as a complete case and engaged in a separate coding process for each in order to substantially understand their unique context. I first engaged in multiple reads and comparative examinations of the data for each family case. During this early stage of analysis, I openly coded the data using both inductive and deductive approaches (Merriam, 2009). I used a deductive approach by identifying key concepts and terms from my funds of knowledge conceptual framework, such as family rituals, transmission of funds, immigration history, familial resources, familial knowledge, and daily practices. I also used inductive analysis to remain open to new and emerging themes (Emerson et al., 2001). To do so, as I read through transcripts, I made annotations at lines in the text that appeared useful in answering my research questions.

Through axial coding, I developed and refined my coding system and connected open codes to broader categories that comprised recurrent patterns within the data (Merriam, 2009). The axial coding process assisted my development of a codebook for each family case (Miles & Huberman, 2005). In order to provide an in-depth understanding of the family cases, I utilized the codebooks to develop a case profile for each family. During this phase, I operationalized the ethnographic construct of microculture, which are systems of cultural knowledge characteristic of subgroups within larger societies (Neuliep, 2012). I engaged the analysis of each family case as a microculture within U.S. society. Members of a microculture can share characteristics, values, and behaviors with the dominant society, but also share common cultural knowledge or a worldview with members of the subgroup (Neuliep, 2012). Using funds of knowledge, I focused on a sociocultural analysis of each case, namely how a microculture functions internally as well as within the U.S education system to navigate college-going.

Next, I began a cross-case analysis. I searched for emergent themes that generally fit each case, although themes varied to some extent from case to case (Merriam, 2009). In this analysis, I developed a cross-case codebook. I first turned to the family codebooks, looking for codes that overlapped across cases and collapsing them within my cross-case codebook. Refining and reducing for inductive coding was more challenging, as these codes were often different within each case. However, by using the definitions and examples provided for each code in the family codebooks, I was able to sort and collapse codes that captured a recurring pattern across cases (Merriam, 2009). Through this process, I refined and reduced my codes from the separate codebooks into one cross-case coding system. This allowed me to link codes that were relevant to the research questions and to compare the ways participants made sense of college preparation.

During the coding process, three themes began to emerge, developing a storyline/core category (La Rossa, 2005; Merriam, 2009). The themes that emerged were college-going legacies, engagement in the home and community, and family/community networks. The primary narrative emerging across cases in these themes reflected how families developed a college-going environment or culture in their home and community. This process interacted with intergenerational, cultural, and social dynamics as well as the transmission of funds of knowledge within families as they engaged in college preparation.

Findings

There were three themes present across cases: college-going legacies, engagement in the home and community, and family/community networks. Findings revealed that families perceived these as important to academic success and college preparation, and that participants' academic motivations and college expectations are situated within familial and cultural contexts.

College-Going Legacies

Families described the motivation for college as part of a larger family effort towards upward mobility and success that is rooted in education. Six of the families have an immigration history initiating with an adult member coming to the U.S. in order to pursue an undergraduate or graduate degree. After becoming pregnant while an international student, Gatwiri Magimbi withdrew from her university to go back to Kenya, but she returned with her son to the U.S. years later as a single mother to complete her bachelor's degree. Adakole Enemari, a Nigerian father, lived away from his wife and five children for nine years while he attained two college degrees in the United States. His family remained in Nigeria during that time until they were finally granted visas to join Adakole. These are examples of educational efforts requiring sacrifices, such as leaving one's home country, financial instability, and years away from loved ones. The value of education was passed on to these first-generation immigrants from their families; likewise, as these parents attained college degrees in the U.S., they could similarly hand down their family's value of education and their own "college-going legacy" to their children.

College-going was not based solely on a desire for individual success, but was part of a larger plan to provide a better life for one's family. Parents explained that entering the U.S. through higher education was a means to achieve that goal. Despite facing challenges with relocation to the U.S., parents were resilient in ensuring they could pass on a college-going legacy. Ruth Obi, a mother from Nigeria, changed her career path after becoming pregnant while in college in the United States. As a single parent, Ruth could not handle the demands of her biochemistry major; she said she realized she could

> either neglect my studies or neglect my child. But I knew my education could provide the best life for my child, so instead of quitting school, I switched to a more flexible major. I gave up my dream of being a pharmacist.

Atieno Amolo's skills as a journalist in Kenya did not transfer to the U.S., but she gave up that career, which she loved, to pursue a master's degree in education in the U.S. because "My focus was that I wanted my kids to grow up here and have the opportunities that are in this country [U.S.]." Parents pursued a higher education in the U.S. for the benefit of their families/children. Thus, it was natural for parents to view this achievement as a resource or value they could provide to their children as a legacy. Adakole Enemari explained,

> Education is our [Enemari family] legacy. It is what my parents provided for me and it is what we as parents provide for the children. It is why we [Enemari family] are here [in the United States] and it is how we will succeed here.

Children grew up hearing their families communicate consistent messages that college is compulsory, and at least one reason they should attend was to contribute to their family's legacy. Children saw or heard stories of their parents' struggles to adjust to life in the U.S. and pursue a college degree. Priscilla Obi expressed that she respected her mother, "Because she was a full-time student and a full-time mom and she was still able to get us a house and all this stuff . . . and it gave me the motivation to try in school." Agaba Enemari explained that his mother sacrificed college so that his father could come to the U.S. for an education. Children described the value of seeing family and community members go to college, and it encouraged them to pursue the same goals. This legacy also connected children to their heritage and family history, because getting an education and going to college was something they could do that was representative of their cultural/familial self—even if they were unable to connect to their African heritage in other ways, such as speaking their parents' native languages or visiting the family's home country regularly.

Engagement in the Home and Community

The interactions children had with adults in their communities influenced their college aspirations. Some parents attended college while their children were young and so acted as college-going role models. Ruth Obi noted,

> She [daughter, Priscilla] was already born when I went through college . . . I think it gives her some sense for her to be proud of me . . . sometimes she would ask me questions to see how college looks like.

Priscilla affirmed,

> When she [mother, Ruth] was getting her master's she was very devoted to it and I saw how she was trying really hard even at the master's degree and it gave me the motivation to try even in middle school.

In addition to being academically motivated through watching family members attend college, children discussed the impact of seeing adult family members engaged in their local community. This included involvement in church and with ethnic organizations. Sarah and Hannah spoke about their mother's Akiba group, a Kenyan women's group that gets together for socializing, but also to engage in financial planning and group savings. Akiba provided opportunities for them to learn about Kenyan culture, such as how to cook Kenyan dishes and speak Swahili. Atieno even gathered Akiba for an intervention with Hannah when she received a report card with bad grades. Hannah explained,

> [They] talked to me about school and were giving me advice and asking me questions about my goals. At the end of the meeting they prayed for me and my well-being. It was overwhelming and I was annoyed the whole time. But . . . how can I complain that my parents care too much or that a whole group of my mom's friends care enough about me to spend a whole evening trying to get me to do the right thing? So I started to get my act together.

While the Amolo children discussed engagement with their U.S. ethnic community, families also described the importance of children engaging with the community "back home." For example, going to Kenya every year is important to Olaf because it gives him the opportunity to connect with his extended family and receive advice that is often focused on his future goals, academic performance, and responsibilities to the family: "The values that I get when I go back [to Kenya], the values that my grandpa and other people tell me help me and I keep them in mind for myself when I'm back in the U.S." While in Kenya three years before our interview, Olaf participated in his tribe's male circumcision ceremony, which "every boy goes through to become a man." He is now expected to set an example for his younger cousins academically and go to college because, "they [adult family members] tell me that when I'm older 'you're going to be the leader of the family.'"

Families discussed the importance of children developing a strong work ethic and having a responsibility to the home. Growing up in a large family taught Agaba about the importance of what he calls "shared responsibility." In the Enemari house, everyone has his or her own chores and responsibilities, and Agaba admitted, "Sometimes I get lazy with it and I just want to watch TV or something. But I know everybody else is working and I have to work too. It can't just be them working, we all have our part." When stepfather Kenneth Amolo began going to Kenya for three to nine months each year for a business opportunity, Atieno sought help from Sara in handling household responsibilities, such as picking up Imani from school. Sara also began working part-time to contribute to the household income because Kenneth's income in Kenya is less than he was making in the U.S., and so family finances are strained. Similar to Sara, Rem Mbai felt an expectation to "take care of my mom" because "since we don't have a man in the household, I had to step up and be the man for my family." Raz and Rem Mbai spoke about times when Rem put family needs before his own. For example, he canceled his plans with friends when Raz was sick to stay home and take care of her, and he got a part-time job to contribute to the money Raz sends to family back in Kenya. Rem explained that he sees the value of "family first" constantly modeled by his mother, who he said, "came here [U.S.] primarily to help her family and to help me." Children consistently saw family members make self-sacrifices to contribute to uplifting the family overall, and thus were strongly socialized to believe they had a responsibility to contribute to their family, whether financially (e.g., working part-time), physically (e.g., engaging in household chores), or academically (e.g., performing well in school and going to college).

Family and Community Networks

Although most families solely included parents and children as participants, they defined themselves beyond the nuclear family, emphasizing the extended family and community. They included individuals of varied educational attainment levels and those who lived in the U.S. and in families' home country. Participants emphasized the importance of family connection; as Gatwiri Magimbi explained, "I've had a lot of support from my family even when they're not here [in the U.S.]. And because we [she and Olaf] stay connected we're never that far away from them." Participants expressed the importance of family working together cohesively for the benefit of the whole. Raz Mbai described her family as a single unit, although many live in Kenya; and relatedly, Judy Nyom, a Cameroonian mother, defined her family as "communal." Moreover, families emphasized community as a cultural worldview. Kenneth Amolo explained that in Kenya, "you are part of the whole group, you are not an individual," and Simon Enemari expressed "In Nigeria, community is part of the system, the tradition, the way people do it."

Family and community networks provided a resource that participants could tap into for help with child-rearing. For example, families generally viewed child-rearing as a community effort, in which all were responsible for children's well-being. Olaf Magimbi explained, "In the African family when something happens with one person, the entire family will know about it. Whenever I do something bad, my whole family will know about it within minutes." Esther Obi, a Nigerian grandmother, suggested that every child in the Obi family is connected to every Obi adult because they "belong to everyone and are the responsibility of everyone [in the family]." While in Maryland, Gatwiri became connected to a Kenyan immigrant community that helped her with childcare and with adjusting to life as a student and single mother in the U.S.: "When I was going to graduate school and even undergraduate, fortunately enough I never needed to hire a babysitter because I had other Kenyans to pitch in. So that's basically how we made it, through people helping out." This responsibility among adults also included ensuring children were achieving academically and on a college pathway. For families, academic/college preparation was not solely experienced between parents and children, but instead reflected involvement from their larger social networks, who helped to normalize college-going in families; as Andi Nyom stated, "It was from all angles, my mom and different people around me telling me about college."

Even members of participants' communities who did not go to college participated in reinforcing the importance of education. Additionally, messages about college were not just transmitted to students from networks living in the U.S., but also from the home country. This involvement reinforced parental expectations and grounded children in college-going culture. Because some children described parental messages about college as "repetitive" or "redundant," these other individuals provided a fresh perspective. Olaf Magimbi explained,

> Like my mom tells me. . . "the opportunity you have to go to school, a lot of kids don't have that in Kenya." I hear that constantly and so sometimes I feel like, "I really don't care at this point." . . . But when we go back to Kenya and I see kids my age in the village or hear my grandpa's stories about his struggles, it's like, "okay, yeah I get it."

Children expressed respecting and trusting these messages they heard from grandparents, siblings, aunts, uncles, cousins, family friends, and other individuals in their familial network.

Discussion

One of the most common reasons for sub-Saharan African immigration to the U.S. is for a postsecondary education (Arthur, 2010; Ogbaa, 2003). Similarly, for most of the families in this study, a major motive for coming to the U.S. was for first-generation immigrants to obtain a college degree, and it was the expectation in all of the families that their children achieve this goal. Although they experienced challenges in navigating the U.S. education system, findings revealed across cases that families emphasized active home-based family involvement, high academic expectations and pressure, the use of cultural and familial obligation, and family/community networks to communicate academic expectations and as college-going strategies.

Funds of Knowledge within the African Immigrant Educational Context

Funds of knowledge is typically used to discuss the adaptive strategies of rural and/or working-class immigrant populations who do not have a family history of (U.S.) college education (Kiyama, 2010, 2011; Moll et al., 1992). Thus, this model may initially appear an unsuitable lens for describing the resources and strategies of the Africans in this study, who primarily reflect a college-educated population living in urban environments. However, I argue this concept is applicable within their context, but their funds of knowledge are different due to their immigration pathway. Obtaining a visa to come to the U.S. for college is one of the primary modes of entry for sub-Saharan Africans (Arthur, 2010; Ogbaa, 2003), and this was the entry mechanism for most first-generation immigrant participants in this study. For these families, going to college in the U.S. reflected a survival strategy/adaptive response. It was one of the only options for entering the U.S., remaining in the U.S., and providing future well-being and economic stability for the family. Learning how to gain access to and navigate college successfully was an integral component for accessing and adapting to life in the United States. Because of this, families' funds of knowledge were more directly related to education and college than might be found in other immigrant groups. Yet, participants' schools still did not recognize or tap into these funds as part of the educational experience.

While families described going to college as a family or cultural value, literature emphasizes additional benefits associated with this perspective. Having parents who are college educated puts students at an advantage in college access (Cabrera & La Nasa, 2000; Hossler, Braxton, & Coopersmith, 1989; Perna, 2000). In the majority of families in this study, at least one parent was college educated, which Massey, Mooney, Torres, and Charles (2007), Bennett and Lutz (2009), and Haynie (2002) identify as common and an advantage for achieving college access among Black immigrants. Some parents described acting as a role model for college because their child grew up seeing them attend. This gave families the opportunity to talk about college and to expose children to the process of pursuing a college degree, and often gave children the opportunity to be on a college campus at a young age—all of which can increase the likelihood of pursuing college (McDonough & Fann, 2007). Much of the college-choice literature would define these factors through the lens of social or cultural capital (Perna, 2000, 2006), which illustrates an important point to be made regarding funds of knowledge and forms of capital. While the participants may possess cultural capital, I argue that exploring their resources and strategies through a funds of knowledge lens provides a more culturally inclusive and relevant approach.

The college degrees that adult family members possessed are a valued credential in U.S. society (institutionalized capital) and can be used as a means of transmitting cultural capital to children. However, accounting for only this credential ignores the host of other unique resources, knowledge, and strategies families relied upon in the U.S. education context. A sole focus on cultural capital overlooks the presence and transmission of funds, such as college-going legacies. Parents' possession of a college degree creates exposure to opportunities for the family, while their stories of "back home" and narratives of struggle to achieve a college degree were cultural/familial/community-based practices of communication and parenting, which socialized children towards college in powerful ways. Because these families' African cultures and immigration histories were not acknowledged or were perceived negatively in school, their familial and cultural strategies for academic success also remained invisible in the school setting.

Families' Funds of Knowledge

Families conceptualized college-going as integral to their existence in the U.S., as it is integrated into their immigration history and goals for family success. Messages about college-going were socialized early in children's lives through family discussions, social networks, daily practices, major events (e.g., graduations), and role modeling. Children received consistent messages on the importance of academic success and going to college from within their family/community network. Furthermore, children saw some of these individuals engaging in academic practices such as studying, which they could learn from and emulate.

These practices can be described through funds of knowledge. For example, college-going legacies were a means of transmitting families' immigration histories, identity, and knowledge across generations (Moll et al., 1992). The legacies "containing ample cultural and cognitive resources" (Moll et al., 1992, p. 134) help families adapt to the U.S. education system. Legacies are deeply rooted within families, offering influential messages to children about the importance of going to college as representative of their familial and cultural self. Thus, legacies act as funds of knowledge because, through narratives and stories passed from adults to children about the family's value of college going, they develop and strengthen "historically accumulated and culturally developed bodies of knowledge and skills" (Moll et al., 1992, p. 133).

The experiences children heard and witnessed were not just exposure to family members' planning, sacrifices, and resilience, but were also resources they could draw upon. For example, families spent years strategizing how to enter or return to the U.S. to further their education and careers. For first-generation parents, intentionality in developing concrete plans for education, immigration, and a career was necessary in being able to pursue life in the U.S. Thus, children learned from their parents the importance of early planning for college beyond just the desire or aspiration to attend. Families knew they could not be successful in the college-going process as passive participants. This is critical to college choice, because enrollment requires not only aspirations, but also planning (Cabrera & La Nasa, 2000). These pre-existing strategies for success were used to foster academic motivation and college-going within families. They also helped build a sense of familial and cultural identity in the children that may have been lost or weakened through immigrating and adapting to life in U.S society.

Strong family and community ties are typical in many African societies (Ogbaa, 2003; Swigart, 2001), and this behavior was evident within the families in this study. Families were strengthened by their networks, which provided funds of knowledge they could utilize in the transition to life in the U.S. (Moll et al., 1992) and engagement in the U.S. education system. Families engaged in reciprocal relationships within these networks, helping one another gain access to resources and navigate the U.S. (Moll et al., 1992; Vélez-Ibáñez & Greenberg, 1992). Participants often defined their family structure as inclusive of extended family and community members. Parents had a major impact on developing a college-going culture within the family. Yet, participants also perceived siblings as well as extended family and community networks playing a major role in reinforcing a college-going culture, assisting in the academic experience, and serving as college-going role models. This reflects the movement in contemporary college access and choice research from a sole focus on parental involvement to an emphasis on "family involvement" (Knight et al., 2004; Tierney & Auerbach, 2005).

Conclusion

In using funds of knowledge, this study acknowledges the diverse ways in which sub-Saharan African families are involved in students' educational experiences and extends the application of the framework to a non-Latino immigrant population. Participants primarily reflect a college-educated demographic. Yet, the ways they developed, communicated, and enacted academic motivations and college preparation do not fit the traditional emphasis in higher education scholarship on parental involvement and measures of social/cultural capital based upon middle/

upper class, White American norms (Kiyama, 2010; Perna, 2006). Instead, their pre-existing knowledge base and strategies for success were situated in family, community, and ethnic cultures that went unacknowledged in school settings (Moll et al., 1992), but that families perceived as valuable and meaningful to their educational experiences. Thus, funds of knowledge provided a fit for unpacking their narratives, and I recommend scholars continue to apply the framework to other diverse communities, particularly those whose socioeconomic or class status may not fully reflect their level of power, voice, or visibility in U.S. society.

While funds of knowledge was useful, I encourage scholars to think innovatively about ways of understanding the pre-college and college experiences of sub-Saharan African immigrants and other under-researched populations in higher education. This study illustrated how participants used networks, resources, and cultural knowledge that are traditionally unexamined in college access and choice literature. Traditional college-choice frameworks, such as Hossler and Gallagher's (1987) combined model, have been criticized for not acknowledging how diverse groups navigate the process (Bergerson, 2010; Freeman, 2005; Hurtado, Inkelas, Briggs, & Rhee, 1997). I agree with this critique, as the narratives families provided were richer and more multifaceted than the three stages of the combined model suggest. For example, families described the college-choice process of a child as being situated within and impacted by the college-choice processes of parents, siblings, and other family members. They utilized family and community networks, both locally and across continents, to navigate college choice and conceptualized the process over a longer time-span that included the family's immigration history. College choice was not limited by spatial or temporal boundaries. Families described the process as more of a reflection of developing and sustaining family belief systems and culture around college-going and academic success than it was about specific milestones or stages. Using nontraditional frameworks or developing new ones can help to expand theory and scholarship beyond its current capacity, particularly regarding family involvement and the use of culture, family, and community as resources for academic achievement and college-going.

It is important that education practitioners tap into African families' pre-existing social networks and resources, such as community-based or religious organizations. These family and community networks have a wide-ranging level of involvement in students' lives that can help to open or close doors to college options and pathways. Thus, providing outreach and education to family and community members about colleges and the college-going process is critical to ensuring that the support these networks provide enhances students' access to college. One way to engage families' communities is by developing a community center within the school that a community organization can host for a few weeks during the school year in order to provide programming and resources within the school. Cultural organizations that work with African immigrants can be targeted for hosting this type of community center initiative to provide opportunities to educate schools about the cultures, histories, and contemporary issues related to the population. Schools, outreach programs, and university staff can also provide training programs for African community leaders, such as religious and community organization leaders, regarding the college preparation process so they can provide effective information to families who often turn to them for support. Although this may require time and resources in the short term, in the long term, K–12 schools and universities can work with families' pre-existing networks as partners in supporting African immigrants within the U.S. education pipeline.

To build relationships, practitioners should use culturally inclusive and responsive practices. The U.S. education system teaches little about sub-Saharan Africa, and what is shown in media often presents a limited, monolithic, and negative view (Awokoya, 2012). Professional development for teachers and staff are necessary to challenge African stereotypes in the curriculum/classroom and to work with African immigrant families in culturally responsive ways (Awokoya, 2012; Harushimana & Awokoya, 2011). These practices can provide an environment that makes families more comfortable in building partnerships with schools and in seeing the school as a resource. Teacher and counselor preparation programs should train practitioners in how to engage in action research and apply funds of knowledge to pedagogy, which can provide tools that can be used as they seek to better understand their students' families and networks, education and immigration histories, and home-based academic support strategies and resources.

Note

1 Funds of knowledge literature often use the term household instead of family (Moll et al., 1992). However, the participants in this study discussed fictive kin and fictive kin living outside the home/abroad as critical to the college-going process, and defined these individuals as family. Therefore, I use the term family, rather than household, to better reflect the participants' lived experiences.

References

Arthur, J. A. (2000). *Invisible sojourners: African immigrant diaspora in the United States.* Westport, CT: Praeger.

Arthur, J. A. (2008). *The African diaspora in the United States and Europe: The Ghanaian experience.* Burlington, VT: Ashgate Publishing Company.

Arthur, J. A. (2010). *African diaspora identities: Negotiating culture in transnational migration.* Plymouth: Lexington Books.

Awokoya, J. T. (2012). Identity constructions and negotiations among 1.5- & 2nd generation Nigerians: The impact of family, school, and peer contexts. *Harvard Educational Review, 82*(2), 255–281.

Baum, S., & Flores, S. M. (2011). Higher education and children in immigrant families. *The Future of Children, 21*(1), 171–193. doi:10.1353/foc.2011.0000

Beitin, B. K. (2007). Qualitative research in marriage and family therapy: Who is in the interview? *Contemporary Family Therapy, 30*(1), 48–58.

Bennett, P. R., & Lutz, A. (2009). How African American is the net Black advantage? Differences in college attendance among immigrant Blacks, native Blacks, and Whites. *Sociology of Education, 82*(1), 70–100. doi:10.1177/003804070908200104

Bergerson, A. A. (2010). *College choice and access to college: Moving policy, research and practice to the 21st century.* San Francisco, CA: Jossey-Bass.

Cabrera, A. F., & La Nasa, S. (Eds.). (2000). *Understanding the college choice of disadvantaged students* (New Directions for Institutional Research, 107). San Francisco, CA: Jossey-Bass.

Capps, R., McCabe, K., & Fix, M. (2011). *New streams: Black African migration to the United States.* Washington, DC: Migration Policy Institute. doi:10.1007/s10591-007-9054-y

Emerson, R., Fretz, R., & Shaw, L. (2001). Participant observation and fieldnotes. In P. Atkinson, A. Coffey, S. Delamont, J. Lofland, & L. Lofland (Eds.), *Handbook of ethnography* (pp. 352–368). Thousand Oaks, CA: Sage.

Freeman, K. (2005). *African Americans and college choice.* Albany: SUNY Press.

George Mwangi, C. A. (2014). Complicating Blackness: Black immigrants & racial positioning in U.S. higher education. *Journal of Critical Thought and Praxis, 3*(2), 1–27.

Griffin, K., del Pilar, W., McIntosh, K., & Griffin, A. (2012). "Oh, of course I'm going to go to college": Understanding how habitus shapes the college choice process of Black immigrant students. *Journal of Diversity in Higher Education, 5*(2), 96–111.

Harushimana, I., & Awokoya, J. (2011). African-born immigrants in U.S. schools: An intercultural perspective on schooling and diversity. *Journal of Praxis in Multicultural Education, 6*(1), 34–48. doi:10.9741/2161-2978.1052

Haynie, A. C. (2002). Not 'just Black' policy considerations: The influence of ethnicity on pathways to academic success amongst Black undergraduates at Harvard University. *Journal of Public and International Affairs, 13*, 40–62.

Hernandez, D. J. (2012). *Changing demography and circumstances for young Black children in African and Caribbean families.* Washington, DC: Migration Policy Institute.

Hossler, D., Braxton, J., & Coopersmith, G. (1989). Understanding student college choice. In F. K. Stage, D. F. Carter, D. Hossler, & E. P. St. John (Eds.), *Theoretical perspectives on college students* (pp. 5–42). Needham Heights, MA: Pearson Custom Publishing.

Hossler, D., & Gallagher, K. S. (1987). Studying student college choice: A three-phase model and the implications for policy makers. *College and University, 2*(3), 207–221.

Hurtado, S., Inkelas, K. K., Briggs, C., & Rhee, B. (1997). Differences in college access and choice among racial/ethnic groups: Identifying continuing barriers. *Research in Higher Education, 38*(1), 43–75.

Kasinitz, P., Mollenkopf, J., Waters, M., & Holdaway, J. (2008). *Inheriting the city: The children of immigrants come of age.* Cambridge, MA: Harvard University Press.

Kiyama, J. M. (2010). College aspirations and limitations: The role of educational ideologies and funds of knowledge in Mexican American families. *American Educational Research Journal, 47*(2), 330–356. doi:10.3102/0002831209357468

Kiyama, J. M. (2011). Family lessons and funds of knowledge: College-going paths in Mexican American families. *Journal of Latinos & Education, 10*(1), 23–42.

Knight, M., Norton, N., Bentley, C., & Dixon, I. (2004). The power of Black and Latina/o counterstories: Urban families and college-going processes. *Anthropology & Education Quarterly, 35*(1), 99–120. doi:10.1525/aeq.2004.35.1.99

La Rossa, R. (2005). Grounded theory methods and qualitative family research. *Journal of Marriage and Family, 67*(4), 837–857.

Massey, D. S., Mooney, M., Torres, K. C., & Charles, C. Z. (2007). Black immigrants and Black natives attending selective colleges and universities in the United States. *American Journal of Education, 113*(2), 243–271. doi:10.1086/510167

McDonough, P., & Fann, A. (2007). The study of inequality. In P. Gumport (Ed.), *Sociology of higher education: Contributions and their contexts* (pp. 53–93). Baltimore, MD: Johns Hopkins Press.

Merriam, S. B. (1988). *Case study research in education: A qualitative approach.* San Francisco, CA: Jossey-Bass.

Merriam, S. B. (2009). *Qualitative research: A guide to design and implementation.* San Francisco, CA: Jossey-Bass.

Miles, M. B., & Huberman, A. M. (2005). *Qualitative data analysis.* Thousand Oaks, CA: Sage Publications.

Moll, L. C., Amanti, C., Neff, D., & González, N. (1992). Funds of knowledge for teaching: Using a qualitative approach to connect homes and classrooms. *Theory Into Practice, 31*(2), 132–141.

Neuliep, J. W. (2012). *Intercultural communication: A contextual approach.* Thousand Oaks, CA: Sage.

Nyang, S. S. (2011). The African immigrant family in the United States of America: Challenges and opportunities. *Irinkerindo: A Journal of African Migration, 5,* 150–171.

Ogbaa, K. (2003). *The Nigerian Americans.* Westport, CT: Greenwood Press.

Perna, L. W. (2000). Differences in the decision to attend college among African Americans, Hispanics, and Whites. *The Journal of Higher Education, 72*(2), 117–141.

Perna, L. W. (2006). Studying college access & choice: A proposed conceptual model. In J. C. Smart (Ed.), *Higher education handbook of theory and research* (Vol. 21, pp. 99–157). Cambridge, MA: Springer.

Portes, A., & Fernandez-Kelly, P. (2008). No margin for error: Educational and occupational achievement among disadvantaged children of immigrants. *The ANNALS of the American Academy of Political & Social Science, 620*(1), 12–36. doi:10.1177/0002716208322577

Rios-Aguilar, C. (2010). Measuring funds of knowledge: Contributions to Latina/o students' academic and non-academic outcomes. *Teachers College Record, 112*(8), 2209–2257.

Rios-Aguilar, C., & Kiyama, J. M. (2012). Funds of knowledge: An approach to studying Latina(o) students' transition to college. *Journal of Latinos and Education, 11*(1), 2–16. doi:10.1080/15348431.2012.631430

Rowan-Kenyon, H., Bell, A. D., & Perna, L. W. (2008). Contextual influences on parental involvement in college going: Variations by socioeconomic class. *Journal of Higher Education, 79*(5), 564–586. doi:10.1353/jhe.0.0020

Simons, H. (2009). *Case study research in practice.* London: SAGE Publications.

Small, M. (2009). How many cases do I need? On science and the logic of case selection in field-based research. *Ethnography, 10*(1), 5–38. doi:10.1177/1466138108099586

Stake, R. E. (1995). *The art of case study research.* Thousand Oaks, CA: Sage.

Swigart, L. (2001). *Extended lives: The African immigrant experience in Philadelphia.* Philadelphia, PA: Historical Society of Pennsylvania.

Terrazas, A. (2009). *African immigrants in the United States.* Retrieved from www.migration information.org/USfocus/display.cfm?id=719

Thomas, K. J. (2010). Household context, generational status, and English proficiency among children of African immigrants in the U.S. *International Migration Review, 44*(1), 142–172. doi:10.1111/j.1747-7379.2009.00801.x

Tierney, W. G., & Auerbach, S. (2005). Toward developing an untapped resource: The role of families in college preparation. In W. Tierney, Z. Corwin, & J. Colyar (Eds.), *Preparing for college: Nine elements of effective outreach* (pp. 29–48). Albany, NY: SUNY Press.

Vélez-Ibáñez, C., & Greenberg, J. (1992). Formation and transformation of funds of knowledge among U.S.-Mexican households. *Anthropology & Education Quarterly, 23*(4), 313–335.

Yosso, T. J. (2005). Whose culture has capital? A critical race theory discussion of community cultural wealth. *Race, Ethnicity, and Education, 8*(1), 69–91. doi:10.1080/1361332052000341006

8

"HACERLE LA LUCHA"

Examining the Value of Hard Work as a Source of Funds of Knowledge of Undocumented, Mexican Ivy League Students

Gloria Itzel Montiel

The phrase "hacerle la lucha" is a Mexican idiom that has been translated to mean "take on the struggle" (see García, 2004). It is composed of the infinitive verb "hacer," meaning to do or to make, and "lucha," the Spanish for struggle or fight. The expression connotes strength and will-power, an attitude of persistence regardless of the difficulty or challenge. The focus of the expression, thus, is not the object or problem against which the person is struggling against, but the determination to overcome. In this sense, the expression closely aligns with the experience of undocumented students who aim at pursuing a postsecondary degree and those already in college. Although it has been estimated that 65,000 undocumented students graduate from high school each year (Passel, 2006), only 200,000 to 225,000 undocumented (including Deferred Action for Childhood Arrivals (DACA) beneficiaries) students are enrolled in college (Teranishi, Suarez-Orozco & Suarez-Orozco, 2015). This accounts for only 10 percent of all undocumented immigrants ages 16 to 24, compared to 30 percent of the general population of the same age (Teranishi, Suarez-Orozco & Suarez-Orozco, 2015). The majority of the undocumented population, therefore, does not enter the higher education system due to various reasons. However, much can be learned from the experience of those students who have persisted in their educational journey.

In 2012, President Obama announced the DACA program, which grants eligible applicants under the age of 30 a two-year deferment from deportation, a work permit, and a social security number. There are an estimated 1,932,000 million individuals eligible for DACA (Migration Policy Institute, 2016). Through the first quarter of 2016, 728,285 individuals have been granted their initial application for DACA (U.S. Citizenship & Immigration Services, 2016b), accounting for 37.7 percent of all eligible individuals. As a result of DACA, between 50,000 and 70,000 undocumented individuals gained legal employment (Pope, 2016). The National UnDACAmented Research Project also reports that among 1,402 young adults surveyed (ages 18 through 31), 61 percent obtained a new job, 38 percent obtained a new credit card, and 61 percent obtained a new driver's license (Gonzales & Terriquez, 2013), all of which signal the entry of this population into the formal United States society and economy.

But more than that, DACA has also positively impacted students' access to higher education. DACA facilitates students' eligibility for in-state tuition in some states, such as South Carolina, with laws prohibiting undocumented students from enrolling in public institutions of higher learning (Gonzales & Terriquez, 2013). Furthermore, higher earnings and better work conditions for DACA recipients also make higher education more viable for this population (Gonzales & Terriquez, 2013). Nonetheless, undocumented students continue to face barriers to higher education after the implementation of DACA. For instance, DACA excludes individuals who are over the age of 30 and those who entered after 2007 (U.S. Citizenship & Immigration, Services, 2016a), even if they meet all other requirements. And those who qualify are not guaranteed these benefits in perpetuity, as the program is not permanent and does not offer a path toward citizenship or permanent residency (Gonzales, Terriquez, & Ruszczyk, 2014). DACA is, therefore, not a complete solution to educational access for undocumented students.

Various stakeholders have responded to the failure of the federal government to address the educational needs of undocumented students. For example, since the first defeat of the DREAM Act in Congress in 2001, a rising number of states have introduced their own legislation allowing undocumented students to enter public colleges and universities and pay in-state tuition rates, and a very limited few have also granted access to state-based financial aid for this population (Rincon, 2010). Through July of 2015, 16 states had passed legislation to offer in-state tuition to undocumented students and four additional states had extended similar benefits through their state university system (National Conference of Legislatures, 2015). One of the most prominent examples is the State of California. Assembly Bill 540 (2001) makes provisions for all students who have graduated from a California high school access to in-state tuition rates, making the cost of a college education more accessible for undocumented students. Assembly Bills 130 (2011) and 131 (2011) also grant undocumented students access to institutional and state-based financial aid, respectively. The most selective private colleges and universities have also opened the doors to higher education for undocumented students for at least a decade, as evidenced by individual accounts of undocumented students in the media (see Hernandez, 2006; Mcardle, 2015).

However, while there has been a number of studies analyzing the effects of in-state tuition on education access of undocumented students (Protopsaltis,

2005; Frum, 2007; Gildersleeve, Ruman, & Mondragon, 2010) and other studies chronicling the experiences of undocumented students at public colleges and universities (e.g., Flores & Horn, 2009; Perez, Espinoza, & Ramos, 2009; Juaregui, Slate, & Brown, 2008; Teranishi, Suarez-Orozco & Suarez-Orozco, 2011), very little is known about the experience of undocumented students at private institutions. Without this empirical knowledge, it is not possible to know the extent to which these institutions serve as a refuge for students and the extent to which they can better structure opportunities for this population. Furthermore, the research that focuses on the experiences of undocumented students in higher education largely focuses on identifying challenges (e.g., Abrego, 2006; Abrego & Gonzales, 2010; Contreras, 2009) or factors that contribute to academic success (Flores & Horn, 2009; Perez et al., 2009) without analyzing the processes through which the latter help undocumented students to navigate through higher education. In so doing, there is a missed opportunity to learn from the strengths of these students who continue on their academic journey regardless of the structural barriers that exist.

Purpose and Research Questions

The purpose of this chapter is to increase our understanding of the college experience of undocumented students in the under-examined context of private colleges and universities. The chapter represents a narrative analysis (Riessman, 1993) of three undocumented Mexican students attending highly selective colleges, guided by the following questions:

1. How do undocumented Mexican students attending Ivy League colleges develop the concept of *hacerle la lucha*, or taking on the struggle (García, 2004), as a source of funds of knowledge (Moll, Amanti, Neff, & González, 1992)?
2. How does this concept influence actions and processes that allow undocumented students to persist in higher education?

In answering these questions, the chapter expands the literature on undocumented students by focusing on the success of undocumented students and analyzing their experience in the context of private colleges, which has remained unexplored in research. It also contributes to the application of funds of knowledge as a conceptual framework that can be used to examine student-strengths in higher education. In the following discussion, I present an overview of the literature on undocumented students. I then present the methodology of the narrative analysis and a discussion of the experiences of three undocumented students attending Ivy League schools. Lastly, I present recommendations for research, policy, and practice.

Undocumented Students in Higher Education

Factors That Limit College Access

Although undocumented students were not federally prohibited from attending institutions of higher education, the Illegal Immigration Reform and Immigrant Responsibility Act (1996) and the Personal Responsibility and Work Opportunity Reconciliation Act (1996) prohibit benefits, such as federal financial aid, from being conferred upon this population, while not directly specifying limitations upon the state to provide such benefits (Frum, 2007). This cost of higher education makes it prohibitive for these students to attend college (Perez, 2010). First, without legal work authorization, it is nearly impossible for undocumented individuals to be employed in jobs other than those that pay minimum wage and require manual or service-oriented labor (Gildersleeve, Rumann, & Mondragón, 2010). Secondly, a lack of understanding of the implications of an undocumented immigration status at various levels of students' pre-college contexts makes it difficult for undocumented students to navigate through the college application process (Gonzales, 2010; Guildersleeve & Ranero, 2010), even in schools of states with policies that make it possible for undocumented students to attend college.

The socialization of undocumented students as a result of their lack of immigration status has also presented hardships for these students in the pre-college and college context. Stigma and other socioemotional stressors associated with being undocumented has been documented as a prevalent barrier to seeking out assistance that may help to put a student on a college track (Abrego, 2011; Gonzales, 2010; Perez, Cortes, Ramos, & Coronado, 2010). At the college level, research has also identified significant barriers to a fully inclusive and welcoming college experience for undocumented students, beginning when students first arrive on campus (Abrego & Gonzales, 2010). At worst, some of these interactions result in outright discriminatory or racist remarks against students, heightening their sense of shame and feelings of not belonging (Huber, 2010). Because of these factors, early literature on higher education access for undocumented students has examined this population through an at-risk lens, that is, a deficit perspective that pays attention to the structural and environmental barriers that predispose students to disappear from the higher education track. Although it was important to identify the shortcomings of structural policies in providing access to higher education for undocumented students (e.g., Ruge & Iza, 2005), such a lens missed focusing on the strengths of students and on advancing creative solutions to the issue of higher education access for this population in the absence of federal policy.

Resilience and Success of Undocumented Students

In recent years, research focused on undocumented students has turned from identifying barriers to identifying the factors that help this population to be academically resilient and successful (see P.A. Perez, 2010; W. Perez, 2012). For the purposes of this discussion, academic success and resilience can be defined as entering and graduating—or being on track to graduate from college (Perez & Perez, 2014). In this definition, however, it should be noted that undocumented students must overcome the "daunting odds" (Perez & Perez, 2014, p. 286) of policies and practices that are not conducive to their persistence in higher education.

In the pre-college context, teachers and counselors have been instrumental in helping students become highly competitive for college (González et al., 2003; Gonzales, 2010). Personal protective factors also contribute to the persistence of undocumented students. For example, in a study of 110 undocumented students attending California high schools and colleges, Perez et al. (2009) found that academic inclination—including valuing school and participating in the Gifted and Talented Education Program—helped undocumented students to obtain higher grade point averages and school awards. In turn, these achievements helped students to be academically eligible to attend college. Tracking into Honors and Advanced Placement (AP) classes, for example, facilitates access to information about college and provides access to adults who they trust will be ready to help (Gonzales, 2010).

There are several factors that help undocumented students to persist once in college. Faculty and staff continue to be an important source of support for undocumented students (Muñoz, 2008). Peers are also one of the greatest sources of support for students, especially on campuses where there are dedicated groups that support undocumented students (Herrera & Chen, 2010). Research has also identified civic engagement and activism as a key contributor to student persistence in college (Perez, 2009; Perez et al., 2010). Civic engagement of undocumented students includes tutoring, volunteer work, and activism (Perez, 2012). This engagement contributes to the reinforcement of a strong political identity and sense of belonging of undocumented students, even though they are excluded from other mainstream political processes such as voting (Gonzales, 2008; Perez, 2012; Perez & Perez, 2014). Undocumented Latino students in college also draw on their parents and families to be sources of support and inspiration in their educational journey (Perez, 2009; Perez & Rodriguez, 2012; Enriquez, 2011). This is an important contrast to the belief that Latino families, especially Mexican families, do not value school (see Valencia & Black, 2002 for an overview of how this myth has been perpetuated in research). In persisting in college, undocumented students present counter stories to the stigmatizing labels of illegality (Muñoz & Maldonado, 2012). Students transform adversity into motivation and use their college identity as a means to resist against a system that excludes them from higher education (Tangalakis & Vallejo Pena, 2016).

Gaps in Literature

While a growing subset of research has focused on how personal and environmental factors help undocumented students to succeed, the focus of the research has been on identifying these resources rather than on examining the processes through which these affect the success of students. Furthermore, available research has predominantly focused on undocumented students in public colleges and universities. In part, the college choice of undocumented students is influenced by financial aid, cost, and socio-environmental factors, including information transmitted in their current networks (Perez, 2010). Given these considerations, community colleges have served as the primary receiving context of undocumented students (Valenzuela, Perez, Perez, Montiel, & Chaparrro, 2015).

However, although private colleges have expressed policies that accept undocumented students, there is virtually no research that examines the experience of this population in these institutions. Anguiano and Najera (2015) explore the theme of deservingness and privilege among seven undocumented Latinos at a single Ivy League institution. Montiel (2016), in a microstudy that was the foundation for this chapter, explores the ways in which funds of knowledge and social capital function in the college experience of undocumented students in three Ivy League institutions. These are the only two published studies that exclusively focus on undocumented students at private universities. However, as more private colleges and universities continue to adopt policies that facilitate the education of undocumented students, there is a significant need to understand the experiences of current and former students in this context in order to draw lessons to help shape institutional policies that continue to foster success for undocumented students. Furthermore, it is necessary to examine the experience of these students from a non-deficit lens to advance the narrative of resilience, resistance, and strength of this population which, despite all barriers, continues to navigate through the most selective institutions in American higher education.

Theoretical Framework

This analysis uses funds of knowledge (Moll, Amanti, Neff, & González, 1992) as a guiding conceptual framework. First, the framework is one that rejects deficit-based inquiry in issues related to underrepresented students by focusing on "historically accumulated and culturally developed bodies of knowledge and said skills essential for household or individual functioning and well-being" (Moll, Amanti, Neff, & González, 1992, p. 133). As such, this framework provides a lens through which it is possible to examine specific knowledge and skills that students possess and the ways in which these forms of knowledge have developed during students' lives. The framework allows for the examination of how students' interactions with their parents and on behalf of their households have provided them with knowledge that is applicable to their educational journey. In addition, and perhaps most importantly for this population given the educational barriers they must overcome, the framework, as expanded by Rios-Aguilar, Kiyama, Gravitt and Moll (2011), also emphasizes the conversion of funds of knowledge into other forms of capital. This discussion explores the ways in which *hacerle la lucha* acts as a form of funds of knowledge in the pre-college context of students' homes, and how such funds of knowledge are transformed into other forms of capital on campus to promote persistence.

Methodology

This is a narrative analysis of themes (Riessman, 1993) drawn from the stories of three individuals originally presented in a microstudy that explores, more generally, how undocumented students used funds of knowledge and social capital to navigate through their Ivy League education (Montiel, 2016). Narrative analysis is concerned with meaning making between stories of participants (Riessman, 1993). This approach allows for a more nuanced analysis of the individual experiences of students, yet without losing the ability to observe commonalities between stories. While the sample size is small, it is worth noting that the discussion is, nonetheless, valuable, in that it focuses on the specific processes by which students use funds of knowledge to be academically persistent. This analysis has been, by and large, missing from the aforementioned literature that focuses on making generalizations about factors that affect the success of undocumented students without examining how these factors interact with one another. The discussion also adds a layer of understanding of the contexts in which undocumented students prevail, which further adds to the empirical stories of educational resistance and resilience of this population.

Data Collection

The analysis draws on in-depth, semi-structured interviews from a microstudy with three 1.5 generation Mexican students attending Ivy League colleges in the spring of 2014 and graduating from their respective colleges between 2014 and 2016. Rumbaut and Portes (2001) define the 1.5 generation as individuals who immigrated to the United States as pre-adolescents or early adolescents but who have familiarity and experience with their country and culture of origin. The first participant was recruited through an e-mail to Harvard's undocumented student group. The two other students were referred by the first.

Interviews were conducted in March of 2014, two via telephone and one via Skype. Interviews lasted between 50 and 65 minutes. Students were provided an overview of the project and structure of the interview at the beginning of the phone call. The interview protocol was developed using concepts of funds of knowledge and social capital. It included a brief demographic questionnaire followed by questions about students' upbringing, their parental occupations, the lessons from home that they drew upon in college, their interactions with different individuals in college, and the benefits of these interactions in terms of information or resources gained.

Data Analysis

The present narrative analysis focuses—in greater detail—on the development and application of *hacerle la lucha* as funds of knowledge, a theme that emerged from the original qualitative study. Original interview data were re-read with exclusive attention to this theme. Each interview narrative was then manually coded for three different categories related to this theme: (1) emergence and development of the concept of *hacerle la lucha*, (2) the function of *hacerle la lucha* as funds of knowledge, and (3) transformation of these funds into other sources of capital, which is concerned with the processes that result in educational benefits for the students (Rios-Aguilar, Kiyama, Gravitt, & Moll, 2011). In so doing, this study purposely selects one single fund as the focus for in-depth analysis that tells the story from its emergence to its conversion.

Participants

Carlos, a Brown University student, arrived in the United States at the age of seven and grew up in a single-parent home after the arrest and deportation of his father. His primary extracurricular activity during high school was helping his mother to take care of his younger brother and to babysit other children. He entered college before the implementation of DACA.

Paula, a Dartmouth College student, also entered college before the implementation of DACA. She was tracked in the Gifted and Talented Education (GATE, also referred to as Honors in some schools) program since the first grade, one year after immigrating to the United States. Paula has two younger brothers, both of whom are U.S. citizens.

Cesar, a Harvard College student, entered college the year DACA was implemented, though he did not become a beneficiary until after his first year of college. He is an only child. His family immigrated to the United States when he was eight years old and has since lived in a house shared by his father's two siblings. Out of his extended family in the United States, only his family is undocumented.

Findings and Discussion

Hacerle la Lucha: *Emergence as a Source of Funds of Knowledge*

For the three participants in this study, the term *hacerle la lucha* or "taking on the struggle" (García, 2004) always carried a connotation of hard work, resourcefulness, and tireless determination to never give up, no matter how many doors closed for them.

To compensate for the loss of the second income, Carlos's mother babysat children living in their same apartment complex, washed dishes at a restaurant—where she was paid in cash, a little less than minimum wage—and also cleaned offices with her sister. In high school, Carlos took an active role in babysitting, especially at times when his mother's schedule at the restaurant did not allow her to get home right after school. There were also times when he accompanied his mom and his aunt to clean offices. On those occasions, the work would be divided equally among the three and he would be paid. He returned the earnings to his mom to help with food or would buy his own clothes and sometimes that of his little brother. He says, "My mom would always say that there was always a way. We just had to, you know, hacerle la lucha—be willing to put in the work."

Similarly, Paula had the official responsibility at home of cooking dinner for her family on a daily basis. She says:

> When my mom asked me to cook for the first time, I would like complain so much. I considered myself a feminist. Like, why did I have to do chores but not my little brothers when I was already at least washing my own plate when I was their age? And so—but then, one day my dad was like, "*no mi hija, todos hay que hacerle la lucha, en lo que te pongan, para salir adelante. Tienes que enseñarte a valer por ti misma.* [No, my daughter, we all have to take on the struggle, in whatever you have to do, to succeed (or get ahead). You have to stand on your own two feet.]" Basically telling me that I needed to be able to stand on my own two feet, and that included cooking and cleaning, I guess.

Carlos and Paula had specific responsibilities within their household. Through these roles, they learned to embody the definition of *hacerle la lucha* and developed skills such as cooking, cleaning, and working with children. Insofar as these skills were passed on to them by their parents and through these skills, and both students contributed to their family's survival and everyday well-being, these skills function as funds of knowledge (Moll, Amanti, Neff, & González, 1992). For both of their parents, *hacerle la lucha* meant an active effort to work hard, as a member of that particular family, and to find a way to succeed or be able to get ahead in their individual life.

Cesar, on the other hand, although not having a specific responsibility at home beyond regular maintenance of his own room and other sporadic chores, nonetheless learned the value of hard work as his parents advised him to continue in the struggle so as to do everything possible for him to achieve his dreams. He says:

> My parents were always, always working hard, extremely hard. I don't know how, but they always made it work for our family. And when I thought maybe I wouldn't go to college or felt I was working for nothing, they would always say "*le tienes que hechar ganas,*" or "*hazle la lucha, tu no sabes lo que va a pasar después. Que no quede en ti no haber logrado tus sueños* [you have to keep wanting it and working toward it. You have to remain in the

struggle. You don't know what will happen later. Don't let it be because of you that you don't make your dreams a reality]."

For Cesar, the concept of *hacerle la lucha* was a recurring theme that emerged from his parents' constant encouragement to not give up. While there was no certainty while he was in high school that he would be able to go to college, he was still encouraged—and to a certain degree expected—to do well as a way to be prepared should any type of immigration relief come in the future. In his experience, the concept of remaining in the struggle came to mean continuing to work hard as a personal responsibility to his own dreams and goals, despite the barriers that presented themselves in his academic journey.

For all three students, *hacerle la lucha* was a concept that they learned at home, through direct advice from their parents. But more than giving advice, each set of parents modeled *hacerle la lucha*, which for them meant working long hours, sometimes at multiple jobs, and making sacrifices for their respective families. This example impressed upon the students the concept that they, too, had to work hard, in all avenues of their life, in order to succeed. Specifically, their parents' example and expectations contributed to their taking the most rigorous courses available in high school and maintaining grade point averages above 4.0, all of which positioned them to become competitive candidates for Ivy League colleges. Acceptance to these colleges meant a scholarship covering full tuition and room and board for the students, which decreased—though not completely eliminated—the financial burden of attending college.

Function of Hacerle la Lucha *as Funds of Knowledge*

Carlos, Paula, and Cesar thus adopted the concept of *hacerle la lucha* and applied it to their unique struggle of pursuing higher education in the United States. In the pre-college context, *hacerle la lucha* functioned as motivation for students, as something that they learned from home and that their family—as a whole—practiced. All students identified their parents' examples of sacrificing their lives in Mexico, crossing the border, and working long hours in any job they could once they arrived to the United States as motivation that propelled them to do academically well. When asked to describe his parents' role in his education, Cesar said:

> I think they were my biggest cheerleaders. They motivated me so much. They weren't able to help me with Calculus homework or AP Chemistry, but they always supported me and didn't let me give up and whatever I needed for school, they got for me, even if it meant like, you know, maybe not buying something for themselves. They always told me that hope is the last thing that dies. But like, I knew that I wasn't allowed to just hope in a very—like—umm . . . like passively. I had to give it my all and if at the end I had failed, I had to try something else.

Similarly, Paula and Carlos both expressed that their parents taught them to work hard, not only to help out at home, but also in their scholastic pursuits. All three participants emphasized the ongoing moral support that their parents provided, a support which served as a primary source of motivation for them. These experiences align with the literature that dispels the negative stereotype that Latino parents do not value education (Chavkin & Gonzalez, 1995; Suarez-Orozco & Suarez-Orozco, 1995; Solorzano, 1997). In fact, the very premise of funds of knowledge lies on identifying the family and household practices that can contribute to the formal educational experiences of students (González et al., 1995; Moll, Amanti, Neff, & González, 1992).

Each of the students in this analysis learned the importance of school at home, and their parents were the most constant source of both encouragement and motivation for them, always portraying what *hacerle la lucha* meant. While parents transmitted to them the realities of the challenges that their immigration status may present, they simultaneously expected them to continue "in the struggle." This expectation was transmitted verbally, but also through their own example and modeling of hard work. This process has been found to positively impact the academic journey of students from immigrant households and can be used to reframe mainstream views of parental involvement (Lopez, 2001). These mainstream perceptions of parental involvement often require parental presence at schools or define it as direct involvement with school work (Scribner, Young, & Pedroza, 1999). However, this type of involvement may be out of reach to immigrant parents due to limited English proficiency as well as intimidating responses from teachers and staff at their child's school (Hyslop, 2000). For Cesar, Paula, and Carlos, their own parents' hard work had the effect of inspiring them in their journeys as students. And each of them translated their parents' example and transmission of *hacerle la lucha* as a demonstration of support of their academic pursuits.

The concept of *hacerle la lucha* functioned as an underlying approach to college for each of these students once they arrived on campus, especially as they contemplated various strategies to finance the incidentals that were not covered by their financial aid packages. Paula says:

> I didn't have a clue how I was going to come up with money for books and for toothpaste and deodorant and detergent, or whatever. I only knew I had to hustle and find a way because my parents couldn't help me anymore than they were already helping me. At the beginning there was no DACA, no way to work, but I always thought, well, my parents are working. They've been doing it all this time. I'll do whatever it takes.

For Paula, "whatever it takes" meant not purchasing course workbooks, resorting to borrowing them from the library for up to three hours at a time in order to complete her reading, often late at night when it was less likely that others would place a request for the workbook. The only textbooks she purchased were the textbooks that did not have a current version in the library, and she would sell them back to the bookstore as soon as the term was over. She notes, however, that one of the benefits of attending her college was that she always had the option of requesting the library to purchase the books that were currently not available.

Carlos considered his moving away to college "a leap of faith," not knowing if he would truly be able to pay all his personal expenses for college, or if he would be able to return home during breaks. Nonetheless, he was confident that he could "figure it out." Carlos was also concerned with leaving his mom without the help he provided during his high school year. On an ongoing basis, he strategized ways to save and earn money while being in school, having to decline invitations from his classmates to go on outings, flying home only once a year, and considering various work options, such as dishwashing at a local restaurant that may be able to pay him in cash or would not be stringent with requiring a valid social security number.

Carlos explains that jobs like dishwashing or doing yard work to earn money would have detracted from his overall campus involvement, but he also says,

> I remember telling myself, "I have to do what I have to do, if that means working all day half of the week or like having no time for clubs and stuff like that." I just knew I had to work as hard as I could so I could graduate in four years.

With obtaining a college degree as an end goal, the concept and value of working hard became Carlos's compass and a guiding filter that helped him to calculate the cost-benefit of various strategies that would allow him to achieve that goal. But, despite limited finances, Carlos and the other two students never doubted that they would finish college in four years—in contrast to many undocumented students in public colleges and universities who do not complete college, in large part because of the lack of any financial aid and lack of guidance in navigating through completion or transfer requirements (Perez, 2010; Terriquez, 2015).

Conversion of Funds into Capital

As their parents before them had made sacrifices and adopted a life of struggle to obtain a better life, Carlos, Paula, and Cesar, too, were firmly resolved to actively work hard and make sacrifices when necessary to ensure that they were able to overcome any financial challenge that could threaten their ability to finish college. They were especially conscious of seeking and pursuing opportunities that would allow them to use the skills they brought with them. When Paula and Carlos entered college, DACA had not yet been implemented, which made their ability to find work difficult.

Carlos enthusiastically responded to a job announcement sent by one of the residence hall staff in need of a tutor. Carlos says,

> I was so happy when I saw that. It took me all of ten minutes to write a short cover letter and send a response. I knew most of my peers here had never had to babysit the neighborhood kids, like I did to help my mom. Some of the kids I know even took a nanny with them on vacation, so I knew I should be able to get the job.

He did. Within a week of sending a response, Carlos was hired to pick up the tutor's son from elementary school, which was around the corner from the college. He would take him to lunch at the college's dining hall and help the child with homework. He was accustomed to such a routine and had the skills to work with children.

Paula was hired to help a new mother with cooking and cleaning in a house that was only a few blocks away from campus: "If my dad had let me off the hook when I complained about doing chores, I wouldn't be standing on my own two feet today. I wouldn't be able to have this amazing educational experience." Paula, like Carlos, incorporated the skills that she learned as part of her role in her family, which positioned her to be able to work once in college. Carlos and Paula were both paid in cash and were able to use that money to offset the incidental costs of college, including a limited social life with friends and the occasional outing.

Cesar entered college in the fall after the announcement of DACA, but he did not apply in his first year of college because he and his family were uncertain of the implications of the program for his safety in the future. Nonetheless, when he received an opportunity to volunteer at a community health center for an HIV program from a professor that worked with this organization, he saw it as an opportunity to "prove himself" by being punctual and by going above and beyond to fulfill his volunteer responsibilities, by helping other volunteers and staff members with tasks that were not directly within his scope of work. Cesar's ethic of hard work continued to be a primary focus for him. Just as it happened with college, he was convinced that in the future, there may be changes in legislation that would facilitate him going to medical school and practicing medicine; but even if there were no such opportunities, he would nonetheless put forth his best effort, because that is the ethic that drove him throughout growing up. That same year, the non-profit organization received a grant that was able to pay him a project-based stipend. When asked about what factors facilitated his being able to have this paid position, he alludes to the essence of *hacerle la lucha* by referencing hard work when saying,

> I had to just work my hardest first as a volunteer, showing that I was like genuinely passionate about what I was doing and do it better than everyone else, not like for competition, but to just prove myself. It was the only way.

In these three experiences, each student was able to convert the funds of knowledge embedded in the value of *hacerle la lucha* into the financial capital that allowed them to contribute to the cost of their education. For Carlos and Paula, this required a direct application of skills that they learned at home from their parents. For Cesar, this conversion was a result of adopting this value as an approach to his college experience, one that was guided by an unwavering determination to work hard, despite any obstacle. And through the conversion between funds of knowledge and financial capital, students created for themselves the roads through which their success was more likely (Rios-Aguilar, Kiyma, Gravitt, & Moll, 2011). Yet, these processes remain under-examined in the literature, even though it is in these conversions of capital that students can draw the most benefit (Rios-Aguilar, Kiyama, Gravitt, & Moll, 2011).

Conclusion and Implications

Paula, Carlos, and Cesar, three Mexican Ivy League students, developed the concept of *hacerle la lucha* (hard work; remaining in the struggle) as funds of knowledge at an early age, taking verbal cues from their parents' expectations and also from their parents' examples. These funds served as motivation for these students during high school, as they considered their options for higher education and learned about the financial barriers that may prevent them from attending. Once they were in college, these funds continued to provide motivation for these students and became an active strategy to find a way to navigate through their college experience. These three students also applied these funds of knowledge as a means to earn money and ameliorate their biggest concern around finances.

While the concept of *hacerle la lucha* may apply to undocumented students attending public institutions, the experiences of Paula, Carlos, and Cesar portray a glimpse of the lives of undocumented students in Ivy League colleges, experiences previously unexplored in the literature. Findings highlight that despite the barriers that the undocumented student population faces in accessing higher education, students also bring with them skills and resources that help them to succeed. This analysis also shows that family, and in particular the parents of these Mexican students, played an important role in the educational trajectory of each of these students, serving as motivation and as examples of "hard work" that Paula, Carlos, and Cesar sought to imitate in their pursuit of higher education.

The experiences of these students hold additional implications for research, policy, and practice. First, it is necessary to continue to examine the processes through which undocumented students develop resilience and become successful. Funds of knowledge, as a lens, can guide this examination through new methodology, including network analysis of families to learn how students and their families learn about jobs, college, and working among households to improve their well-being; and conducting a more extensive analysis of the types of funds of knowledge that exist among undocumented students, and the processes through which these help them become academically successful. Additionally, there is a need to continue to examine the experiences of undocumented students at private institutions. Although the majority of undocumented students attend public colleges and universities, a growing number of private institutions have openly committed to serving this population. Having an understanding of the experiences of current or even previous students at similar institutions can be greatly beneficial to implement admissions, financial aid, and student services policies and practices that are student-centered and truly meet the needs of this population. Additionally, although all three students interviewed eventually became DACA recipients, two of them entered school before DACA and the last student did not readily apply. These differing circumstances are but a microscopic depiction of the variability among students in regard to DACA or other types of temporary relief, pointing to the need for a more permanent immigration solution for the undocumented population as a whole. Lastly, because DACA is not a permanent solution to the immigration status of beneficiaries, there is much uncertainty about the future of beneficiaries in the coming year, at the change of the federal government administration. Ivy League students responded to the 2016 election results by organizing and petitioning their schools to become "sanctuaries" and to commit to protecting undocumented students (Svrluga & Anderson, 2016). This points to a growing number of undocumented students at these institutions who are willing to speak about their experience. It also presents a unique opportunity for these institutions and other private colleges to acknowledge the presence of undocumented students by acting on their behalf through providing safe campuses and proactively advocating for them. In so doing, they will contribute to expanding opportunities for this population and facilitating their academic and professional trajectories.

References

Abrego, L. J. (2006). "I can't go to college because I don't have papers": Incorporation patterns of Latino undocumented youth. *Latino Studies, 4*(3), 212–231.

Abrego, L. J. (2011). Legal consciousness of undocumented Latinos: Fear and stigma as barriers to claims-making for first and 1.5 generation immigrants. *Law & Society Review, 45*(2), 337–370.

Abrego, L. J., & Gonzales, R. G. (2010). Blocked paths, uncertain futures: The postsecondary education and labor market prospects of undocumented Latino youth. *Journal of Education for Students Placed at Risk, 15*(1/2), 144–157.

Anguiano, C. A., & Nájera, L. G. (2015). Paradox of performing exceptionalism: Complicating the deserving/underserving binary of undocumented youth attending elite institutions. *Association of Mexican American Educators Journal, 9*(2), 45–56.

Chavkin, N. F., & Gonzalez, D. L. (1995). *Forging partnerships between Mexican American parents and the schools.* Charleston, WV: ERIC Clearinghouse on Rural Education and Small Schools.

Contreras, F. (2009). Sin papeles y rompiendo barreras: Latino students and the challenges of persisting in college. *Harvard Educational Review, 79*(4), 610–632.

Enriquez, L. (2011). "Because we feel the pressure and we also feel the support": Examining the educational success of undocumented immigrant Latina/o students. *Harvard Educational Review, 81*(3), 476–500.

Flores, S. M., & Horn, C. L. (2009). College persistence among undocumented students at a selective public university: A quantitative case study analysis. *Journal of College Student Retention: Research, Theory & Practice, 11*(1), 57–76.

Frum, J. L. (2007). Postsecondary educational access for undocumented students: Opportunities and constraints. *American Academic, 3*(1), 81–108.

García, A. M. (2004). *Narratives of Mexican American women: Emergent identities of the second generation.* Walnut Creek, CA: Altamira Press.

Gildersleeve, R. E., & Ranero, J. J. (2010). Precollege contexts of undocumented students: Implications for student affairs professionals. *New Directions for Student Services, 2010*(131), 19–33.

Gildersleeve, R. E., Rumann, C., & Mondragón, R. (2010). Serving undocumented students: Current law and policy. *New Directions for Student Services, 131*(1), 5–18.

Gonzales, R. G. (2008). Left out but not shut down: Political activism and the undocumented student movement. *Nw. JL & Soc. Pol'y, 3,* 219.

Gonzales, R. G. (2010). On the wrong side of the tracks: Understanding the effects of school structure and social capital in the educational pursuits of undocumented immigrant students. *Peabody Journal of Education, 85*(4), 469–485.

Gonzales, R. G., & Terriquez, V. (2013). *How DACA is impacting the lives of those who are now DACAmented.* Los Angeles, CA: Center for the Study of Immigrant Integration and Immigration Policy Center.

Gonzales, R. G., Terriquez, V., & Ruszczyk, S. P. (2014). Becoming DACAmented assessing the short-term benefits of Deferred Action for Childhood Arrivals (DACA). *American Behavioral Scientist, 58*(14), 1852–1872.

González, N., Moll, L. C., Tenery, M. F., Rivera, A., Rendon, P., Gonzales, R., & Amanti, C. (1995). Funds of knowledge for teaching in Latino households. *Urban Education, 29*(4), 443–470.

González, M. S., Plata, O., García, E., Torres, M., & Urrieta Jr., L. (2003). Testimonios de inmigrantes: Students educating future teachers. *Journal of Latinos and Education, 2*(4), 233–243.

Hernandez, J. C. (2006, June 7). For student immigrants, a secret life. The double life of an undocumented immigrant at Harvard. *The Harvard Crimson.* Retrieved from www.thecrimson.com/article/2006/6/7/for-student-immigrants-a-secret-life/

Herrera, A., & Chen, A. (2010). Strategies to support undocumented students. *Transitions, 5*(2), 3–4, 10–11.

Huber, L. P. (2010). Using Latina/o critical race theory (LatCrit) and racist nativism to explore intersectionality in the educational experiences of undocumented Chicana college students. *The Journal of Educational Foundations, 24*(1/2), 77–96.

Hyslop, N. (2000). *Hispanic parental involvement in home literacy.* Bloomington, IN: ERIC Clearinghouse on Reading, English, and Communication.

Jauregui, J. A., Slate, J. R., & Brown, M. S. (2008). Texas community colleges and characteristics of a growing undocumented student population. *Journal of Hispanic Higher Education, 7*(4), 346–355.

Lopez, G. (2001). The value of hard work: Lessons on parent involvement from an (im)migrant household. *Harvard Educational Review, 71*(3), 416–437.

McArdle, E. (2015, August 24). What about the dreamers? *Harvard Ed. Magazine*. Retrieved from www.gse.harvard.edu/news/ed/15/08/what-about-dreamers

Migration Policy Institute (2016). *DACA-eligible populations and application rates by country of origin, 2016*. Retrieved from www.migrationpolicy.org/programs/data-hub/deferred-action-childhood-arrivals-daca-profiles

Moll, L. C., Amanti, C., Neff, D., & González, N. (1992). Funds of knowledge for teaching: Using a qualitative approach to connect homes and classrooms. *Theory Into Practice, 31*(2), 132–141.

Montiel, G. I. (2016). Navigating the Ivy league: Funds of knowledge and social capital of undocumented Ivy league students. *Harvard Journal of Hispanic Policy, 28*, 64.

Muñoz, S. M. (2008). *Understanding issues of college persistence for undocumented Mexican immigrant women from the new Latino Diaspora: A case study*. ProQuest.

Muñoz, S. M., & Maldonado, M. M. (2012). Counterstories of college persistence by undocumented Mexicana students: Navigating race, class, gender, and legal status. *International Journal of Qualitative Studies in Education, 25*(3), 293–315.

National Conference of Legislatures (2015). *Tuition benefits for immigrants*. Retrieved from www.ncsl.org/documents/immig/InStateTuition_july212015.pdf

Passel, J. S. (2006). The size and characteristics of the unauthorized migrant population in the US. *Pew Hispanic Center, 7*.

Perez, P. A. (2010). College choice process of Latino undocumented students: Implications for recruitment and retention. *Journal of College Admission, 206*, 21–25.

Pérez, P. A., & Rodríguez, J. L. (2012). Access and opportunity for Latina/o undocumented college students: Familial and institutional support factors. *Association of Mexican American Educators Journal, 5*(1), 14–21.

Perez, W. (2009). *We are Americans: Undocumented students pursuing the American dream*. Sterling, VA: Stylus Publishing.

Perez, W. (2012). *Americans by heart: Undocumented Latino students and the promise of higher education*. New York, NY: Teachers College Press.

Pérez, W., Cortés, R. D., Ramos, K., & Coronado, H. (2010). "Cursed and blessed": Examining the socioemotional and academic experiences of undocumented Latina and Latino college students. *New Directions for Student Services, 2010*(131), 35–51.

Perez, W., Espinoza, R., Ramos, K., Coronado, H. M., & Cortes, R. (2009). Academic resilience among undocumented Latino students. *Hispanic Journal of Behavioral Sciences, 31*(2), 149–181.

Perez, W., & Perez, I. G. (2014). Factors that impact the academic success and civic engagement of undocumented college students. In L. A. Lorentzen (Ed.), *Hidden lives and human rights in the United States: Understanding the controversies and tragedies of undocumented immigration* (pp. 283–292). Santa Barbara, CA: Praeger.

Pope, N. G. (2016). The effects of DACAmentation: The impact of Deferred Action for Childhood Arrivals on unauthorized immigrants. *Journal of Public Economics, 143*(2016), 98–114.

Protopsaltis, S. (2005, April 1–14). Undocumented immigrant students and access to higher education: An overview of federal and state policy. *The Bell Policy Center*.

Riessman, C. K. (1993). *Narrative analysis* (Vol. 30). Newbury Park, CA: Sage.

Rincon, A. (2010). !Si se puede!: Undocumented immigrants' struggle for education and their right to stay. *Journal of College Admission, 206*, 13–18.

Rios-Aguilar, C., Kiyama, J. M., Gravitt, M., & Moll, L. C. (2011). Funds of knowledge for the poor and forms of capital for the rich? A capital approach to examining funds of knowledge. *Theory and Research in Education, 9*(2), 163–184. doi:10.1177/1477878511409776

Ruge, T. R., & Iza, A. D. (2005). Higher education for undocumented students. The case for open admission and in-state tuition rates for students without lawful immigration status. *Immigr. & Nat'lity L. Rev.*, *26*, 383.

Rumbaut, R. G., & Portes, A. (2001). *Ethnicities: Children of immigrants in America*. Berkeley, CA: University of California Press.

Scribner, J. D., Young, M. D., & Pedroza, A. (1999). Building collaborative relationships with parents. In P. Reyes et al. (Ed.), *Lessons from high-performing Hispanic schools: Creating learning communities* (pp. 36–60). New York, NY: Teachers College Press.

Solórzano, D. G. (1997). Images and words that wound: Critical race theory, racial stereotyping, and teacher education. *Teacher Education Quarterly*, *24*(3), 5–19.

Suarez-Orozco, C., & Suárez-Orozco, M. M. (1995). *Transformations: Immigration, family life, and achievement motivation among Latino adolescents*. Stanford, CA: Stanford University Press.

Svrluga, S., & Anderson, N. (2016, November 15). Ivy league students, professors, alumni ask schools to be sanctuaries for undocumented students. *The Washington Post*. Retrieved from www.washingtonpost.com/news/grade-point/wp/2016/11/15/ivy-league-students-professors-alumni-ask-schools-to-be-sanctuaries-for-undocumented-immigrants/?utm_term=.065a97d667ff

Tangalakis, C., & Peña, E. V. (2016). Academic identity development of undocumented college students. *Journal of Student Affairs*, *25*, 53.

Teranishi, R. T., Suárez-Orozco, C., & Suárez-Orozco, M. (2011). Immigrants in community colleges. *The Future of Children*, *21*(1), 153–169.

Teranishi, R. T., Suárez-Orozco, C., & Suárez-Orozco, M. (2015). In the shadows of the ivory tower: Undocumented undergraduates and the liminal state of immigration reform. *The UndocuScholars Project: The Institute for Immigration, Globalization, & Education, University of California*, Los Angeles.

Terriquez, V. (2015). Dreams delayed: Barriers to degree completion among undocumented community college students. *Journal of Ethnic and Migration Studies*, *41*(8), 1302–1323.

U.S. Citizenship & Immigration Services. (2016a). *Consideration of Deferred Action for Childhood Arrivals (DACA)*. Retrieved from USCIS website www.uscis.gov/childhoodarrivals

U.S. Citizenship & Immigration Services. (2016b). *Deferred Action for Childhood Arrivals process (Through Fiscal Year 2016, 2nd Quarter)*. Retrieved from USCIS website www.uscis.gov/sites/default/files/USCIS/Resources/Reports%20and%20Studies/Immigration%20Forms%20Data/All%20Form%20Types/DACA/I821d_performancedata_fy2016_qtr2.pdf

Valencia, R. R., & Black, M. S. (2002). "Mexican Americans don't value education!"—On the basis of myth, mythmaking, and debunking. *Journal of Latinos and Education*, *1*(2), 81–103.

Valenzuela, J. I., Perez, W., Perez, I., Montiel, G. I., & Chaparro, G. (2015). Undocumented students at the community college: Creating institutional capacity. *New Directions for Community Colleges*, *2015*(172), 87–96.

PART 3

Funds of Knowledge as a Pedagogical Tool for Student Success in Higher Education

9

ALIGNING PRACTICE WITH PEDAGOGY

Funds of Knowledge for Community College Teaching

Juana Mora and Cecilia Rios-Aguilar

Unlike my K–12 counterparts, I, Dr. Mora, have never been required to take a class that teaches me how to teach. Instead, I earned my Master of Arts degree, secured adjunct teaching positions at two- and four-year institutions, and after almost eight years of "freeway flying," I interviewed and was offered a tenure-track position at a community college not far from the working-class residential neighborhood where I was raised. Admittedly, I am simplifying the process, but my point is to emphasize that not at any moment before, during, or leading up to securing a full-time and tenure-track position was I required to learn how to teach. Even as I worked toward tenure, there was no expectation to improve my teaching. I was naively vested in the assumption that I was a good professor because I cared about my students. I also unwisely believed that my students were solely responsible for their academic success.

I do not recall the exact moments when I internalized the notions of what it meant to be a "good" college professor, but I do very clearly remember walking in to teach my first college class. I imitated what had been my experience: I handed out the syllabus (a syllabus that I had adopted from a friend who was teaching a similar course), reviewed what was in it, took attendance, and dismissed the class. At the following class session, I began doing what I understood to be the role of the professor—to lecture. In preparation for every class session, I would spend countless hours mulling over how to fill every minute of class time. I was religious about my preparation time, and as long as I kept adding new content to my course lectures, I felt that I was doing my part to be relevant and effective. I even considered my teaching to be student-centered. After all, I felt that I was vested in my students' academic success, and I felt that I connected with them. I, too, had been a community college student, and I was a Latina with immigrant parents. I assumed that was enough to connect and convince my students that I cared about their academic achievement, so I was often disheartened when so many students failed to complete the class or just straight failed the course. I found some reassurance and solace in knowing that I was not the only one. My colleagues and I commiserated about low student achievement and unwittingly relied on deficit explanations to understand our low success rates. For example, we cited lack of student motivation, poor academic preparation, and lack of family support, but we genuinely wanted our students to do better; and because we wanted our students to succeed, we could not recognize how attached we had become to using deficit thinking to engage with our students.

After several years of community college teaching and defaulting into deficit frameworks, I was finally able to clearly see the connection between pedagogy, practice, and student academic achievement. I had enrolled in a graduate class, taught by Dr. Rios-Aguilar, titled "Funds of Knowledge," and while in the beginning of the course I doubted its relevance, by the end I was committed to adapting funds of knowledge to community college teaching. In the following pages, I provide context on how I, as a community college faculty member, came to understand that student success and achievement is a collective undertaking, and how a funds of knowledge approach could help me to: (1) design and conduct scholarship that builds on students' funds of knowledge, and (2) connect students' funds of knowledge to my teaching practices to become a more effective instructor. I share the process of how and why I re-contextualized the seminal study by Moll, Amanti, Neff, and González (1992) to a community college setting, and I highlight some of the key findings of my dissertation study. I unreservedly recognize the limitations of my own study, but I am hopeful about the potential of using funds of knowledge to innovate and shift the way community college faculty understand their roles and responsibilities and alter their teaching practices as we *educators* engage with our students.

Funds of Knowledge and Community College Teaching

Applying funds of knowledge to community college teaching requires understanding the multiple obligations of community colleges that, while seemingly congruent, often contradict each other in practice (Brint & Karabel, 1989; Cohen & Brawer, 2003; Beach, 2011; Desai, 2012). Within each community college, there are policies and processes that administer academic and transfer curriculum, vocational and occupational training, remediation and developmental support, and community service (Beach, 2011; Desai, 2012). According to Desai (2012), the comprehensive nature of community colleges "results in a dilution of focus and concentration on the foundations of community colleges providing students access to four-year institutions through transfers" (p. 120). Transferring to four-year colleges and universities is imperative for students seeking to increase their socio-economic status through higher educational attainment (Chapa & Schnink, 2006). While Desai (2012) rightfully critiques the "dilution of focus," community colleges remain the most democratizing element in a hierarchically stratified American higher education system (Alfonso, 2006; Cox, 2009).

Bearing this in mind, community colleges are uniquely situated to provide access to postsecondary education for students identified as nontraditional.[1] For the great majority of these students, which in states like California tend to be Latino (Campaign for College Opportunity, 2013), community colleges are the only route toward a baccalaureate. Yet the low rates of academic achievement among nontraditional students in community colleges diminish the chances at degree attainment (Alfonso, 2006; Chapa & Schnink, 2006). This is particularly disconcerting at a time when the U.S. job market requires a more educated workforce, and the population that is projected to continue growing is Latino (Chapa & Schnink, 2006; Excelencia in Education, 2015).

Degree attainment from four-year colleges and universities has long been accepted as the path toward social and economic mobility for nontraditional students (Darder, Torres, & Gutíerrez, 1997; Gándara & Contreras, 2009). Yet it is well documented that few manage to successfully transfer from a two-year college into a four-year institution (Rosenbaum, Deil-Amen & Person, 2006; Dowd, 2007; Beach, 2011; Nuñez & Elizondo, 2013). The Campaign for College Opportunity (2013) found that only four out of ten degree-seeking students completed an associate degree, certificate, or transferred to a four-year institution after six years. Chapa and Schnink (2006) attribute the degree of underrepresentation in academic attainment to "massive leaks in the [educational] pipeline" (p. 49) and urge community colleges and their four-year counterparts to focus on increasing Latino transfer and baccalaureate attainment.[2]

As a response to the low rates of transfer and degree completion among nontraditional students, national and state initiatives are improving policy and practice in postsecondary education to increase college completion (Excelencia in Education, 2015). For example, in 2012, the California legislature passed the Student Success Act (SB1456), which is a reform initiative aimed at increasing educational outcomes for students in California community colleges, and that same year the California Community College Chancellor's Office (CCCCO) began releasing scorecards for each California community college to increase transparency and accountability on student progress.[3]

If the community college system, the open-access and low-cost tier of American higher education, is the path to social mobility for nontraditional students, then it is imperative to understand what causes the "leaks in the pipeline." Although it is beyond the scope of this chapter to address all the complexities and contradictions endemic throughout the community college system that lead to gaps in the process, it is feasible to focus on one under-examined area—the pedagogical approaches and practices of community college faculty.

Community college professors may unwittingly alter their pedagogical approaches and practices to align with their perceptions of nontraditional students. Cox (2009) explains that faculty members make assumptions about what students should know and how they should perform. This enhances the tendency for faculty to develop curriculum and adopt pedagogical approaches that reinforce a dominant narrative that attributes the achievement and outcome of nontraditional community college students to cultural deficiency (Yosso, 2005; Ochoa, 2013). This presupposes that "educational outcomes cannot be changed unless families and cultures are altered" (Ochoa, 2013, p. 37).

In resistance to deficiency frameworks, the intent of my study was to redirect attention to the community college classroom and, more specifically, to the community college professor. The underlying rationale stemmed from the assumption that students' classroom experiences can be significantly enhanced when faculty learn about the everyday lived contexts of their students' lives and find ways to connect their students' realities with pedagogical practices (Bensimon, 2007; Umbach & Wawrzynski, 2005; Barnett, 2010). In this context, pedagogy extends beyond what faculty do in the classroom, becoming a practice that prioritizes how individuals experience life, how they learn, and how knowledge is produced (González et al., 2005). A funds of knowledge approach can potentially mediate between students' lived realities and the dominant constructs of a college classroom. Concisely, funds of knowledge, understood as the strategic and cultural resources that households contain (Vélez-Ibáñez & Greenberg, 1992), can be harnessed to transform the community college students' classroom experience.

The Study

Since the academic success of community college students is predicated upon their academic performance in the classroom, it is reasonable to direct attention toward the approaches and practices of community college faculty to understand the choices they make with respect to how they teach content. Not dismissing other elements that contribute to community college student success and achievement, this study simply maintains that the pedagogical approaches and practices of community college professors deserve closer examination. Too often, determinants of higher student achievement focus solely on students' academic preparation (Barnett, 2010; Pascarella & Terenzini, 2005; Hurtado & Carter, 1997), and this insular view impedes effective institutional change. Consequently, institutional efforts are directed toward "changing" students and inculcating in them the appropriate behaviors and requisite skills for student achievement (Bailey & Alfonso, 2005). The community college classroom, by contrast, remains consistently under-examined.

The research design in this study re-conceptualizes an approach used by Moll, Amanti, Neff, and González (1992). Moll et al. (1992), with the intent to develop innovations in teaching that integrated students' funds of knowledge into classroom instruction, designed a qualitative research project with three interrelated activities: ethnographic analysis of household dynamics, examination of classroom practices, and after-school study groups with teachers. They argued that by understanding the sociopolitical and economic contexts of households, the teachers would be better positioned to identify the funds of knowledge that children bring to school (Moll et al., 1992). The teacher, using qualitative methods to study household knowledge, can then access this knowledge to develop participatory pedagogy and establish more symmetrical relationships with the parents of the students. This relationship, as Moll et al. (1992) note, "can become the basis for the exchange of knowledge about family or school matters, reducing the insularity of classroom, and contributing to the academic content and lessons" (p. 139).

In conceptualizing the current study, I redesigned elements of the original study as certain activities were not practical. For instance, the faculty participants immediately rejected the suggestion of household visits. They considered household visits to be intrusive of student privacy and too demanding of faculty time. In lieu of household visits, the faculty made suggestions on how to learn about their students' funds of knowledge. The faculty study groups, the hour-long sessions of dialogue on selected readings about funds of knowledge, proved to be instrumental in furthering the dialogue about the feasibility of a funds of knowledge pedagogy for community college teaching (Mora, 2016).

Data Collection and the Faculty

The faculty that volunteered for this study were recruited from Peaks College (a pseudonym).[4] There were eight faculty participants, and all were members of the Social Sciences Department. Each participant agreed to two classroom observations, two structured interviews, and four one-hour-long faculty study groups that were conducted during the academic year of 2015–2016. (Mora, 2016). This research design allowed for an exploratory process about funds of knowledge for community college teaching, and allowed for a more complete understanding of how community college faculty develop their pedagogical approaches and practices. The following section highlights the key findings of the study.

Findings and Discussion

Community college professors have a pedagogical approach to teaching, but they cannot describe it and they rarely talk about it. Why? It has simply not been necessary for community college faculty to attach a name to their teaching practices. Nonetheless, faculty's pedagogical approaches and practices in the classroom are incontrovertibly informed by a "philosophical" belief about how best to teach. The three are interconnected: pedagogy, practice, and philosophy. It became evident that faculty wanted to have these discussions and to expand their conceptions of what it means to be a community college professor.

The questions asked of each faculty member during the second interview were to explain what they do in the classroom and why. Their responses varied slightly, but the answers to why were uniform. Simply put, faculty teach how they teach because that is what they know; it is the way they learned:

> No one trains you on this stuff. . . . So, you go in front of the classroom and you lecture. It is very traditional. You are up on the podium, and you are giving them a bunch of information. And you send them off.
>
> *(Irene, Adjunct Faculty Member)*

The college classroom experiences for the faculty participants were traditional and lecture-based. It was a disconnected and sterile relationship between professor and student. This type of teaching environment relied on strict and traditional notions and expectations of a "good college student." However, community college professors, given the dynamics and complexities of the community college system—too many to address within the space of this research—were obligated to re-think the traditional approach.

Valeria, a tenured faculty member, candidly admits that her teaching "shifts," or as she explains, "it starts out one way and then it changes." She changes her approaches and practices when she does not feel that students are engaged and when they do not respond to the questions she poses.

> I tend to lecture, but I don't want to. . . . I use group work, I really think they need to be in small groups talking to each other. It works sometimes, but again it doesn't work when three-fourths of the people in the group haven't done the reading.

Despite her efforts to be flexible and accommodate her students' needs on any given day, there was a notable tone of frustration in Valeria's speech when it came to instances when student participation, which she believed was vital to their success, was low. She attributed such moments to lack of student preparedness. Not all instructors were as willing as Valeria to make changes, but those who were noted that there was no proper support or training on how to be more effective in the classroom. Instead, as faculty mentioned, students are encouraged to participate in workshops that teach them to become better students.

Deficit Model Approach to Teaching

A deficiency framework places the blame on students and their families (Solorzano & Yosso, 2001; Ochoa, 2013). According to this rationale, it was not pedagogical methods but the students who had failed by lacking preparation, motivation, ability, readiness, or seriousness in regards to their education. Thus, using this framework, it is reasonable to direct resources to changing student behavior and practices rather than asking faculty to reconsider their classroom practices.

The classroom observations in this study did not suggest that professors had taken the time to consider the complexities of content delivery and student achievement. Instead, the relationship between instructor and student appeared to be static, and this relationship relied on deficit explanations for student behavior. These contradictions are difficult to reconcile. Despite faculty participants' seeking to further their students' learning, they have nonetheless been inculcated by the values of higher education, which historically excludes and denigrates nontraditional students. Within this system, it is acceptable and normal to operate from a deficiency framework. Thus, conversations about students' academic achievement and outcomes are shaped by a paradigm that judges students as either having or lacking the "right" skills and attitudes.

> The first day of class, I don't know what they expect, but I tell them what the class is going to be like. I point out some things. I always write the number eight on the board because percentage-wise, only 8% of you are going to graduate with a bachelor's degree. You are going to have crappy teachers and some great teachers. This might be a good class or a horrible class. It doesn't matter. You have to get through us all. And then I tell them that intelligence has nothing to do with you graduating or not. It's all about the hard work.
>
> *(Horacio, Tenured Faculty Member)*

From the faculty perspective, underperforming students are deficient in the skills, attitudes, and behaviors requisite for higher educational attainment. Thus, faculty instructors incorporate lessons on the characteristics of a successful college student into their courses. The most notable lesson, as supported in this study, focused on efficient and effective note taking. It is not the lesson itself that is problematic, but the assumption that once students learn to be "good college students," they will fare well. This deficit framework fails to recognize the previous educational experiences and contexts of students' lives. Moreover, it refuses to consider that such teaching practices may be antithetical to student success and achievement.

The lack of alternative pedagogical approaches further exacerbates the issue. Instead, deficit model approaches were unconsciously reinforced. Most recently, Peaks College sponsored a professional development workshop, advertised as a chance for faculty to learn how to promote reasoning, creativity, insightfulness, and perseverance in students. The underlying assumption is that "unsuccessful" students lack these characteristics. Table 9.1 provides a synthesis of some of the more common remarks made by faculty during the faculty study group sessions that reflect these underlying assumptions.

Although faculty freely acknowledged that students face numerous barriers, this did not translate into considering alternative teaching practices. Rather,

TABLE 9.1 Examples of Deficit Discourse

Deficit Discourse	Underlying Assumptions
It is not fair to other students . . .	The students are just making excuses for not completing the work, so they should not be granted preferential treatment. All students should be treated the same.
The students don't come from families with college degrees . . .	Students just do not know or understand the value of higher education.
It doesn't matter where you come from . . .	If students work hard enough, then there should be no excuses for them not to succeed.
If I could do it, then so can they . . .	Every student has the ability to make the right choices. Look at me. I did not have it easy, and I did it.
These students just don't care . . .	Students are just lazy.
Some students don't even try . . .	Students are just lazy.
We didn't do this when we were in college . . .	I did my work when I was in college.

the reality of students' difficulties led faculty to challenge a funds of knowledge approach to community college teaching. They understood funds of knowledge as simply a pedagogical strategy that emphasizes learning about students' lives, rather than a chance to gain knowledge about how students' experiences, skills, and knowledge can potentially increase their learning and improve student achievement and outcomes.

While the faculty participants understood the concept of funds of knowledge, they expressed hesitation towards it as a viable pedagogical approach. As they read and later discussed the selected articles on funds of knowledge during the faculty study groups, they did not see a connection between the funds of knowledge approach and community college teaching. Faculty participants challenged the viability of funds of knowledge in the community college classroom given its concentration predominantly in the K–12 system. However, as the study group discussions evolved, it was evident that they already used funds of knowledge to a limited extent.

The faculty talked about using different strategies to keep students engaged, and one of those techniques was the use of storytelling. One faculty member shared stories about his sibling, and another recounted his dating experience. They shared their personal stories as a way to connect and interact with their students, but it was one-directional. There were two faculty members in particular who asked students to include personal experiences in their responses to essay prompts. Another faculty member said that she uses "quick-writes" in her class to keep students focused. She explains that she does not want students to just sit and not be invested in the class: "Your body just being there is not enough. You have to be engaged. Be a part of it, somehow" (Valeria).

Prior to this study, some faculty had already adopted activities in their classroom with the intent of becoming better acquainted with their students. One participant implemented a survey, while another reported asking students to write something unique about themselves on notecards that he hands out on the first day of class.

> One of the things we do in the learning community . . . we give the class a survey. We ask them questions about how many units they are taking, how did they place into English 101, which is a very telling item . . . we ask them if they are working. So we ask them that. And another very telling question, has anyone is your family ever gone to college? Who is it? Where did they go? And then what is your GPA? So, what I do, it is primarily done to inform us about the students.
>
> *(Maribel, Tenured Faculty Member)*

During class, as noted in the classroom observations, the faculty shared personal stories about their lives and experiences. They also used humor to connect with the class and to break the monotony of lecture. They are conscious of the need to connect with students, but they do not have the tools or support to break from the deficiency framework.

Instead, they remained frustrated about the lack of student engagement in class. To address this challenge, some faculty said that they used small-group discussions, but with a limited success. They noted that many students still hesitated to participate and largely remained quiet. Faculty interpreted minimal participation as lack of student preparation or student interest. An additional explanation offered by most faculty participants was that students failed to read assigned material ahead of time. In only one instance did a faculty member question the students as to why they were not participating. She did so by asking if they had done the reading; after a brief moment of silence with no responses, she continued with the lecture. In other words, the faculty did not know with certainty why students are not more engaged and active.

Funds of Knowledge Approach to Community College Teaching

Despite the faculty's reticence to visit students' homes to collect funds of knowledge, the faculty participants offered alternatives. They suggested that students collect their own funds of knowledge, but they did not specify how this might be concretely achieved. They considered using Facebook to learn more about students' lives, but wondered whether Facebook presents an inaccurate portrayal of people. Another suggestion was to solicit assistance from the college's institutional research department and request that they present demographic data about students, including self-reported family income, educational background, and racial or ethnic identity. Maribel, one of the tenured faculty participants, noted that the college had a fantastic research department who might be willing to develop a survey instrument and run the data.

Interestingly, faculty participants were interpreting funds of knowledge as an approach that advocates preferential treatment of students based on the severity of the personal challenges the students face. Faculty objected to the idea of extending special treatment to students because they perceived it as a disservice to students who they believe must learn to successfully adapt and navigate the system of higher education. In an exchange between Maribel and Horacio, Maribel considered the value of using a funds of knowledge approach to teaching. She recognized that the community college was a unique institution.

> I think that perhaps [funds of knowledge approach] might be a useful tool because it is a unique institution. The community college is a unique institution . . . we are teaching a whole set of skills and we don't know what experiences they have . . . it might seem like something that we would do in a K–12 setting, but that is our population. I often struggle with the notion that just to say they are college students and they have to act like such.

Once they understood more clearly the intent of using a funds of knowledge approach to teaching, they became more open to the idea of learning a new pedagogical practice.

From Practice to Pedagogy

A funds of knowledge approach to community college teaching should start by creating a space for faculty to dialogue and reflect on their teaching practices. The faculty participants in this study could not name or sufficiently explain their pedagogical approach, which indicates that they may not know or attach value to specific philosophies of teaching. However, faculty participants were capable of discussing their teaching practices, even if those practices did not align with any identified pedagogy. Thus, funds of knowledge for community college teaching needs to start with the faculty learning about themselves—the study groups are the central component of this process.

In addition, the faculty, on select occasions, should invite other faculty to observe their classroom practices with the intent of documenting what happens in the classroom. The faculty being observed can review and discuss their impressions with their colleagues. Another method to promote self-reflection is to ask faculty to journal about their experiences in their classrooms and to write about their processes, assignments, setbacks, and other classroom dynamics. Faculty should even be encouraged to journal about their observations of students and to write about what they perceive to know about the students they teach. The purpose is to encourage faculty to assess their classroom practices and determine whether those approaches are conducive to student success and achievement. If the faculty finds that a deficiency framework informs their approach to students, they may be more easily persuaded to actively work toward a new pedagogical approach that "far exceeds in quality the rote-like instruction that [students] commonly encounter in schools" (Moll et al., 1992, p. 132).

Implications for Policy and Practice

Community colleges are at the center of the most recent accountability movement in higher education (Alexander, 2000). While it is easy to become disheartened, given the ebb and wane of past accountability measures in higher education, the most recent higher education initiative in California is using language that denotes a commitment to institutional and structural change (CCCCO, 2017). The use of the terms equity and justice, and the insistence on action research, all indicate a shift in paradigm.

The Student Success Act of 2012 established funding for the Student Success and Support Program (SSSP) (CCCCO, 2017). The intent of SSSP was to assess and develop processes and programs that ensure student academic success. Community colleges were obligated to examine their admission policies, orientation processes, assessment and testing, and counseling services, and restructure components that thwarted student academic achievement. To this end, community colleges were also required to develop student equity plans. A condition of receiving SSSP funding was that community college districts maintain a student equity plan and submit them to the CCCCO. These plans urged colleges to identify their high-need student populations as well as develop specific goals and outline activities that would mitigate the disproportionate impact on these students. In addition to SSSP funding, community colleges were provided funds to implement the activities listed in the student equity plans (CCCCO, 2017).

One factor common to both the CCCCO's commitment to student equity and a funds of knowledge approach is the endeavor to challenge and shift existing educational paradigms and practices in the best interest of student success. Including a funds of knowledge approach within ongoing student equity initiatives can redirect attention to the community college classroom. Both SSSP and Student Equity policies address the macro-level changes essential to increasing academic outcomes, but there is a lag in developing support systems for community college faculty to assess the effectiveness of their teaching practices. While it is crucial to improve student services to disproportionately impacted student populations, it is equally vital to create faculty-training programs. Faculty need to be introduced to varied pedagogical approaches with the intent to innovate practices that increase student success. In sum, a funds of knowledge framework can shape policy and practice to promote a discourse that replaces the deficiency framework with an approach that validates the student experience and draws on their funds of knowledge to transform the classroom.

Future Research

The classroom practices and pedagogical approaches of community college faculty as an area of study remain under-examined. Further research is necessary to identify those classroom practices and develop a pedagogical approach that supports higher academic achievement among nontraditional students. This study considers the funds of knowledge approach as the pedagogy with the higher potential to support and increase student success. The parameters of this study sought only to begin the process of delineating a funds of knowledge approach for community college teaching; thus, future research needs to build on this sort of dialogue and continue to provide opportunities for faculty to self-assess and reflect.

Moreover, using a funds of knowledge framework, future research should also endeavor to determine the extent of unconscious or unintended racial bias informing faculty attitudes of students. This can be addressed as faculty learn about their students' funds of knowledge, and in response to develop innovative teaching strategies. As faculty innovate and implement a funds of knowledge approach, future research should also attempt to evaluate the success of the courses in which this approach is applied. To this end, the community college students' experience needs to be documented as well. Students should be encouraged to collect their own funds of knowledge using varied methodological approaches, such as ethnography and oral history. The voices and experiences of students are a vital component to any research seeking to develop pedagogical approaches in a community college environment, particularly those that empower students to affirm their commitment to higher educational attainment.

Conclusion

This study represents an opportunity to better understand the factors that shape and influence pedagogical choices and practices among community college faculty. Seldom does a researcher gain access to the community college classroom to observe the method of content delivery and level of student engagement. Seldom does a researcher have the trust of faculty to facilitate serious discussions about pedagogy and practice, and the extent that those approaches reflect faculty's perceptions of the students in their classes.

Since very little is known about the experiences that shape faculty practices (Bensimon, 2007), it is increasingly difficult to develop pedagogy that better supports student success and simultaneously challenges the dominant paradigm that views students as culturally deficient. This research, grounded in a funds of knowledge framework, also expands the potential of using a funds of knowledge pedagogy in the community college classroom. A funds of knowledge approach, applied almost exclusively in the K–12 educational setting (Moll et al., 1992), can also work for community college instruction. The concept of funds of knowledge, based on the assertion that "people are competent, they have knowledge, and their life experiences have given them that knowledge" (González, Moll, & Amanti, 2005, p. ix), can potentially inform and expand normative conceptions of teaching and learning.

Notes

1 Nontraditional students are those who come from working-class backgrounds, are older, work at least half-time while simultaneously attending college, are predominantly from communities of color, have family responsibilities, are the first generation in their family to attend college, and in California, likely to be Latino (Cox, 2009; Campaign for College Opportunity, 2013; Jain, 2015).
2 Chapa and Schnick (2006) also explain that the economic value of an associate degree in comparison to the bachelor's degree is significantly less, and they contend that community colleges often emphasize vocational education over preparation for transfer, which hinders students' chances for economic and social mobility.
3 The California Community Colleges Board of Governors established Student Success Scorecards as a performance measurement system that tracks students' success at all 113 community colleges throughout California. The scorecard provides data on remedial instruction, job training programs, and student retention, graduation, and completion rates (http://scorecard.cccco.edu/scorecard.aspx).
4 Peaks College is a community college in Southern California that reflects the enrollment patterns among Latino college students, and it is designated as a Hispanic-Serving Institution.

References

Alexander, F. E. (2000). The changing face of accountability: Monitoring and assessing institutional performance in higher education. *Journal of Higher Education, 71*(4), 411–431.

Alfonso, M. (2006). Hispanic educational attainment in sub-baccalaureate programs. *Latino Educational Opportunity, 133,* 17–26.

Bailey, T. R., & Alfonso, M. (2005). *Paths to persistence: An analysis of research on program effectiveness at community colleges.* New York: Community College Research Center, Teachers College.

Barnett, E. A. (2010). Validation experiences and persistence among community college students. *Review of Higher Education, 34*(2), 193–230.

Beach, J. M. (2011). *Gateway to opportunity? A history of the community college in the United States.* Sterling, VA: Stylus Publishing, LLC.

Bensimon, E. M. (2007). The underestimated significance of practitioner knowledge in the scholarship on student success. *Review of Higher Education, 30*(4), 441–469.

Brint, S., & Karabel, J. (1989). *The diverted dream: Community colleges and the promise of educational opportunity in America, 1900–1985.* New York, NY: Oxford University Press.

Campaign for College Opportunity. (2013). *The state of Latinos in higher education in California.* Sacramento, CA. Retrieved from www.collegecampaign.org/files/6013/8361/4629/State_of_Higher_Education_Latino_FINAL.pdf

CCCCO. (2017). California Community Colleges Chancellor's Office. Retrieved from http://www.cccco.edu

Chapa, J., & Schnink, W. (2006). California community colleges: Help or hindrance to Latinos in the higher education pipeline? *Latino Educational Opportunity*, *2006*(133), 41–50.

Cohen, A. M., & Brawer, F. B. (2003). *The American community college*. San Francisco, CA: Jossey-Bass.

Cox, R. D. (2009). *The college fear factor: How students and professors misunderstand one another.* Cambridge, MA: Harvard University Press.

Darder, A., Torres, R. D., & Gutiérrez, H. (1997). *Latinos and education: A critical reader.* New York, NY: Routeledge.

Desai, S. A. (2012). Is comprehensiveness taking its toll on community colleges? An in-depth analysis of community colleges' missions and their effectiveness. *Community College Journal of Research and Practice*, *36*(2), 111–121.

Dowd, A. C. (2007). Community colleges as gateway and gatekeepers: Moving beyond the access 'saga' toward outcome equity. *Harvard Educational Review*, *77*(4), 407–419.

Excelenica in Education. (2015). *Helping or hindering? State policies & Latino college completion*. Washington, DC: D. A. Santiago & E. C. Galdeano.

Gándara, P., & Contreras, F. (2009). *The Latino education crisis: The consequences of failed social policies*. Cambridge, MA: Harvard University Press.

González, N., Moll, L. C., & Amanti, C. (2005). *Funds of knowledge: Theorizing practices in households, communities, and classrooms*. Mahwah, NJ: Erlbaum.

Hurtado, S., & Carter, D. F. (1997, October). Effects of college transition and perceptions of the campus racial climate on Latino college students' sense of belonging. *Sociology of Education*, *70*(4), 324–345.

Jain, D. (2015). Women community college student leaders of color: An examination of student involvement theory. In L. S. Kelsay & E. M. Zamani-Gallaher (Eds.), *Working with students in community colleges: Contemporary strategies for bridging theory, research, and practice*. Washington, D.C. and Sterling, VA: ACPA Books co-published with Stylus Publishing.

Moll, L. C., Amanti, C., Neff, D., & González, N. (1992). Funds of knowledge for teaching: Using a qualitative approach to connect homes and classrooms. *Theory Into Practice*, *31*(2), 132–141.

Mora, J. (2016). *Aligning pedagogy with practice: Funds of knowledge for community college teaching* (unpublished doctoral dissertation). Claremont Graduate University, Claremont, California.

Núñez, A., & Elizondo, D. (2013). Closing the Latino/a transfer gap: Creating pathways to the baccalaureate. *Perspectivas: Issues in Higher Education Policy and Practice*, *2*. Retrieved from www.academia.edu/4105129/Closing_the_Latino_a_Transfer_Gap_Creating_Pathways_to_the_Baccalaureate

Ochoa, G. L. (2013). *Academic profiling: Latinos, Asian Americans, and the achievement gap*. Minneapolis, MN: University of Minnesota Press.

Pascarella, E. T., & Terenzini, P. T. (2005). *How college affects students: A third decade of research, Vol. 2*. San Francisco, CA: Josey-Bass.

Rosenbaum, J. E., Deil-Amen, R., & Person, A. E. (2006). *After admission: From college access to college success*. New York, NY: Russell Sage Foundation.

Solorzano, D. G., & Yosso, T. J. (2001). From racial stereotyping and deficit discourse toward a critical race theory in teacher education. *Multicultural Education*, *9*(1), 2–8.

Stanton-Salazar, R. D. (2001). *Manufacturing hope and despair: The school and kin networks of U.S. Mexican Youth*. New York: NY: Teachers College Press.

Umbach, P. D., & Wawrzynski, M. R. (2005). Faculty do matter: The role of college faculty in student learning and engagement. *Research in Higher Education, 46*(2), 153–184.

Vélez-Ibáñez, C., & Greenberg, J. (2005). Formation and transformation of funds of knowledge. In N. González, L. C. Moll, & C. Amanti (Eds.), *Funds of knowledge: Theorizing practices in households, communities, and classrooms* (pp. 47–70). Mahwah, NJ: Lawrence Erlbaum Associates.

Yosso, T. J. (2005). Whose culture has capital? A critical race theory discussion of community cultural wealth. *Race, Ethnicity, and Education, 8*(1), 69–91. doi:10.1080/1361332052000341006

10

LEARNING FROM STUDENTS' CAREER IDEOLOGIES AND ASPIRATIONS

Utilizing a Funds of Knowledge Approach to Reimagine Career and Technical Education (CTE)

Rebecca Colina Neri

Policy conversation in higher education has become increasingly focused on the promise of Career and Technical Education (CTE) to both meet the demands of the labor market and ensure every student has the chance to obtain a high-paying, high-skilled job (Duncan, 2011). However, through its rhetoric and discourse, CTE has largely been reduced to high-quality job training opportunities for underrepresented students that support business growth by responding to shifting demands of the labor market (Jocson, 2015). Furthermore, CTE discourse focused on improving the educational and career trajectories of underrepresented students has largely been based on human capital frameworks that focus on a set of skills and traits that these students and their families lack (English & Mayo, 2012) rather than what they bring to and aspire to do with their educational and career preparation. In its current state, CTE is a more polished reflection of the vocational education of the past. While it has gone great lengths to meet the shifting demands of a 21st century labor market by addressing issues of alignment, credentialing, and streamlining coursework and vocational pathways (Bailey, Jaggars, & Jenkins, 2015), it has not fully considered, nor addressed in a meaningful way, the needs, aspirations, and expectations of its students. This inattention to students' aspirations leads to missed opportunities for CTE to improve educational and vocational student outcomes. One such missed opportunity can be learned from the field of vocational aspiration, where scholars have found that while sociopolitical barriers may constrain underrepresented youths' connection to the world of work, low-income Youth of Color have also been found to have a sociopolitical development, or a critical consciousness and aspiration to change their social realities by addressing sociopolitical inequalities (Diemer, 2009). Students' sociopolitical development has been found to increase their educational and occupational persistence, participation, engagement, and completion as well as raise the level of employment for which they aspire (Diemer et al., 2010). Traditional frameworks for studying underrepresented students' aspirations do not reveal these important, and potentially powerful, resources for reimagining and redesigning CTE. For these reasons, CTE must first see aspiration as a resource for reform, and second, employ non-deficit approaches, such as funds of knowledge (Rios-Aguilar & Kiyama, 2012), for studying the educational and career aspirations of underrepresented students.

Career and Technical Education

Since its implementation in 1917, vocational education has been heavily critiqued for serving businesses at the expense of students' intellectual development and educational and employment mobility by tracking underrepresented students into occupational training programs that offer a narrow curriculum and credentials that have limited and expiring marketability (Oakes, 1985; Rogers, Kahne, & Middaugh, 2008; Jocson, 2015). In recent years, the U.S. Department of Education has recognized the need to reimagine and remake CTE, and therefore embarked on a $1.4 billion reform mission to ensure that all students earn a postsecondary degree and are qualified and prepared for the 21st century workforce (Duncan, 2011). Most recently, in September of 2016, the House Committee on Education and the Workforce passed H.R. 5587, the *Strengthening Career and Technical Education for the 21st Century Act*, which reauthorizes and reforms the *Carl D. Perkins Career and Technical Education Act*. This bipartisan bill promises to be a landmark step towards closing our nation's skills gap by ensuring "that students, especially historically disadvantaged and underserved students, are prepared for success in high-demand jobs that offer living wages, employer benefits, and opportunities for meaningful career advancement" (162 Cong. Rec. H4185, 2016). The bipartisan legislation will, among other objectives, increase CTE's alignment to a 21st century labor market and enhance CTE's focus on employability skills and meaningful credentialing.

While the need to reform CTE has been recognized, subsequent efforts have largely been reduced to high-quality job training opportunities for underrepresented students based on economic growth and shifting demands of the labor market. Simply put, CTE reform and rhetoric has largely been focused on the user needs of businesses and much less effective at addressing the user needs of its students. Under current CTE legislation, human capital frameworks too narrowly define criteria for success as those that result in material production. Human capital frameworks, based on a "rigorous and unforgiving ideology of individual accountability" (Apple, 2005, p. 15), frame individual success or failure in terms of entrepreneurial virtues or personal failings (Harvey, 2007). This ideology of individual accountability tends to reproduce schooling inequities and social hierarchies as it fails to address systems of oppression facing students of color and low-income students. In CTE, we see this in the form of low-ability tracking and technical training at the expense of academic preparation and human development. As Jocson (2015) explains, when productivity is cast solely through human capital investment, CTE misses other forms of productivity, such as one's contribution towards transformative change in society or the struggle for the political, social, or cultural. In light of such negative consequences, the question too quickly becomes whether or not vocational education has a place in schools. As recent legislation has only solidified, and in many ways strengthened, CTE's role in students' educational and occupational trajectories, the better question would be how to reconceptualize the role of CTE in education and society. To answer this question, it may be helpful to return to the writings of John Dewey from the early 1900s.

According to Dewey, vocational education should be the type of education that prepares students and workers to be more than "appendages to their machines" (Dewey, 1900, p. 22). "By utilizing the factors of industry to make school life more active, more full of immediate meaning, more connected with out-of-school experience" (Dewey, 1916, p. 324), vocational education should help students understand the origins and purpose of their work and develop their industrial intelligence—the ability to locate their work within its historical, economic, and social bearings (Rogers et al., 2008). This industrial intelligence allows for the readaptation to continuously changing conditions that is necessary for workers to realize an infinite variety of callings rather than become fossilized in one specialized vocation. Vocational education should also require that intelligence be linked to activity and calls for a reconnection between thought and bodily activity, an individual's conscious development and associated life, theoretical culture and practical behavior, and making a livelihood and the enjoyment of leisure (Dewey, 1916, p. 326). Through these reconnections, students are encouraged and prepared to imagine their current situations in light of future conditions under the broader goal of building community. Inherent in Dewey's conception of vocational education are commitments to human flourishing, civic participation, and social transformation—notions that are largely absent from current rhetoric in CTE based majorly on employability skills in a 21st century global marketplace and meeting the shifting demands of the labor market. In a sense, Dewey was calling for the type of education that would help students develop a critical consciousness, or what vocational aspiration literature refers to as a sociopolitical development.

Vocational Aspiration

Vocational aspiration literature argues that the construction of one's occupational self-concept is mediated by both a larger social structure and one's social environment (Super, 1990). Within this mediation process, sociopolitical barriers—under-resourced schools, racism, limited structures of opportunity, poverty—play a large role in the perpetuation of disparities between the vocational aspirations and outcomes of low-income Youth of Color and their White counterparts (Hotchkiss & Borow, 1996; Blustein, McWhirter, & Perry, 2005; Brown, 2002; Hill & Torres, 2010). Scholars have found that awareness of these barriers can make it difficult for low-income Youth of Color to realize their aspirations in their future world of work (Wilson, 1996); lead them to aspire for lower-paying, lower-status jobs (Diemer, 2009); and, in some cases, disengage entirely from educational and occupational systems (Conchas, 2001; Fine, 1991). However, Diemer (2009) argues that while these findings are significant, students' desire, agency, and capacity to negotiate and alter these conditions of oppression remain under-examined.

In his work, Diemer (2009) found that underrepresented students often have a sociopolitical development, or a critical consciousness and motivation to change one's social reality and help others by addressing sociopolitical inequalities through community action (Ginwright & Cammarota, 2002; Watts & Flanagan, 2007). He found that the sociopolitical development of underrepresented youth could serve as a powerful asset or "antidote to oppression" (Watts, Griffith, and Abdul-Adil, 1999, p. 255 as cited in Diemer, 2009). Using this lens to examine students' vocational aspirations revealed that students' sociopolitical development can be a successful means for students to: (a) implement their occupational self-concept in the world of work; (b) increase the clarity of their vocational identities; (c) realize their vocational expectations; (d) expect to attain higher-paying, higher-status occupations; and (e) enhance their ability to critically assess and act upon the sociopolitical barriers of their lived realities (Diemer, 2009; Diemer & Blustein, 2006).

Asset-based approaches, like the one above, to studying the aspiration of under-represented students can offer important new understandings for CTE. For too long, CTE has used a narrow human capital lens to improve students' outcomes that often portrays students as static individuals lacking the skills, knowledge, aspiration, and disposition to be successful in the 21st century workforce. Subsequent reform efforts have resulted in banking method approaches to educational and career preparation that constrain the participation, learning, and outcomes of underrepresented students. Instead, CTE must widen its view to consider (a) what students bring to their learning—funds of knowledge, (b) student agency and capacity to negotiate and address sociopolitical barriers facing their lives, and (c) the type of education and career preparation students desire. One asset-based approach that has not been given enough consideration in CTE, and that has the potential to accomplish these objectives, is the funds of knowledge framework.

Funds of Knowledge: A Non-Deficit Approach to Studying Student Aspirations

Funds of knowledge (FK) are the historically-accumulated skills and cultural resources that students use to navigate their daily lives (Moll, Amanti, Neff, &

González, 1992). Incorporating students' FK into classroom practices has been found to challenge deficit approaches of education, increase students' engagement and academic outcomes, improve teacher-student relationships, and enhance teachers' pedagogical understandings and practices (González, 2005; Zipin, 2009; Esteban-Guitart & Moll, 2014; Moll, Soto-Santiago & Schwartz, 2013). The FK approach has also been used to study the educational and career aspirations of students and their families (Kiyama, 2010; Rios-Aguilar & Kiyama, 2012; Zipin, Sellar, Brennan, & Gale, 2015). Rios-Aguilar and Kiyama (2012) argue that there are other resources, beyond measures of academic achievement and individual attributes, affecting Latina/o college preparation that have not been given serious consideration. To explore these resources, the authors use a funds of knowledge approach through which they examine how students' FK have contributed to their educational and occupational aspirations and ideologies. They argue that this approach is ideally situated to study college and career aspiration as, by exposing students' cultural resources, it (a) challenges deficit views of underrepresented students and their families as not valuing education and having low career aspirations; and (b) helps educational organizations better understand their role in perpetuating these deficit perspectives. Zipin et al.'s (2015) work on student aspiration and FK supports this argument. The authors found that students' aspirations are future-oriented as students "desire, imagine, articulate and pursue community futures that exceed, rather than reproduce, historically received social—structural limits" (Zipin et al., 2015, p. 238). They argue, alongside Rios-Aguilar and Kiyama (2012) and Diemer (2009), that "it is of vital socioethical value if agency among the less powerful is capacitated to imagine, voice and proactively pursue futures other than what their inherited worlds might seem to hold in store for them" (p. 243).

In order to move away from the historical practice of technical training that has been proven to reproduce social inequity, CTE programs must learn to see students' diversities as assets that "contain valuable knowledge and experiences that can foster . . . educational development" (Moll & González, 1997, p. 98). Using a non-deficit approach, such as the FK framework, to study and leverage students' educational and career aspirations, therefore holds great promise for CTE across multiple levels. On an individual level, recognizing and leveraging students' funds of knowledge and career aspirations can increase students' engagement, sense of belonging, and persistence in and through CTE programs. Furthermore, as CTE is charged with building a diverse and prepared workforce, utilizing an FK approach can support CTE programs in exploring ways to respect, take seriously, and learn from this diversity to improve educational and training practices. On a broader level, redesigning curriculum and pedagogy to provide students with an opportunity to explore their FK in the context of their future work can lead to the creation of new ideals and ends for the workforce. In the case of the CTE program that is the context of this study, this could lead to solutions for building worker capacity in ways that reimagine and potentially improve policing practices and community-police relations.

Method

The CTE program that is the context of this study is a dual-enrollment, police-oriented CTE program. As recent tragedies across our country have put a strain on already tenuous relationships between police and underrepresented communities (Giroux, 2014; Coates, 2015), reconceptualizing the role of a CTE program that trains a future cohort of officers takes on unprecedented importance. At a time when policy reform, and specifically the design of new models for educating and training a diverse policing workforce, has become a top priority in our country, this particular CTE program becomes a momentous context to rethink the purpose of CTE reform. CTE reforms based solely on entrepreneurial virtues and personal failings will fall short of imagining ways to leverage and learn from the cultural resources and vocational aspirations of a student body that has the potential to offer great insight into some of the most pressing issues currently facing our nation. Utilizing an asset-based approach to study student aspiration in CTE, such as the FK approach, can provide insights that lead to more humanizing and social justice-oriented reform efforts in CTE and workforce partners. Building from the work of Rios-Aguilar and Kiyama (2012), this study uses an FK approach to explore CTE students' career aspirations as utilities for improving CTE programs through attempting to answer the following questions:

1. What is the relationship between CTE students' funds of knowledge and the development of their career aspirations?
2. In what ways are students' career aspirations aligned to the curriculum, pedagogy, and goals of their CTE program?

Setting

The police-oriented CTE program that is the context of this study is a dual-enrollment CTE program meant to prepare young adults for a career with their local police department. Its purpose beyond providing police training and a pathway to an associate's degree is to support the development of a homegrown community police force that improves the relationship between the police and the communities it serves. The 103 students who participated in this study are in a unique position to offer important insights for methods aimed at strengthening community policing and police diversity efforts. Participants are approximately 60 percent male and 40 percent female; 93 percent Latino, 3 percent White, 2 percent Black, and 2 percent Asian/Pacific Islander; 17–19 years of age; and nearly all students come from low-income communities of color that historically lack trust with the police.

Study Design

From 2013–2015, students from this police-oriented CTE program and researchers from a public university engaged in youth participatory action research (YPAR)—a "research methodology in which young people study their own social contexts to understand how to improve conditions and bring about greater equity" (Akom, Cammarota, & Ginwright, 2008, p. 5). The purpose of the collaboration was to provide a space for students to leverage their funds of knowledge in their education and training, and for researchers to learn more about students' funds of knowledge and career aspirations as they related to student engagement and persistence in the program. During the weekly sessions, students engaged in discussion, activities, and tasks—including autobiography, critical media literacy, and role play—through which they individually and/or collectively explored their funds of knowledge in relation to law enforcement overall, and the education and training they were receiving in their CTE program specifically. Interviews and focus groups were conducted to better understand (a) students' career aspirations, funds of knowledge, and the relationship between the two; (b) the alignment, or lack thereof, between students' aspirations and the education and training they received in their CTE program; and (c) the type of education and training students desired.

Data Collection and Analysis

Several forms of data were collected throughout this project. For the purposes of this chapter, the data that will be discussed here included 20 student interviews, three focus groups, 102 student law enforcement autobiographies, and approximately 30 hours of ethnographic fieldnotes. The interviews and focus groups were semi-structured and focused on the development of students' career aspirations. The student law enforcement autobiographies asked students to tell their story about the role that law enforcement has played in their lives, starting from their first interaction with an officer through their decision to join the police-oriented CTE program. Included in the autobiographies were the development of students' and their families' ideologies and experiences regarding law enforcement. The 30+ hours of ethnographic fieldnotes included the transcription of 10 YPAR meetings and 10+ hours of CTE program operation observation, including administrative meetings, classroom observation, and day-to-day functioning.

Using qualitative data analysis, initial coding was used in the first cycle of data analysis to create a list of codes. Next, axial coding (Saldaña, 2015) was used to not only make comparisons across data sources, but also to begin to synthesize the codes into categories that provided insight into how students' funds of knowledge mediated the ongoing development of students' aspirations to join law enforcement and the moments when the context of policing or CTE (a) recognized and/or leveraged students' FK; and (b) challenged or supported students' aspirations. Axial coding was also used to form categories about students' and their families' specific ideologies about and experiences with law enforcement that influenced the development of students' career aspirations. The final round of coding analyzed more specifically (a) students' sociopolitical development; and (b) how students believed their sociopolitical development drove their persistence, belongingness, and academic and career performance.

Findings and Discussion

Using a FK framework to better understand students' career aspirations revealed several important findings. CTE reform frames education as a means for supporting economic growth and providing high-skilled, high-quality job training opportunities. Students' educational and career aspirations complicate this framing of CTE. Students desired a type of education that would provide them with the knowledge, skills, and tools to solve complex problems facing their communities and their future career in policing. As demonstrated in Table 10.1 students chose to pursue CTE as an opportunity to use their funds of knowledge to reimagine the role of policing, or utilize their sociopolitical development.

Table 10.1 speaks to the complexity of students' funds of knowledge and how these inform their educational and vocational aspirations. While job stability and economic advancement were also important factors in students' decisions to pursue CTE, in most cases they were not the main driving factors. The main drivers were students' sociopolitical development or the desire to address and transform the problems of their social reality. Therefore, when attending to challenges such as increasing student engagement, persistence, and completion, CTE must widen their view to consider more humanizing and problem-centered approaches. The following stories of Mateo and Yareli demonstrate how leveraging, or neglecting, students' FK in the design of curriculum and pedagogy can affect student engagement and persistence in CTE.

Navigating Boundaries: Mateo's Story

The most common theme in the development of students' career aspirations and reasons for pursuing CTE, with more than 80 percent of students indicating these factors, was the desire to use their education and training to help people and make a change in their communities. Significantly, over 60 percent of students reported that the aspiration to help others (i.e. family, neighborhood, schools, friends, the homeless, abuse victims, people suffering with addictions, and victims of bullying) was the strongest driving factor for pursuing a career in policing. Students explained that their life experiences afforded them an ability to "see" people and situations from multiple perspectives. The following epigram explores factors that

TABLE 10.1 The Relationship Between Students' Funds of Knowledge and Vocational Aspirations

Funds of Knowledge	Vocational Aspirations
Immigration history Being undocumented, Sonia's family feared the police and therefore did not call on them in their times of need.	*Improve trust between undocumented people and police* Sonia wants to become an officer to build trusting relationships with her community and find new ways to inform undocumented people of their rights so that they might feel safer calling upon and using their local police force.
Employment Jordan worked at his father's liquor store in high school. Many of his regular customers were homeless. Jordan learned that homeless people were often mistreated by officers.	*Improve police interactions with vulnerable populations* Jordan desires to become a police officer to "improve how police communicate and interact with homeless so things don't get out of hand and so homeless people get resources they need."
Language Bella speaks English, Spanish, and Zapoteco. She often serves as a language broker between her community and doctors, teachers, and police officers.	*Improve communication between Latinos and local police* In her experience language brokering, Bella realized that "there is a lot of really important information that can be misunderstood when people don't speak the same language." Bella desires to become an officer to improve communication between her community and local police.
Community knowledge Neto watched his neighborhood change due to gentrification. He believes that officers are more concerned with protecting businesses than building relationships with the community.	*Help build a local, community police force* Neto recalled that while he was growing up, before his neighborhood was gentrified, the local police officers were a common presence in his neighborhood. Neto explained that "the officers back then knew me and my family. One of them even grew up with my [uncle]. He was a mentor to me. I'm here today to be like him and help the kids in my community."
Sports Rodolfo was the captain of his soccer team. He enjoyed being a leader for his team, "someone who his teammates respected and trusted."	*Do the job honorably and be a leader* Rodolfo explained that he would like to use his leadership skills as an officer to respond to serious, at times dangerous, situations and be responsible for the safety of his team.
Dark funds of knowledge[i] Patricia's uncle was killed by a rival gang member. According to Patricia, losing him was like losing a father for her.	*Interact with people respectfully and empathetically* Patricia explained that some of the more difficult experiences she faced throughout her life were the main reasons she wanted to become an officer. She watched people in her neighborhood be treated "like they weren't human beings." She explained that she wants to be an officer who prevents and stops crime, but also treats people respectfully while doing so.

TABLE 10.1 (Continued)

Funds of Knowledge	Vocational Aspirations
Religion Soraya is an active member of her church. Her church organizes outreach events to provide the community with resources—food, toys, clothes, and tutoring. Her church also provides support for victims of domestic violence.	*To serve and protect the community; to be a resource for those in need* Soraya explained that her church taught her about problems facing her community and the importance of helping others. She also explained that "officers do not always handle calls for domestic violence in the best way and then victims don't want to ask for help and or can even be put in more danger." She hopes that becoming an officer will provide her with new tools to help her community.

¹Zipin (2009) describes dark FK as students' "dark lifeworld experiences" that include experiences of crime, addiction, mental illness, family separation, and so on. In his work using the FK approach, he found that students' darker life-world experiences opened the door for deep and transformative student and teacher learning. However, he also noticed teachers' great hesitancy to engage students' darker life-world experiences.

attributed to the career aspirations of a community college freshman, Mateo. This excerpt also reveals the misalignment between why Mateo pursued CTE and the type of education and training Mateo is presently receiving.

> When I was [. . .] maybe like 6 years old [. . .] my uncle started bringing these guys to the house and spending all this time in the garage. I found out from my cousin that he was dealing drugs out of our house. I always respected him and he always looked out for me so I was kind of confused about it all. Anyway, he got really addicted to drugs [. . .]. He was living sometimes on the street and sometimes he would sleep on our porch. [. . .] My aunt felt bad for him one day and let him come in the house. [. . .] I was like 13 at the time. The police came and I remember having mixed feelings about my uncle getting arrested. [. . .] I knew that this wasn't him, you know, his addiction was bad. [. . .] Those years of my life made me want to be an officer. I want to work in narcotics or help victims of domestic violence. I have seen things that most people haven't so I understand [he pauses] or like, I get it, I get people.
>
> (Student Interview, 04–14–16)

In this epigram, we learn that Mateo's career aspirations were largely influenced by having exposure to dark or difficult funds of knowledge. By watching his uncle, who he respected very much, sell drugs, become addicted to them, and end up on the streets, Mateo began to form a sociopolitical development to address issues related to narcotics and domestic violence. His sociopolitical development is what drove him to purse CTE, where he believed he would learn how to address problems of his social reality. However, what he experienced in his CTE program was very different than the education and training in which he hoped to engage.

> I still want to be an officer, but now, I am not so sure that I want to continue in this program, but I feel like I have to because what am I going to do? [. . .] It's just this program doesn't really talk about real problems. It's like all procedures and Physical Training. I know those are important parts of the job, but the only time we talk about hard problems is in Sociology and maybe, Community Relations, and even in those classes it's all about stopping crime before it happens or getting rid of the [Mateo signals quotations marks] problem people. I get that's the point, but I'm also here to help people like my uncle and my family in a different way, not just locking people up.
>
> *(Student Interview, 04–14–16)*

Mateo's experience supports Jocson's (2015) analysis of the paradoxical rhetoric of CTE. For Mateo, pursuing CTE was a humanizing mission, in contrast to the economic growth rhetoric of CTE reform. Growing out of this paradox, boundaries have been constructed between the practices of his CTE program and Mateo's sociopolitical development. Navigating these boundaries has led to great confusion for Mateo about what it means to be a police officer; what it means to help people; the value of his life experiences, and the value of his education. The narrow education of his CTE program, based largely in technical training and deficit frameworks (i.e. culture of poverty (Lewis, 1961) and broken windows theories (Wilson & Kelling, 2003)) has also led Mateo to question his continued participation in his CTE program. Since Mateo is a leader who his peers greatly respect, Mateo's CTE program would be impacted heavily were he to leave. However, if his CTE program were able to learn from Mateo's FK and design curriculum and pedagogy that allowed him to exercise his sociopolitical development, as can be seen in Yareli's story below, Mateo's and his peers' engagement and persistence might improve.

"We Could Be the Teachers": Yareli's Story

Yareli's decision to attend her CTE program and become a police officer largely stemmed from her deep understanding of mental illness. Over the last four years, Yareli has been helping her mother care for her brother, who suffers from paranoid schizophrenia. Her experiences caring for her brother, learning about his illness, and witnessing several negative interactions between the police and her brother contributed to the formation of her sociopolitical development. She desired to become an officer to effectively and respectfully handle situations with people suffering from mental illness. In response to a discussion in YPAR about a national news story reporting on a deadly interaction between an officer and a mentally ill homeless man, Yareli shared her story with the class. The discussion revealed that many of her classmates knew very little about people suffering from mental illness. Yareli asked if she could do a presentation for not only her class, but the entire program, around interacting with people with paranoid schizophrenia. Fortunately, her program agreed, and we were able to organize a presentation for her program that included the attendance of active-duty officers and officers in training. Yareli explained that "for the first time, I felt like I made the right decision coming here. I haven't even become an officer yet and maybe I have already helped people." Yareli plans on not only finishing her program, but now also desires to transfer to a four-year college to pursue a bachelor's degree in Criminal Justice.

Conclusions and Implications

Arguing that student aspiration be used as a resource for CTE improvement, this study used the funds of knowledge framework to better understand students' career aspirations as they related to their participation in and evaluation of their learning. In addition to extending the FK framework into higher education and specifically CTE, this study is significant as it expands our understanding of students' aspirations in ways that challenge narrow framings of CTE as investment towards economic growth and employability skills for the global marketplace. Using a FK framework revealed the FK (i.e. difficult life experiences, speaking multiple languages, community organizing, diverse communication skills, empathy for others, leadership skills) that students bring to their learning. Students' FK overwhelmingly contributed to the formation of a sociopolitical development, or critical consciousness, to address the sociopolitical barriers facing their lives. Pedagogical and curricular designs that tapped into students' sociopolitical development, as seen in the case of Yareli, increased student engagement and persistence, but when ignored, as seen in the case of Mateo, led students to question their engagement in their CTE program. Therefore, reimagining and redesigning pedagogy and curriculum in a way that takes up important problems facing students' social realities and future careers holds great promise for increasing student persistence and completion in CTE. Engaging students' sociopolitical development takes on unprecedented importance in Human and Public Service clusters of CTE, such as law enforcement. Currently, police reform that addresses sociopolitical inequities is not only needed, but is being mandated by our federal government. Mateo and Yareli not only understand this need to reimagine policing; their main reasons for pursuing CTE are to learn how to enact such reform efforts. However, the type of education and training provided by their CTE program does not always address, and in many cases counteracts, such reform efforts. CTE has the potential to be a space of learning that not only prepares students to enter high-paying, high-skilled jobs, but also develops their agency to address socio-political barriers and problems facing their own lives, communities, and future careers. The funds of knowledge framework is a promising, non-deficit approach to begin this important and humanizing work in CTE.

References

Akom, A. A., Cammarota, J., & Ginwright, S. (2008). Youthtopias: Towards a new paradigm of critical youth studies. *Youth Media Reporter, 2*(4), 1–30.

Apple, M. (2005). Education, markets, and an audit culture. *Critical Quarterly, 47*(1/2), 11–29.

Bailey, T. R., Jaggars, S. S., & Jenkins, D. (2015). *Redesigning America's community colleges.* Cambridge, MA: Harvard University Press.

Blustein, D. L., McWhirter, E. H., & Perry, J. C. (2005). An emancipatory communitarian approach to vocational development theory, research, and practice. *The Counseling Psychologist, 33*(2), 141–179.

Brown, D. (2002). The role of work and cultural values in occupational choice, satisfaction, and success: A theoretical statement. *Journal of Counseling & Development, 80*(1), 48–56.

Coates, T. (2015). The myth of police reform. *The Atlantic.* Retrieved from www.theatlantic.com/politics/archive/2015/04/the-myth-of-police-reform/390057/

Conchas, G. Q. (2001). Structuring failure and success: Understanding the variability in Latino school engagement. *Harvard Educational Review, 71*(3), 475–504.

Dewey, J. (1916). Democracy and education. *MW, 9,* 316–330.

Dewey, J. (1990). *The school and society.* Chicago, IL: The University of Chicago Press (Original work published 1900).

Diemer, M. A. (2009). Pathways to occupational attainment among poor youth of color the role of sociopolitical development. *The Counseling Psychologist, 37*(1), 6–35.

Diemer, M. A., & Blustein, D. L. (2006). Critical consciousness and career development among urban youth. *Journal of Vocational Behavior, 68*(2), 220–232.

Diemer, M. A., Wang, Q., Moore, T., Gregory, S. R., Hatcher, K. M., & Voight, A. M. (2010). Sociopolitical development, work salience, and vocational expectations among low socioeconomic status African American, Latin American, and Asian American youth. *Developmental Psychology, 46*(3), 619.

Duncan, A. (2011). *The new CTE: Secretary Duncan's remarks on CTE* [Press release]. Retrieved from www.ed.gov/news/speeches/new-cte-secretary-duncans-remarks-career-and-technical-education

Esteban-Guitart, M., & Moll, L. C. (2014). Funds of identity: A new concept based on the funds of knowledge approach. *Culture & Psychology, 20*(1), 31–48. doi:10.1177/1354067X13515934

Fine, M. (1991). *Framing dropouts.* Albany, NY: State University of New York Press.

Ginwright, S., & Cammarota, J. (2002). New terrain in youth development: The promise of a social justice approach. *Social Justice, 29*(4), 82–95.

Giroux, H. A. (2014). *The militarization of racism and neoliberal violence.* [Blog]. Published by truth-out.org, 18 August 2014. Retrieved from www.truth-out.org/opinion/item/25660-the-militarization-of-racism-and-neoliberal-violence

González, N. (2005). Beyond culture: The hybridity of funds of knowledge. In N. Gonzales, L. C. Moll, & C. Amanti (Eds.), *Funds of knowledge: Theorizing practices in households, communities, and classrooms* (pp. 29–46). Mahwah, NJ: Lawrence Erlbaum Associates.

Harvey, D. (2007). *A brief history of neoliberalism.* Oxford: Oxford University Press.

Hill, N. E., & Torres, K. (2010). Negotiating the American dream: The paradox of aspirations and achievement among Latino students and engagement between their families and schools. *Journal of Social Issues, 66*(1), 95–112.

Hotchkiss, L., & Borow, H. (1996). Sociological perspective on work and career development. In D. Brown & L. Brooks (Eds.), *Career choice and development* (3rd ed., pp. 281–336). San Francisco, CA: Jossey-Bass.

Jocson, K. M. (2015). "I want to do more and change things": Reframing CTE toward possibilities in urban education. *Urban Education,* 1–28. doi:10.1177/0042085915618714

Kiyama, J. M. (2010). College aspirations and limitations: The role of educational ideologies and funds of knowledge in Mexican American families. *American Educational Research Journal, 47*(2), 330–356. doi:10.3102/0002831209357468

Lewis, O. (1961). *The children of Sanchez: Autobiography of a Mexican family.* New York, NY: Random House.

Moll, L. C., Amanti, C., Neff, D., & González, N. (1992). Funds of knowledge for teaching: Using a qualitative approach to connect homes and classrooms. *Theory Into Practice, 31*(2), 132–141.

Moll, L. C., & González, N. (1997). Teachers as social scientists: Learning about culture from household research. In P. M. Hall (Ed.), *Race, ethnicity, and multiculturalism: Policy and practice* (Vol. 1, pp. 89–114). New York: Garland.

Moll, L. C., Soto-Santiago, S., & Schwartz, L. (2013). Funds of knowledge in changing communities. In K. Hall, T. Cremin, B. Comber, & L. Moll (Eds.), *International handbook of research on children's literacy, learning, and culture* (pp. 172–183). West Sussex: Wiley-Blackwell.

Oakes, J. (1985). *Keeping track: How schools structure inequality.* New Haven, CT: Yale University Press.

Rios-Aguilar, C., & Kiyama, J. M. (2012). Funds of knowledge: An approach to studying Latina(o) students' transition to college. *Journal of Latinos and Education, 11*(1), 2–16. doi:10.1080/15348431.2012.631430

Rogers, J., Kahne, J., & Middaugh, E. (2008). Multiple pathways and the 'future of democracy'. In J. Oakes & M. Saunders (Eds.), *Beyond tracking: Multiple high school pathways that prepare students for college, career, and civic participation* (pp. 153–169). Boston, MA: Harvard Education Press.

Saldana, J. (2015). *The coding manual for qualitative researchers.* Los Angeles, CA: Sage.

Super, D. E. (1990). A life-span, life-space approach to career development. In D. Brown & L. Brooks (Eds.), *Career choice and development: Applying contemporary theories to practice* (2nd ed., pp. 197–261). San Francisco, CA: Jossey-Bass.

Watts, R. J., & Flanagan, C. (2007). Pushing the envelope on youth civic engagement: A developmental and liberation psychology perspective. *Journal of Community Psychology, 35*(6), 779–792.

Watts, R. J., Griffith, D. M., & Abdul-Adil, J. (1999). Sociopolitical development as an antidote for oppression—Theory and action. *American Journal of Community Psychology, 27*(2), 255–271.

Wilson, J. Q., & Kelling, G. L. (2003). Broken windows: The police and neighborhood safety. In E. McLaughlin, J. Muncie, & G. Hughes (Eds.), *Criminological perspectives: Essential readings.* Trowbridge, Wiltshire: Cromwell Press.

Wilson, W. J. (1996). *When work disappears: The world of the new urban poor.* New York, NY: Random House.

Zipin, L. (2009). Dark funds of knowledge, deep funds of pedagogy: Exploring boundaries between lifeworlds and schools. *Discourse: Studies in the Cultural Politics of Education, 30*(3), 317–331. doi:10.1080/01596300903037044

Zipin, L., Sellar, S., Brennan, M., & Gale, T. (2015). Educating for futures in marginalized regions: A sociological framework for rethinking and researching aspirations. *Educational Philosophy and Theory, 47*(3), 227–246.

11

FUNDS OF KNOWLEDGE AS A CULTURALLY RESPONSIVE PEDAGOGY IN HIGHER EDUCATION

Judy Marquez Kiyama, Cecilia Rios-Aguilar, and Regina Deil-Amen

The important work of Gloria Ladson-Billings (1995) has taught us that cultur-ally responsive pedagogy encourages student achievement in K–12 education. Culturally responsive pedagogy includes the following three criteria:"an ability to develop students academically, a willingness to nurture and support cultural com-petence, and the development of a sociopolitical or critical consciousness" and includes "three conceptions regarding self and other, social relations, and knowl-edge" (Ladson-Billings, 1995, p. 483). Thus, culturally responsive pedagogy situ-ates student learning and academic success within the broader social and cultural contexts in which students and their families live, work, and function in everyday life. And, by drawing upon students' cultural ways of knowing and being, their learning and engagement is enhanced (Brockenbrough, 2014; Ladson-Billings, 1995). According to Ladson-Billings (1995), she built upon the term "culturally responsive," rather than culturally appropriate, culturally congruent, or culturally compatible, for the following reason: "only the term *culturally responsive* appears to refer to a more dynamic or synergistic relationship between home/commu-nity culture and school culture" (p. 467). Therefore, an essential conceptual and pedagogical foundation is established when considering funds of knowledge as a culturally responsive pedagogy.

Literature is limited, however, when it comes to the role that culturally respon-sive pedagogy, like funds of knowledge, plays in higher education classrooms. Two examples within postsecondary scholarship are important to note, the lessons of which will be woven into this chapter. The first pushes us to rethink pedagogy in diverse college classrooms (Howell & Tuitt, 2003), and the second encour-ages us to reflect on what inclusive college environments can and should look like (Osei-Kofi, Richards, & Smith, 2004). Yet, it is not often that literature on teaching and learning in postsecondary settings takes the same critical examination that Ladson-Billings' (1995) culturally responsive pedagogy offers us from a conceptual standpoint.

Building off of the notion of lived experiences within the funds of knowledge framework, in this chapter we push readers to move beyond learning about students' lived experiences and explore how cultural knowledges, lived experiences, and home practices can be validated, incorporated, and developed into culturally responsive pedagogy in higher education curriculum and programming. We offer a critical lens from which to build pedagogy that is humanizing and decolonizing in efforts to offer inclusive classroom and learning spaces. In doing so, we are informed by Weiler (2003), who summarizes that incorporating lived experiences into the classroom offers an opportunity for students' narratives while also challenging students (and faculty) to examine the sociohistorical and sociocultural practices that create such narratives. The goals of utilizing funds of knowledge as a culturally responsive pedagogy are to foster student success in a familiar and collective manner while also challenging larger social issues.

A Brief Review of Literature and Guiding Questions

Curricular transformation within higher education is hardly a new or novel goal (Tuitt, 2003). Pedagogical models utilizing inclusive frameworks have sought to transform higher education curriculum since the 1960s (Tuitt, 2003). Yet, creating culturally responsive pedagogy that promotes the academic success of underserved students and facilitates structural transformation remains a challenge. Creating a culturally responsive pedagogy takes time and, bringing in a funds of knowledge framework, as has been established throughout this volume, requires investment on the part of the instructor. To understand the lived experiences of students in higher education requires the instructor to invest time and energy and to engage in dialogue with others (Osei-Kofi et al., 2004). Similarly, Osei-Kofi and colleagues (2004) stress that creating inclusive and culturally responsive pedagogy requires interrogating and understanding ourselves; merely having information about other groups does not constitute culturally responsive pedagogy.

Culturally responsive pedagogy lends itself to multiple goals. As previously stated, one of those goals is transforming lived experiences into knowledge and academic success.

> If students are not able to transform their lived experiences into knowledge and to use the already acquired knowledge as a process to unveil new knowledge, they will never be able to participate rigorously in a dialogue as a process of learning and knowing.
>
> *(Freire & Macedo, 2003, p. 196)*

TABLE 11.1 Summary of Practices for Inclusive Pedagogy

Recognize students' experiences as worthy knowledge
Elicit and build on students' funds of knowledge
Invite students to share their knowledge in multiple ways
Collaborate with students as co-constructors of knowledge
Establish critical dialogues with students
Incorporate noncompetitive, collaborative assignments and group work
Facilitate large and small group discussions
Use formative assessments, such as journal writing and portfolios
Include assignments such as life history interviews, personal stories of survival, and
    autobiographical writing that will diversify and personalize learning
Engage students in debate, student-led discussion, read-alouds, and experiential learning
    activities
Foster student choice

(adapted from Salazar, Norton, & Tuitt, 2010, pp. 211–212)

Another goal includes engaging in the politics of knowledge and challenging the structures that continue to privilege certain students (Osei-Kofi et al., 2004). What Osei-Kofi et al. (2004) describe is the process of using culturally responsive pedagogy to go beyond recognizing and celebrating different (in other words, beyond the *valuing* of funds of knowledge) to facilitating transformative action.

Salazar, Norton, and Tuitt (2010) suggest that including students' funds of knowledge is one consideration when creating culturally responsive pedagogy. Table 11.1 summarizes these practices.

By creating more inclusive spaces within higher education settings, culturally responsive pedagogy can facilitate the transformative goal noted above and interrupt "the cycle of inequity" (Salazar et al., 2010, p. 220).

Informed by the literature around culturally responsive and inclusive pedagogies in higher education, we consider the following guiding questions when encouraging a funds of knowledge approach to postsecondary classrooms:

1. How is the researcher/instructor located in pedagogical exploration? This question is adapted from Ladson-Billings (1995) and leads us to consider not only theoretical foundations of culturally responsive pedagogy, but culturally responsive methodological practices as well, in our attempt to gather information about students' social and cultural contexts.

2. How can (culturally responsive) pedagogy promote the kind of student success that engages larger social–structural issues in a critical way (Ladson-Billings, 1995, p. 469)?

3. In attempting to become culturally responsive, what should the role of teacher versus facilitator be (Freire & Macedo, 2003, p. 189)? We would add: What role do the students take on within the community of learners that is being developed?

4. How do we make sure to create a dialogue as a process of learning and knowing rather than a dialogue as conversation that mechanically focuses on the individual's lived experience? (Freire & Macedo, 2003, p. 193)?
5. Finally, adapted from Osei-Kofi et al. (2004, p. 61), what do my teaching practices say about my assumptions, values, and beliefs about teaching? What constrains my view of what is possible in teaching?

It is with these questions in mind that we begin exploring the role of funds of knowledge as a pedagogy in higher education.

Implementing a Culturally Responsive Pedagogy in Higher Education

In this section, we present three cases that offer specific examples for implementing funds of knowledge into higher education pedagogy. The first is an example of a college outreach program that operates from a funds of knowledge framework and incorporates weekly workshops delivered through a funds of knowledge pedagogical lens. The second is a rationale and proposed process for collecting and integrating funds of knowledge into community college classrooms. And the third case is an example of utilizing existing pedagogical tools found in participatory action research methods to integrate funds of knowledge into higher education classrooms. The collection of cases presents a multitude of prospects for creating more culturally responsive pedagogy in postsecondary classrooms.

Case 1:   Culturally Responsive Pedagogy in College Outreach Programs for Parents

In Chapter 6, I (Kiyama) shared the results of a multiple-case study research project where I documented the funds of knowledge and college ideologies of Mexican-American families participating in a university outreach program. At the time of data collection in 2007, the children who were part of these families were in grades K–6. Now ten years later, I have had the opportunity to follow up with 19 families, including the majority of those who participated in the original 2007 study, who were part of the initial outreach program cohorts. The children are now moving through the college-choice and transition process, and many have matriculated into postsecondary institutions. I approached this follow-up study with the intent of exploring the following research questions: (1) How has the "funds of knowledge" framework been incorporated into a college outreach program? (2) How has the long-term influence of the household setting (i.e., family funds of knowledge and college ideologies) been impacted by the outreach program? (3) What are the college-going practices of former participants of the college outreach program?

I conducted interviews with 48 participants, including ten Spanish-speaking families, nine English-speaking families, six current college students, and ten program and university administrators. For the purposes of this chapter, I share examples of the ways in which funds of knowledge has been incorporated as a pedagogical tool in this ten-week outreach program for parents. The examples that follow demonstrate culturally responsive pedagogy for adult learning.

Physics y de campo

Consider this conversation between a mother, Consuelo, who had participated in the college-access outreach program over ten years ago, and the interviewer. In this exchange, the interviewer asked Consuelo to reflect on specific examples of workshops or artifacts that she recalled from her participation in the program. Consuelo begins by sharing an experiment that the Physics faculty presenter demonstrated and moved to describing how she learned that families have the necessary "laboratories" for learning in their own kitchens.

Consuelo: Muy suave, muy, muy suave. El globo cuando se infló y así muchas cosas. Experimentos.
[It was very cool! Very cool!! The balloon when it was inflated and so many things. Experiments.]

Interviewer: *Sí, creo que ese globo es de física y todavía tenemos el mismo profesor que nos ayuda. Y todos así, bien emocionados, guau.*
[Yes, I believe it was the balloon from Physics and we still have the same professor who helps us. And everyone was very excited, wow.]

Consuelo: *Como estamos puestos nada más que los laboratorios que tenemos aquí, en la cocina, a mezclar productos, pero no es lo mismo que ir allá y que te enseñen. Y las bacterias, cuando pusimos el gel y nos pasaron por los rayos, vimos las bacterias, todas las que había, muchas, muchas.*

Interviewer:

[And we were more then set with the laboratories we have here in the kitchen, mixing products, but it is not the same as going there and having them teach you. And the bacteria, when we put the gel and we went through the rays, we saw the bacteria, everything that was there, many, many.]

Interviewer: *O sea, que se que sí que se divirtieron.*
[That is, you did enjoy yourself.]

Consuelo: *Mucho, sí, sí. Aparte de que uno también hace vida de campo pero a la vez también conociendo. Sí, muchas cosas, muchas cosas, muy bonito, muy suave, algo nuevo para uno siempre.*
[A lot, yes, yes. Besides the fact that one comes from the country life yet also knowing. Yes, many things, many things, very beautiful, very cool, there was always something new.]

What is particularly noteworthy is not only the connection Consuelo made to her own kitchen laboratory, but her statement at the end of the conversation, "hace vida de campo." She was explaining her family's background from country life, yet also knowing. This process of teaching and learning is the epitome of what funds of knowledge as a culturally responsive pedagogy can look like within adult learning and college classrooms. The Physics faculty member connected science curriculum with the families' home and cultural knowledge, and in doing so, validated their "vida de campo" as responsive, rich with learning, and important. Although the Physics faculty member may not have knowingly drawn from a funds of knowledge pedagogy, he certainly was intentional about connecting with the families in culturally responsive and respectful ways. Likewise, as mentioned, the program itself is built upon a funds of knowledge framework, and when inviting the faculty to present to families, program administrators select faculty who share the equity lens promoted by the program. That is, the program taps into a critical agency network (Kiyama, Lee, & Rhoades, 2012) of individuals, a network that is built upon shared social justice values and shared relationships. As shared by Kiyama, Lee, and Rhoades (2012), the administrators, faculty, and staff involved with this program "worked through trust, mutual respect, and persuasion" (p. 289) and included faculty who had familial, cultural, and/or geographic ties to the local community who participated in the program. What manifested then, as a result of these mutual and trusting relationships, was the integration of faculty presenters who understood the local ecologies and social and cultural contexts of the family participants. As readers should recall, each of these factors is critical in the framework of funds of knowledge and in becoming driving forces in the creation of outreach curriculum that is culturally responsive.

Parents as Graduates

This second example captures parents' reflections on the culminating event that occurred as part of the college outreach program. The program held a graduation ceremony for the parents who completed the program. As each parent (or grandparent) participant was called to the stage, they were honored with a completion diploma and a graduation cap, and they stood proudly before the many pictures being taken by their own children and grandchildren. In that moment, what was cemented for grandparents, parents, and the children was the idea that college was possible. The administrator at the partnering school district described it in this way:

> There is this grandmother who has the cap on her grandson and I think like a first grader, and those two things, seeing your child as a graduate, whether it's a college graduate or a high school graduate . . . but that, to me is what it's all about.

Indeed, one of the mothers, Tania said,

> I have the diploma—both of ours [mother and father]—and the big picture that we took. . . . And I kept saying, "I'm going to take out the picture, and I'm going to frame it." And Maria [daughter] was like, "You should. You should just put it out. It was a proud moment." . . . See, I'm a graduate.

From a funds of knowledge perspective, the learning that occurs can be further developed through the use of symbols (Kiyama, 2010). In this case, the outreach program has built in the symbolism of the graduation ceremony and accompanying artifacts—caps, diplomas, a stage, and the like. What is even more significant is the symbolism of the parents and grandparents as graduates. The graduates become the literal exhibition of college as a possibility, and a possibility that, according to my recent follow-up study, does in fact become a reality. Therefore, not only is the curriculum of the program being delivered in culturally responsive ways, the events and artifacts that make up the program are also culturally responsive.

Case 2: A Proposed Approach to Examine Culturally Responsive Pedagogy in Community College Classrooms

Classrooms and pedagogies in community colleges are under-investigated and under-theorized in research on educational opportunity. Existing conceptions of the typical college student are idealized and based on a traditional, imagined norm of someone who begins college immediately after high school, enrolls full-time, lives on campus, and is prepared to begin college-level classes. In community college classrooms in particular, students' diverse cultural, work, and family backgrounds, and prior experiences, should inform how educators and scholars think about how students approach learning and the educational process generally. The reality of today's diverse students consists of beginning their postsecondary academic trajectories at a community college (Deil-Amen, 2015).

In this example, we (Rios-Aguilar and Deil-Amen) contend that the pedagogical choices faculty make are determined by their specific (often negative) perceptions of their students. Faculty make assumptions about what students know and how they expect them to perform in the classroom (Cox, 2009). Frequently, faculty design curriculum by adopting "remedial pedagogy[ies]" (Grubb, 2013) that reinforce dominant narratives of community college students as incapable of learning complex material. Deil-Amen (2011) finds that two-year college students' decisions to persist are shaped by socio-academic integrative moments—interactions within and just outside the classroom with instructors and peers who enhance belonging and encourage/reinforce students' academic identity. Thus, it is necessary to examine classroom dynamics and more closely understand the role of faculty in community college students' success. More specifically, we should explore what faculty do in the classroom.

In this case example, we seek to identify specific funds of knowledge (FK) that exist in community colleges and their relationship to teaching and student outcomes—as a culturally responsive pedagogy. The underlying rationale for carrying out this project, as it was for the original FK study (see Moll, Amanti, Neff, & González, 1992), stems from the assumption that the educational process in schools (including community colleges) can be greatly enhanced when teachers learn about the everyday lived contexts of their students' lives, and find ways to connect their students' realities and FK with their pedagogical practices (González, Moll, & Amanti, 2005; Moll et al., 1992). In this context, pedagogy becomes more than just what faculty do in the classroom. Rather, pedagogy is the culturally responsive practice that values and incorporates how individuals experience life, how they learn, and how knowledge is produced (González, 2005). A FK approach can potentially mediate between students' lived realities and the dominant constructs of a college classroom. In our particular version of how faculty can learn from students' contexts, ethnographic research methods may help uncover the broad range of FK available for community college teaching. As was done in past research on FK, faculty-ethnographers in the proposed project will venture into their students' family and community lives, not as "teachers" attempting to deliver content, but as "anthropological learners" seeking to understand the ways in which people make sense of their everyday lives (González et al., 2005). In addition to this qualitative component, and unlike most available scholarship on FK, the proposed project will also utilize quantitative methods, including student surveys, to learn about existing FK in the households of working-class, under-represented, and marginalized community college students.

Therefore, we believe that a culturally responsive pedagogy can be understood in the community college context by exploring the following goals: (a) to identify and explore the pedagogical practices used by community college faculty, (b) to identify the repertoire of FK available to faculty, (c) to examine the relationship between students' FK and student outcomes, and (d) to identify the institutional conditions that enable/hinder faculty to utilize students' FK in their classrooms. By shifting attention to the pedagogical practices of community college faculty, one can more comprehensively understand the factors that affect students' persistence and success. Moreover, by allowing the space for community college faculty to engage in discussions and reflect on teaching approaches, the result can be an increase in innovations in culturally responsive pedagogy that better align with diverse community college students.

Case 3: Participatory Action Methods as Culturally Responsive Pedagogical Tools

When considering culturally responsive pedagogies, we should not be confined to school settings (Brockenbrough, 2016). What this allows us to consider then is the role that students themselves play in collecting and documenting home and cultural knowledges in an effort to integrate funds of knowledge into postsecondary learning. Participatory action research is defined as "a social process of collaborative learning realized by groups of people who join together in changing the practices through which they interact in a shared social world" (Kemmis & McTaggart, 2005, p. 563). Participatory action research incorporates the participants, or in this case the students, as co-researchers (Irizarry & Brown, 2014). Participatory action research involves exploring and incorporating actual, not abstract, practices (Kemmis & McTaggart, 2005). Given that the transmission of funds of knowledge often occurs during the experimentation of the "actual," and in hands-on learning moments with children, the methods associated with participatory action research offer helpful tools when considering translating funds of knowledge pedagogy into college classrooms. Similarly, participatory action research aligns with funds of knowledge in its recognition of social practices (i.e. communication), social structures (i.e. cultural/symbolic, sociopolitical), social media (i.e. language/discourses), and participants' knowledge (Kemmis & McTaggart, 2005). Specifically, Irizarry and Brown (2014) highlight that participatory action research assumes that "local people possess expert knowledge about the conditions of their lives that outsiders cannot access on their own" (p. 64).

There are three attributes that are recognized in participatory action research that differ from traditional research. The first is "shared ownership of research projects"; the second is "community-based analysis of social problems"; and the third is "an orientation toward community action" (Kemmis & McTaggart, 2005, p. 560). A key feature of participatory action research includes the method of a spiral of self-reflection. This spiral often includes planning, acting and observing, reflecting, replanning, acting and observing again, and reflecting again (Kemmis & McTaggart, 2005).

For example, take into account Dworin's (2006) work with the Family Stories Project. Dworin (2006) describes a process with fourth-grade children that is similar to participatory action methods that can be utilized for higher education students. The Family Stories Project was an assignment in which students in a biliteracy classroom were asked to write a collection of family stories. Children collected the stories from family members and wrote them in both English and Spanish. Funds of knowledge was used as a framing so that students could draw on their home and community knowledge when writing the stories. Ultimately, the students wrote and published an anthology of the family stories and worked through a process of peer review, feedback, creating illustrations, and incorporating their families' edits and revisions. Similar to participatory action methods, the students (as opposed to the teacher or researcher) were empowered to research and document their own family resources, *cuentos*, and history (Dworin, 2006). Likewise, the students did so through a process of continuous planning, reflecting, feedback, and replanning—with each stage of the spiral being student led. An assignment such as this one could easily be translated into a writing assignment within a college classroom.

Participatory action research can help facilitate the goals of culturally responsive pedagogy as it provides students a means to incorporate their home and cultural knowledges and is based on the principles of sociopolitical justice and equity, with the ultimate goal of action (i.e. social transformation) (Irizarry & Brown, 2014). Participants, or students, can realize that action in many forms—workshops, rallies, art exhibits, co-curricular development (Irizarry & Brown, 2014). Irizarry (2009) compiled the ways in which youth participatory action research advanced multicultural education. One example included high school student researchers who examined legislation around teacher qualifications. What resulted was the development of student-created educator qualifications inclusive of culturally responsive learning communities and bridging with students' families (Irizarry, 2009). In another example, urban youth created a community-based curriculum based on their lived experiences and issues facing their local communities. The development of the curriculum allowed for partnership amongst faculty, staff, students, and community members (Irizarry, 2009). In all of the examples, the students are both the knowledge holders and the knowledge producers (Irizarry, 2009).

Participatory action research creates space that encourages students to generate curriculum and counterstories, assess and refine policies, and collectively promotes cross-cultural understanding (Irizarry, 2009)—all while honoring the funds of knowledge present within students and their communities. Participatory action research, like culturally responsive pedagogy, is itself an ideology representing a paradigmatic shift (Irizarry & Brown, 2014). Just as participatory action research requires a shift in understanding about researcher and participant relationships, culturally responsive pedagogy requires a similar shift in the understanding about instructor and student. Both humanize students and honor cultural knowledge (Irizarry & Brown, 2014).

Culturally Responsive Communities of Learners

The connection between home knowledge, cultural knowledge, and school knowledge is not straightforward, nor is it linear (González, McIntyre, & Rosebery, 2001). What each of the three cases illustrate are the opportunities presented when educators in higher education embrace the pedagogical complexity of culturally responsive teaching via funds of knowledge. When González and colleagues first wrote about integrating funds of knowledge into college classrooms in 2001, and later in the original *Funds of Knowledge* book in 2005, they indicated that

> it [the formation of a learning community] involves an acknowledgement that all knowledge has elements of the abstract and the concrete, theory and practice, the particular and the universal. Forming learning communities then becomes an exercise in drawing from these multiple knowledges in a way that is accessible to students.
>
> *(González, McIntyre, & Rosebery, 2001, p. 121)*

When considering the idea of forming communities of learners through a culturally responsive lens, understanding and integrating students' cultural and social contexts becomes even more imperative. The postsecondary classroom can become a space where power dynamics are minimized, where teaching and learning are equitably shared amongst the community, and where students' home knowledges become the base from which course content is developed. We believe the results can be not only enhanced academic success (Ladson-Billings, 1995; Salazar et al., 2010), but a powerful development and demonstration of student agency and active participation in the pedagogical process.

References

Brockenbrough, E. (2016). Becoming queerly responsive: Culturally responsive pedagogy for Black and Latino urban queer youth. *Urban Education, 51*(2), 170–196.

Cox, R. D. (2009). *The college fear factor: How students and professors misunderstand one another.* Cambridge, MA: Harvard University Press.

Deil-Amen, R. (2011). Socio-academic integrative moments: Rethinking academic and social integration among two-year college students in career-related programs. *Journal of Higher Education, 82*(1), 54–91.

Deil-Amen, R. (2015). The "traditional" college student: A smaller and smaller minority and its implications for diversity and access institutions. In M. Stevens & M. Kirst (Eds.), *Remaking college: The changing ecology of higher education* (pp. 135–165). Stanford, CA: Stanford University Press.

Dworin, J. E. (2006). The family stories project: Using funds of knowledge for writing. *The Reading Teacher, 59*(6), 510–520.

Freire, P., & Macedo, D. P. (2003). A dialogue: Culture, language, and race. In A. Howell, & F. Tuitt (Eds.), *Race and higher education: Rethinking pedagogy in diverse college classrooms* (pp. 189–214). Cambridge, MA: Harvard Education Publishing Group.

González, N. (2005). Beyond culture: The hybridity of funds of knowledge. In N. Gonzales, L. C. Moll, & C. Amanti (Eds.), *Funds of knowledge: Theorizing practices in households, communities, and classrooms* (pp. 29–46). Mahwah, NJ: Lawrence Erlbaum Associates.

González, N., McIntyre, E., & Rosebery, A. (2001). Seeing, believing, and taking action. In E. McIntyre, A. Rosebery, & N. González (Eds.), *Classroom diversity: Connecting curriculum to students' lives* (pp. 115–122). Portsmouth, NH: Heinemann.

González, N., Moll, L., & Amanti, C. (2005). *Funds of knowledge: Theorizing practices in households, communities, and classrooms.* Mahwah, NJ: Lawrence Erlbaum Associates.

Grubb, N. (2013). *Basic skill education in community colleges: Inside and outside of classrooms.* New York, NY: Routledge.

Howell, A., & Tuitt, F. (2003). *Race and higher education: Rethinking pedagogy in diverse college classrooms.* Cambridge, MA: Harvard Education Publishing Group.

Irizarry, J. (2009). Reinvigorating multicultural education through youth participatory action research. *Multicultural Perspectives, 11*(4), 194–199.

Irizarry, J., & Brown, T. M. (2014). Humanizing research in dehumanizing spaces: The challenges and opportunities of conducting participatory action research with youth in schools. In D. Paris & M. T. Winn (Eds.), *Humanizing research: Decolonizing qualitative inquiry with youth and communities* (pp. 63–80). Los Angeles, CA: Sage Publications.

Kemmis, S., & McTaggart, R. (2005). Participatory action research: Communicative action and the public sphere. In N. K. Denzin & Y. S. Lincoln (Eds.), *The Sage handbook of qualitative research* (3rd ed., pp. 559–603). Thousand Oaks, CA: Sage Publications.

Kiyama, J. M. (2010). College aspirations and limitations: The role of educational ideologies and funds of knowledge in Mexican American families. *American Educational Research Journal, 47*(2), 330–356.

Kiyama, J. M, Lee, J. J., & Rhoades, G. (2012). A critical agency network model for building an integrated outreach program. *The Journal of Higher Education, 83*(2), 276–303.

Ladson-Billings, G. (1995). Toward a theory of culturally responsive pedagogy. *American Educational Research Journal, 32*(3), 465–491.

Moll, L. C., Amanti, C., Neff, D., & González, N. (1992). Funds of knowledge for teaching: Using a qualitative approach to connect homes and classrooms. *Theory into Practice, XXXI,* 132–141. doi:10.1080/00405849209543534

Osei-Kofi, N., Richards, S. L., & Smith, D. G. (2004). Inclusion, reflection, and the politics of knowledge: On working toward the realization of inclusive classroom environments. In L. I. Rendón, M. García, & D. Person (Eds.), *Transforming the first-year experience for students of color* (pp. 215–242). Monograph No. 38. Columbia, SC: University of South Carolina, National Resource Center for the First-Year Experience and Students in Transition.

Salazar, M. C., Norton, A. S., & Tuitt, F. (2010). Weaving promising practices for inclusive excellence into the higher education classroom. In L. B. Nilson & J. E. Miller (Eds.), *To improve the academy: Resources for faculty, instructional, and organizational development* (pp. 208–226). San Francisco, CA: Jossey-Bass.

Tuitt, F. (2003). Afterword: Realizing a more inclusive pedagogy. In A. Howell & F. Tuitt (Eds.), *Race and higher education: Rethinking pedagogy in diverse college classrooms* (pp. 243–268). Cambridge, MA: Harvard Education Publishing Group.

Weiler, K. (2003). Freire and a feminist pedagogy of difference. In A. Howell & F. Tuitt (Eds.), *Race and higher education: Rethinking pedagogy in diverse college classrooms* (pp. 215–242). Cambridge, MA: Harvard Education Publishing Group.

12

CONCLUSION

The Future of Funds of Knowledge in Higher Education

Judy Marquez Kiyama and Cecilia Rios-Aguilar

In 2012, we proposed funds of knowledge as a new approach to study Latina/o students' transition in and out of college (Rios-Aguilar & Kiyama, 2012). We acknowledged that "although we have gained a new perspective on the meaning of various funds of knowledge, we are still restricted in our knowledge of how these funds of knowledge are applied to the transitions into and out of college" (Rios-Aguilar & Kiyama, 2012, p. 13). This limitation of our own research at that time is what compelled us to further explore the ways in which funds of knowledge could be useful in the study of issues of college access and success; pedagogy and curriculum development; and as a framework for policy and practice within the context of higher education. To that end, the goal of this edited volume was not to repeat work done previously, but to elaborate a funds of knowledge approach for the context of higher education. In doing so, we advanced an understanding of funds of knowledge by relating it to other key conceptual frameworks used in the field of education, including the forms of capital, critical race theory, community cultural wealth, and critical pedagogy. We strived to offer a perspective that takes into consideration both the strengths and the weaknesses of a funds of knowledge approach to higher education research. As demonstrated throughout the volume, we did not suggest that funds of knowledge was the cure-all strategy to the problems related to college access and success for all underrepresented students. Instead, in this book, we carefully examined what funds of knowledge can (and cannot) do to improve researchers' and practitioners' understanding of underrepresented students' educational trajectories and experiences in college.

In preparing for this book, we asked each author to consider the following questions:

1. How does the chapter extend the concept of funds of knowledge, either methodologically or conceptually?
2. What are the challenges and opportunities of using a funds of knowledge framework in higher education?
3. What are the implications for policy and practice of using funds of knowledge in higher education?
4. What can be the future of funds of knowledge in higher education?

Methodological and Conceptual Extensions

When combined with other frameworks, funds of knowledge becomes a powerful conceptual foundation from which to understand and study issues of educational equity for marginalized populations. In Chapter 3, Kiyama, Rios-Aguilar, and Sarubbi presented an extensive content analysis of over 300 articles that have utilized the frameworks of funds of knowledge, social capital, and/or cultural capital in education-related research studies. Employing the process of content analysis, the authors demonstrated that one characteristic of this literature is that the conceptual tools of funds of knowledge and forms of capital are presented with a lack of clarity regarding theoretical origins, utility, definitions, and mechanisms to explain why educational inequities persist. Thus, the authors spent significant time in both Chapters 2 and 3 reviewing the conceptual origins of the three frameworks. An important contribution of Chapters 2 and 3 is reconnection to the ways in which Bourdieu's social and cultural capital provide us a framework from which to study and understand broader issues of power and domination in school settings. When pairing this theory of power with funds of knowledge, we are provided with the tools from which to also understand the culturally-based practices of diverse students and their experiences as members of families, communities, and larger systems. The result of the analysis is a complementary framework of funds of knowledge and forms of capital. This refinement can help scholars and educators to conduct research that is more powerful and meaningful.

In Chapter 4, Giraldo, Huerta, and Solórzano drew upon critical race theory while specifically combining community cultural wealth and funds of knowledge to explore the experiences of previously incarcerated, formerly gang-involved men and women who are now attending community colleges. Not only does the chapter offer insight into a population that is severely missing from the literature and often depicted in deficit ways, it conceptually bridges community cultural wealth and funds of knowledge. The connections between funds of knowledge and community cultural wealth have only been mentioned peripherally in previous literature. This chapter represents one of the first to integrate the two frameworks, highlighting their complementarity, and applying the complementary framework to a study of critically important populations. In doing so, the authors highlight how previously incarcerated, formerly gang-involved community college students use their funds of knowledge and different forms of aspirational, navigational, and familial capital to traverse their academic experiences and combat issues of racial injustice in community colleges.

García, in Chapter 5, offered the concept of creative resistance as an art-based learning tool. García described the process through which creative resistance as a pedagogical framework developed from students' home knowledge, sociopolitical circumstances, and issues of race and racism to highlight both students' funds of knowledge and combat oppressive conditions in school settings. The author did so by combining funds of knowledge pedagogy with the theoretical frameworks of critical race theory, critical pedagogy, and funds of knowledge. One result was the student-led redesign of the game La Lotería, which drew from the home knowledge and capital of his students. The creation of La Lotería elicited many of the funds of knowledge found in Moll and colleagues' original study, that of familial history, occupational history, household knowledge, and cultural knowledge. Thus, the project itself became a source of cultural knowledge for his students. García's contribution of creative resistance extends funds of knowledge as a pedagogical framework to consider the ways in which students take the lead for classroom learning and engage in this process as a means to protect themselves from oppressive environments.

Challenges and Opportunities of Using Funds of Knowledge in Higher Education

Parts 2 and 3 of this book offer examples of the ways in which funds of knowledge has been used as a framework to study college access and persistence in higher education, and as a developing pedagogy in postsecondary classrooms. Although often applied to studies of Latina/o families, George Mwangi (Chapter 7) utilizes the framework when exploring the college-going opportunities for sub-Saharan African immigrants. Her work represents some of the only research to use funds of knowledge when studying this particular community. Montiel (Chapter 8) applies funds of knowledge to the study of undocumented Mexican Ivy League students. Again, her research represents the only of its kind to use funds of knowledge to explore student experiences at Ivy League institutions. Kiyama's chapter (Chapter 6) was the first to apply funds of knowledge to studying college outreach programs for Mexican-American families. Each chapter in this section represents original contributions in their use of funds of knowledge.

Funds of Knowledge as a Theoretical Framework

There have been many calls to integrate a more culturally-responsive curriculum into outreach initiatives for families of color. Most notably, Tierney and Auerbach

(2004) urged for the use of cultural integrity models that honored the home languages and home cultures of diverse families. In Chapter 6, Kiyama explored the educational ideologies and funds of knowledge of Mexican-American families participating in a university outreach program. The program itself was in the early stages of implementing funds of knowledge as a curricular framework from which program content was delivered to family participants. Kiyama demonstrated how families' college knowledge, social networks, and college cultural symbols served as the basis from which college ideologies were formed. These ideologies both contributed to the reasons why families participated in the outreach program and were further cultivated by the outreach program. Thus, Kiyama's contribution is unique as funds of knowledge were used both to understand families' college-going knowledge and educational ideologies, and to understand (and offer additional recommendations to) the framework of the outreach program. The challenges Kiyama identified highlighted the difficulties that outreach programs face when attempting to develop culturally-relevant curriculum when financial and human resources are limited.

Chapter 7 explored the college-going aspirations, expectations, and access strategies of sub-Saharan African immigrant families. George Mwangi was specifically interested in pre-existing knowledge related to college preparation. She drew upon funds of knowledge to understand family and community contexts, and how funds of knowledge within these contexts served as academic motivators. Importantly, George Mwangi extends the application of funds of knowledge beyond a Latina/o immigrant population. One particular fund of knowledge George Mwangi highlighted was the college knowledge transmitted through college-going legacies, knowledge that was passed on in family contexts where navigation of a new country was key to their survival. The struggles to achieve a college degree were narrated to kids as a means of passing on cultural, familial, and community-based funds of knowledge. George Mwangi notes the challenges of continuing to (attempt to) apply normative college-choice models (i.e. Hossler & Gallagher, 1987) to the college-going processes of diverse families, and specifically sub-Saharan African families. She aptly points out that families in her study offered experiences that were more complex than a three-stage college-choice model.

In Chapter 8, Montiel examined the college experiences of undocumented, Mexican students at Ivy League institutions. She conceptualized their experiences through the concept of *hacerle la lucha* (taking on the struggle) and identified it as a source of funds of knowledge. Montiel accomplished many things in this chapter. Not only did she extend the literature on undocumented students, she did so through the use of funds of knowledge that positioned the students' contributions as strengths within higher education contexts. She illustrated how *hacerle la lucha* as a fund of knowledge was converted into forms of social, cultural, and economic capital. Unlike any other chapter within this volume, Montiel traces a fund of knowledge from emergence to conversion. A challenge and future opportunity reflect the fact that this study reflects the need to better understand the processes that undocumented students face through an asset-based lens, particularly at private Ivy League institutions, as these students are often treated as invisible within these contexts.

Implications for Policy and Practice

To understand the opportunities funds of knowledge offers for educational policy and practice, we focus on the contributions of Chapters 9 and 10. Chapter 9 positions funds of knowledge as a powerful pedagogy in community college classrooms, and Chapter 10 demonstrates how career and technical education policies can be understood and influenced by a funds of knowledge lens.

Funds of Knowledge as a Pedagogy

Funds of knowledge offers the opportunity to transform college classrooms. In Chapter 9, Mora and Rios-Aguilar demonstrate how funds of knowledge can promote teaching discourse that replaces remedial pedagogies in the classroom with models that validate student experiences and increase student success. The authors studied the pedagogical choices and practices among community college faculty and documented the ways in which they grappled with, applied, and/or resisted a funds of knowledge pedagogy. Important to this chapter are the implications for policy and practice on how funds of knowledge can be implemented in community college spaces. Yet, an important challenge that Mora and Rios-Aguilar noted was the resistance of some of the faculty to consider the utility of a funds of knowledge pedagogy, suggesting that more normative teaching practices were pervasive in community college classrooms and difficult to break out of.

Extending Policy and Practice Through a Funds of Knowledge Lens

Neri, in Chapter 10, critiques that the traditional frameworks that have been used to study students' aspirations do not provide the tools necessary for redesigning policy and practice for career and technical education. Specifically, Neri was interested in the career aspirations of underrepresented students, and argued that career and technical education must account for the funds of knowledge students bring into their learning processes, student agency when navigating sociopolitical barriers, and students' requests for their career paths. Neri argues that funds of knowledge provides a lens from which reform and policy work around career and technical education can be more humanizing and social justice-oriented. Neri challenges the "narrow framings" of career and technical education, suggesting that most often it is viewed as a means for developing economic growth. Her exploration of students' funds of knowledge shows that cultural and home knowledge significantly ad..d to students' learning and development of career aspirations beyond employable skills.

The Future of Funds of Knowledge in Higher Education

As established, funds of knowledge can be a creative tool when developing curriculum in postsecondary settings; a powerful tool when combined with frameworks that interrogate larger issues of power and systems of domination within education contexts; and a culturally-relevant lens from which to value and understand the diverse resources students bring with them into college settings. There remains additional work to be done. We return to the recommendations we laid out in 2012 and extend upon them here.

Refining units of analysis when studying funds of knowledge. Future research must begin to incorporate into analyses of funds of knowledge and college access the role that siblings, extended families' members, and communities play in this process (Rios-Aguilar & Kiyama, 2012, p. 14). The chapters in this volume have begun to explore how, collectively, families and communities influence the college-going paths of their children and insist on more equitable educational opportunities for their communities. Future work by emerging scholars like Janette Mariscal (University of Arizona) will examine how families themselves become the agents for creating college-going opportunities for other families within their communities. Important here are the ways in which families move outside of and beyond the organization, enacting their funds of knowledge and developing it in others.

Examining the variation in households' funds of knowledge. Future research on funds of knowledge needs to continue using both qualitative and quantitative methodologies to study different dimensions and variations of funds of knowledge as they apply to academic preparation and college access among Latina/o students. Further research should expand upon this quantitative approach (Rios-Aguilar & Kiyama, 2012, p. 14). There has not yet been a quantitative funds of knowledge instrument distributed to students within higher education contexts. Future research that examines specific units of analysis of funds of knowledge and analyzes the ways in which those funds are connected to student success in college will help to methodologically extend the framework even further. It will also provide a more culturally-relevant way to understand how student success is conceptualized and supported within postsecondary contexts. This survey is currently under development at the Higher Education Research Institute at the University of California, Los Angeles (UCLA) in collaboration with Delma Ramos (University of Denver) and will change the way we capture postsecondary students' funds of knowledge in both community colleges and four-year institutions.

Understanding the role of funds of knowledge in college access and the development of career aspirations. Future college access research should examine how families construct the processes of getting into and getting out of college, as well as how families develop career aspirations for their children (Rios-Aguilar & Kiyama, 2012, p. 14). Thus far, much of the research on the role of funds of knowledge in higher education focuses on getting in and experiences while in. There remains little research on the process of getting out and the connections to career goals. Rebecca Neri is one of the first to examine funds of knowledge and career aspirations, and her emerging research agenda will offer the next dimension of funds of knowledge research.

Conclusion

This volume presents the most recent available scholarship on funds of knowledge in higher education. This work is important, meaningful, and very much needed in our field. We hope you learn that to combat deficit thinking with a *funds of knowledge* approach requires, as Zipin (2009) suggests, conceptual and analytic depth, creativity, courage, rare support, and we add *confianza* (Moll & González, 1997) and *respeto* (Valdés, 1996). We must continue to expand this work and to elaborate on it. Multiple opportunities exist to expand this work. The living conditions of students, families, and communities throughout the United States have changed considerably in the last few years. Some dynamics are particularly concerning. For instance, income inequality in the U.S. is rising at a rapid pace, and at the same time, college persistence and completion rates remain painfully low for many underrepresented students. Similarly, higher education institutions are experiencing significant challenges, including pressure to do more with less resources, a high turnover of leadership, and a lack of focus on teaching and learning. These new realities bring more complexity to our field. However, our book is an invitation to not forget that *all* students, and especially historically underrepresented students, bring a wealth of resources to higher education institutions, and that we must utilize them strategically to give them more opportunities to succeed academically and in life.

References

Hossler, D., & Gallagher, K. S. (1987). Studying student college choice: A three-phase model and the implications for policymakers. *College and University, 62*(3), 207–222.

Moll, L. C., & González, N. (1997). Teachers as social scientists: Learning about culture from household research. In P. M. Hall (Ed.), *Race, ethnicity, and multiculturalism: Policy and practice* (Vol. 1, pp. 89–114). New York, NY: Garland.

Rios-Aguilar, C., & Kiyama, J. M. (2012). Funds of knowledge: A proposed approach to study Latina/o students' transition to college. *Journal of Latinos and Education, 11*(1), 2–16.

Tierney, W., & Auerbach, S. (2004). Toward developing an untapped resource: The role of families in college preparation. In W. Tierney, Z. Corwin, & J. Colyar (Eds.), *From high school to college: Evaluating access*. Albany: State University of New York Press.

Valdés, G. (1996). *Con respeto: Bridging the distance between culturally diverse families and schools.* New York: Teachers College Press.

Zipin, L. (2009). Dark funds of knowledge, deep funds of pedagogy: Exploring boundaries between lifeworlds and schools. *Discourse: Studies in the Cultural Politics of Education, 30*(3), 317–331. doi:10.1080/01596300903037044

CONTRIBUTORS

Regina Deil-Amen is a Professor of Higher Education and Sociology at the University of Arizona, and an expert on qualitative research methods and college student transitions. Her book, *After Admission*, details how two-year colleges use different institutional approaches to prepare students for sub-baccalaureate careers. She completed a longitudinal study of Chicago students' transition from high-poverty high schools into college. Her other research analyzed strategies, challenges, and success among lower-income university students, including Latino students' social networks and career decision-making. More recently, she and Cecilia Rios-Aguilar explored how community college students use social media to create community and enhance their success.

Luis-Genaro García is a PhD candidate in the School of Educational Studies at Claremont Graduate University. Luis' research connects the fields of public art, critical art education, and public education to explore the effectiveness of the arts in transforming the academic outcomes for working-class students of color. Luis is also a local community artist and educator. He teaches art at his alma mater, Thomas Jefferson High School, in South Los Angeles. As an educator, Luis teaches art through a social justice curriculum incorporating ethnic, personal, and historical experiences of students in order to challenge the current institutional barriers that exist for students of color. He uses an art-based methodology of civic engagement along with Paulo Freire's theory of critical pedagogy as a contemporary form of critical learning and student empowerment.

Chrystal A. George Mwangi is an Assistant Professor of Higher Education at the University of Massachusetts Amherst. Her scholarship broadly centers on (1) structures of opportunity and educational attainment for underrepresented populations along the P–20 education pipeline; (2) impacts of globalization and migration on U.S. higher education at the student, institution, and policy levels; and (3) African and African Diaspora populations in higher education. She brings expertise in the educational experiences of Black immigrants, specifically related to identity development, college access, and college persistence. Her work in this area has been published in journals including *Diversity in Higher Education* and the *Journal of Student Affairs Research & Practice*.

Luis Gustavo Giraldo is the Director of Equity, Diversity and Cultural Competency at Santa Barbara City College. His research stems from his work at Homeboy Industries in Los Angeles. Homeboy Industries is the largest gang rehabilitation community in the world. Dr. Giraldo uses critical race theory coupled with funds of knowledge and community cultural wealth to examine the higher education experiences of previously incarcerated and formerly gang-involved men and women—particularly focusing on how these students experience racial microaggressions. His research also focuses on the experiences of students of color in higher education and the impact that transformative resiliency has on the educational trajectory of these students. Dr. Giraldo earned his PhD from Claremont Graduate University, his MA in Higher Education and Organizational Change from the University of California, Los Angeles (UCLA), and his BA in Human Development and Social Change from Pacific Oaks College.

Adrian H. Huerta is a postdoctoral scholar at the Higher Education Research Institute at the University of California, Los Angeles (UCLA). Dr. Huerta has published on college access, transition, and criminal justice for Latino males in the K–20 educational pipeline. He is a Research Affiliate with Project Males at the University of Texas, Austin.

Judy Marquez Kiyama is an Associate Professor in the Higher Education Department at the University of Denver's Morgridge College of Education. Dr. Kiyama's research examines the structures that shape educational opportunities for underserved groups through an asset-based lens to better understand the collective knowledge and resources drawn upon to confront, negotiate, and (re)shape such structures. Her research is organized in three interconnected areas: the role of parents and families; equity and power in educational research; and underserved groups as collective networks of change.

Luis C. Moll is Professor Emeritus in the Language, Reading and Culture Program of the Department of Teaching, Learning and Sociocultural Studies, College of Education, University of Arizona. His main research interest is the connection among culture, psychology, and education, especially as it relates to the education of Latino children in the U.S. Among other studies, he has analyzed the quality of classroom teaching, examined literacy instruction in English and Spanish, studied how knowledge is produced in the broader social contexts of household and community life and, in collaboration with teachers, attempted to establish pedagogical relationships among these domains of study. Among his honors, he was elected to membership in the National Academy of Education (1998), named a Kappa Delta Pi Laureate (2013), elected to the Reading Hall of Fame (2014), and awarded the Medal for Distinguished Service by Teachers College, Columbia University (2015). He was also named Fellow (2009), and received the Presidential Citation Award (2010) and the Palmer O. Johnson Award (2011), all from the American Educational Research Association.

Gloria Itzel Montiel is a 2017 doctoral candidate in Education Policy, Evaluation and Reform at the Claremont Graduate University, School of Educational Studies. Her dissertation research focuses on the identity and college experience of undocumented students attending selective private colleges. She also serves as the Grants and Contracts Coordinator at Latino Health Access and at the Human Resources Partners at A-Z Techs LLC, both in Orange County, California. Gloria holds a BA in English and American Literature and Language from Harvard College, and an EdM in Learning and Teaching from the Harvard Graduate School of Education. Born in Guerrero, Mexico, she became a DACA recipient in 2013.

Juana Mora is an Associate Professor of Chicana/o Studies and Faculty Coordinator of Student Equity at Rio Hondo College. Dr. Mora has been a faculty member at Rio Hondo College since 2006 and received tenure in 2010. Prior to 2006, Dr. Mora was a "free-way flyer" teaching at two-year and four-year colleges and universities. Dr. Mora's research examines the pedagogical practices of community college faculty and their connection to student persistence and success. Dr. Mora earned her PhD in Education from Claremont Graduate University, her MA in Political Science from Claremont Graduate University, her MA and BA in Chicana/o Studies from California State University Northridge, and her AA in Liberal Arts from Mt. San Antonio College.

Rebecca Colina Neri is a PhD student in the Urban Schooling Division of the Graduate School of Education and Information Studies (GSEIS) at the University of California, Los Angeles (UCLA). Her research focuses on improving the trajectories of foster youth into and through community college. More broadly, she is interested in studying and developing inter- and trans-disciplinary approaches for addressing student trauma to improve educational and career outcomes. Rebecca also has extensive experience working in schools. She taught Algebra for 12 years across middle school, high school, and community college levels. She also works with school instructional leaders to develop more equitable teaching and learning practices.

Cecilia Rios-Aguilar is an Associate Professor of Education and Director of the Higher Education Research Institute in the Graduate School of Education and Information Studies at the University of California, Los Angeles. Dr. Rios-Aguilar's research is multidisciplinary and uses a variety of conceptual frameworks—funds of knowledge and the forms of capital—and of statistical approaches—regression analysis, multilevel models, geographic information systems (GIS), and social network analysis—to study the educational and occupational trajectories of underrepresented minorities. Dr. Rios-Aguilar's research interests include critical quantitative research methods, big data, social media, community colleges, and educational policies. She obtained her PhD in Education Theory and Policy from the University of Rochester, her MS in Educational Administration from the University of Rochester, and her BA in Economics from the Instituto Tecnológico Autónomo de México (ITAM).

Molly Sarubbi is a PhD student in Higher Education at the University of Denver. She holds a master's degree in Higher Education from the University of Rochester and a bachelor's degree in Psychology from Nazareth College. Her diverse professional experiences continue to utilize asset-based frameworks to examine the bridges between higher education and the public good. Grounded in a commitment to social justice and equity in education, her current research and practice focuses on access for traditionally underserved students and families, and specifically on educational pathways for former foster care youth and the resulting imperatives for higher education.

Daniel Solórzano is the director of UC/ACCORD and a Professor of Social Science and Comparative Education in the Graduate School of Education and Information Studies (GSEIS) at the University of California, Los Angeles (UCLA). He is also a Professor in the Chicana and Chicano Studies Department and Women's Studies Department. His teaching and research interests include critical race theory and gender studies on the educational access, persistence, and graduation of underrepresented minority undergraduate and graduate students in the United States. Solórzano has authored more than 60 articles, book chapters, and reports on issues of educational access and equity for underrepresented minority populations in the United States. In 2007, he was awarded the UCLA Distinguished Teacher Award. Solórzano received his PhD in Sociology of Education from Claremont Graduate School.

INDEX

Note: Page numbers followed by *n* refer to notes.